Supervising Practices for Postgraduate Research in Art, Architecture and Design

Edited by

Brent Allpress, Robyn Barnacle,
Lesley Duxbury and Elizabeth Grierson
Royal Melbourne Institute of Technology (RMIT) University,
Melbourne, Australia

SENSE PUBLISHERS
ROTTERDAM/BOSTON/TAIPEI

A C.I.P. record for this book is available from the Library of Congress.

PLYMOUTH UNIVERSITY

9 0094 9 8 2 4 8

ISBN: 978-94-6209-017-0 (paperback)
ISBN: 978-94-6209-018-7 (hardback)
ISBN: 978-94-6209-019-4 (e-book)

Published by: Sense Publishers,
P.O. Box 21858,
3001 AW Rotterdam,
The Netherlands
https://www.sensepublishers.com/

Printed on acid-free paper

Cover Image: The Turn On, plaster sculptural pieces, Pia Ednie-Brown, 1998, artist's collection.

All Rights Reserved © 2012 Sense Publishers

No part of this work may be reproduced, stored in a retrieval system, or transmitted in any form or by any means, electronic, mechanical, photocopying, microfilming, recording or otherwise, without written permission from the Publisher, with the exception of any material supplied specifically for the purpose of being entered and executed on a computer system, for exclusive use by the purchaser of the work.

TABLE OF CONTENTS

MICHAEL A. PETERS

FOREWORD

Creative Practice, Creative Economy

It is quite remarkable how the creative, design and expressive arts once marginal and marginalised have become central to the mission of the university. Indeed, under the ideology of the creative economy the so-called cultural industries have taken centre stage and in some senses displaced or eclipsed the role and place of the traditional humanities. The modern university was built around philosophy and literature. Kant talked of the "conflict of the faculties", Hegel occupied the first chair of philosophy at the University of Berlin in 1811, and Henry Newman crafted the Idea of the university around a body of literature. In 2010 The United Nations released its *Creative Economy: A Feasible Development Option,* which details evolving concepts of creativity, cultural and creative industries and aspects of the "creative economy", its multiple dimensions and cross-sectoral linkages. Its first *Creative Economy Report* was released in 2008 concluding that the creative industries were among the most dynamic sectors of the world economy and offered new, high growth opportunities for developing countries. As Supachai Panitchpakdi, Secretary-General of United Nations Conference on Trade and Development, and Helen Clark of United Nations Development Programme note in their joint Foreword to the 2010 report:

> This report builds on the earlier analysis of its predecessor, with new and improved data, showing how creativity, knowledge, culture, and technology can be drivers of job creation, innovation, and social inclusion. It suggests that world trade in creative goods and services remained relatively robust at a time when overall levels of international trade fell. It analyzes the rapid growth in the creative economy sectors across the South and the growing share of creative sector trade which is coming from the South.

Which university or nation can afford to ignore the ideas and analysis behind this report? The ten key messages (summarised and truncated here) are (pp. xxiii–xxv):

1. Even in times of crisis "the creative industries hold great potential for developing countries that seek to diversify their economies and leapfrog into one of the most dynamic sectors of the world economy".
2. "The world economy has been receiving a boost from the increase in South-South trade".
3. "A right mix of public policies and strategic choices are essential for harnessing the socio-economic potential of the creative economy for development gains".
4. "Policy strategies to foster the development of the creative economy must recognise its multidisciplinary nature – its economic, social, cultural, technological and environmental linkages".

5. "A major challenge for shaping policies for the creative economy is related to intellectual property rights: how to measure the value of intellectual property, how to redistribute profits and how to regulate these activities".
6. "The creative economy cuts across the arts, business and connectivity, driving innovation and new business models".
7. "The creative economy is both fragmented and society-inclusive. It functions through interlocking and flexible networks of production and service systems spanning the entire value chain".
8. "Policies for the creative economy have to respond not only to economic needs but also to special demands from local communities related to education, cultural identity, social inequalities and environmental concerns".
9. "In the aftermath of the crisis, the firmness of the market for creative products is a sign that many people in the world are eager for culture, social events, entertainment and leisure".
10. "Each country is different, each market is special and each creative product has its specific touch and splendor".

This is considered the new development mantra and its principles for the United Nations' development programme. It is a powerful reassertion of the notion of the knowledge economy still couched within a theory of international trade and oriented towards a development paradigm and without the neoliberal recipe enshrined in the Washington consensus. Yet it also provides a philosophy and ethos for 'development' across the board and for developed countries.

It is in the context of this evolving understanding of development that the contribution of *Supervising Practices for Postgraduate Research in Art, Architecture and Design* edited by Brent Allpress, Robyn Barnacle, Lesley Duxbury, Elizabeth Grierson, from Royal Melbourne Institute of Technology University, Australia can be appreciated. *Supervising Practices for Postgraduate Research* makes clear the fundamental shift towards a model of applied practice-led research which, as the editors explain in their introduction, "offers an effective means to conduct research on knowledge both embodied in, and discovered through discipline-specific art, architecture and design practices". And they themselves note the centrality of such a conception to the "creative economy".

The shift can be contextualised as a response by the academy to global changes in knowledge generation. Today productive and creative forms of applied and situated knowledge are being validated for their contribution to innovation economies with universities and industry working in close partnership to forge a practice-focused research and innovation nexus.

The emphasis is on a form of creative practice harnessed to project-based knowledge work that encourages intensive knowledge exchanges between teacher and student (or should I say co-investigators or co-creators), and between university and industry where the emphasis is on *knowledge as enactment, knowledge as doing*. Yet the element of criticality is not to be forgotten in the market or in trading knowledges that demand an applied and entrepreneurial context. These are critical models of social and public entrepreneurship.

The emphasis on knowledge as a social practice has taken a long time to mature from its early formulations in the work of Wittgenstein and in Bourdieu, before it begins to get institutionalised in the doctrine of the reflective practitioner with Donald Schön and Chris Argyris in the 1970s, and accounts of "practitioner cultures".

What this new collection does so well is to adopt a creative approach to the notion of supervision in art, architecture and design and to examine, as the editors phrase it, "emerging modes of postgraduate research and supervisory practice".

This is a very astute and valuable contribution to the literature on supervision in the applied arena with a series of excellent discussions on creative practice-based research, pedagogical practices of supervision, creative writing and the creative work in process, "generative praxis", distance supervision, doctoral exhibitions, supervision of designers, and a range of related issues and concerns. I particularly like the phrase of Linda Daley who talks of "Pedagogies of Invention".

It is a path-breaking, path-finding book that will be of great assistance to all kinds of professionals and students across a wide range of disciplines and with important lessons for all doctoral supervision. It is an exciting and accessible book and a great achievement for a group of colleagues in a leading institution.

REFERENCES

United Nations (2008) *Creative Economy Report.* Retrieved May 10, 2012, from http://unctad.org/en/docs/ditc20082cer_en.pdf

United Nations (2010) *Creative Economy: A Feasible Development Option.* Retrieved May 10, 2012, http://www.intracen.org/uploadedFiles/intracenorg/Content/About_ITC/Where_are_we_working/Multi-country_programmes/CARIFORUM/ditctab20103_en.pdf

NOTES ON CONTRIBUTORS

Brent Allpress is the research coordinator in the discipline of architecture in the School of Architecture and Design at RMIT University. His teaching, postgraduate supervision and research focuses on contested and informing relationships between design practices and discourses, particularly in the context of emerging digital design technologies. He was the founding editor of the project-based design research journal, *Architectural Design Research*, an international first in the field.

Dr Robyn Barnacle is a Senior Research Fellow in the School of Graduate Research at RMIT University where she runs a seminar series and course on supervision of higher degrees by research pedagogy and practice. She also leads, and is otherwise involved in a variety of other research projects and quality improvement initiatives in the area of research education. Robyn's research interests focus on research education and pedagogy, research practice and knowledge generation, ontology, embodiment and learning. She has published widely in these areas and supervises higher degree by research candidates in a range of fields, such as education and design. Robyn holds a Ph.D. in philosophy from Monash University.

Dr Catherine Cole is Professor of Creative Writing and Deputy Dean, Faculty of Creative Arts, Wollongong University, NSW, Australia, and previously of RMIT. She has published numerous novels, non-fiction books, anthologies, poetry, short stories, essays and reviews. She is currently leading a research project on creative communities, which examines the role of UNESCO's Cities of Literature in conjunction with Melbourne, Iowa and Norwich. She has extensive experience of teaching in a number of Australian universities, and has been a Writing and Research Fellow at the University of East Anglia, UK, a resident of the Keesing Studio, Cité International des Arts in Paris, and an Asialink writer-in-residence in Hanoi, Vietnam. As a former member of the Committee of Management and the Executive of the Australian Society of Authors, Catherine has links with Australian writers, publishers and critics.

Dr Linda Daley is a senior lecturer in literary and communication studies in the School of Media and Communication, RMIT University where, until recently, she was a Director for Higher Degrees by Research. She supervises candidates undertaking research degrees by project and thesis. Her recent publications focus on the intersection of continental philosophy with literature, photography and film, and with a particular emphasis on invention, pedagogy and sense-making.

Dr Peter Downton is Professor of Design Research, RMIT University. His research includes the production of knowing and knowledge through designing and making, models in thinking, and people's relations with physical environments. Having begun in 1974, he currently supervises Ph.Ds. covering aspects of design in architecture, fashion, industrial design, interior design, landscape architecture, and other fascinating domains. His books include, *Design Research* (RMIT Press, 2003); *Studies in design research: Ten epistemological pavilions* (RMIT Press, 2004); and with Mark Burry, Michael Ostwald, and Andrea Mina (eds.) three books under the generic title *Homo Faber* (Archadia Press, 2007, 2008, 2010).

Dr Lesley Duxbury is the Deputy Head, Research and Innovation in the School of Art at RMIT University. She is an artist who uses print media to emulate and recreate experiences and perceptions of the natural environment, especially the atmosphere and its phenomena, and her current projects and publications address climate change action and mitigation. She has exhibited for over 25 years in Australia and the UK, with solo exhibitions in Melbourne, Perth and Sydney, and more than 50 selected group exhibitions in Australia, Korea, Austria and Hong Kong. She is the recipient of Australia Council Visual Arts Board funding (2011 and 1996) and has completed public art commissions in Perth (2004 and 1996). Her work is held in all major public collections in Australia.

Dr Pia Ednie-Brown, Associate Professor at RMIT University's School of Architecture and Design, is a design researcher, educator and theorist with a research practice, *onomatopoeia* (http://onomatopoeia.com.au/practice/). Based in the architecture programme and the Spatial Information Architecture Laboratory (SIAL), she has directed numerous creative research projects involving multiple disciplines across the arts and sciences. Her book *Plastic green: Designing for environmental transformation* (RMIT Press, 2009) offers an account of one of these projects. From 2009 to 2011 she led an ARC Discovery research project seeking to re-theorise innovation for contemporary design practices in terms of coupled ethical and aesthetic concerns therein.

Dr Elizabeth Grierson is Professor of Art and Philosophy at RMIT University, and for seven years Head of the School of Art (2005–2012). She is a research leader of RMIT Design Research Institute and Fellow of the Royal Society of Arts UK, and has a long experience of supervising and examining postgraduate degrees. She was a practising artist and theorist in NZ for over 20 years, Visiting Research Fellow at University of Brighton, UK (1997–98), and since 2001 executive editor, *ACCESS: Critical Perspectives on Communication, Cultural & Policy Studies*. Her books include, *Designing sound for health and wellbeing* (co-author, ASP, 2012), *A life in poetry: Nicholas Lyon Gresson* (ASP, 2011), *Doctoral journeys in art education* (ed., ASP, 2010), *Creative arts research* (co-author, Sense, 2009), *A skilled hand and cultivated mind* (co-author, RMIT Press), *Thinking through practice* (ed., RMIT Press, 2007), *The arts in education* (ed., 2003).

Dr Philip Samartzis lectures in the School of Art, RMIT University, and researches in the areas of sound art, acoustic ecology and spatial sound practices, with a specific focus on climate change and environmental sustainability. His Ph.D., *Surround sound in installation art*, examined the place of sound in contemporary art practice through a range of site determined sound art projects. In

2010 Philip was awarded fellowships by the Australia Council for the Arts, and the Australian Antarctic Division to document the effects of extreme climate and weather events on the human condition at Davis Station in Eastern Antarctica, and Macquarie Island.

Dr David Thomas was born in Belfast, N. Ireland. He studied art at the University of Melbourne, Monash University and RMIT University where he is an Associate Professor of Painting. His paintings, photopaintings and installations employ monochromes and painted reflective surfaces to address issues of the perception of time and space. His work is exhibited in Australia, New Zealand, Asia, USA and Europe, and is held in numerous private and public collections including the: National Gallery of Victoria; Australian National Gallery, Canberra; Art Bank; Museum of Modern Art at Heide; Chartwell Collection; Auckland Art Gallery, NZ; and Kunstmuseum Bonn, Germany. He also curates and writes on contemporary art.

Dr Laurene Vaughan is an Associate Professor in the School of Media and Communication at RMIT University and Research Leader in the RMIT Design Research Institute. She has melded a career of practising artist, designer and educator in Australia and internationally. Her current research is investigating the historical and cultural evolution of vernacular artefacts: their making and their meaning. Laurene supervises masters and Ph.D. students with a focus on research through practice. In 2011 she was awarded an Australian Learning and Teaching Council Citation Award for her sustained contribution to this teaching practice.

Kevin White is Associate Professor and Deputy Head, International Development, in the School of Art, RMIT University and has a major role in supervising doctoral candidates in the Asian region. He is a ceramic artist whose current research focuses on interpreting the porcelain traditions of Japan and the Japonisme seen in British ceramics of the nineteenth century. In 1978 he was awarded a prestigious Japanese Ministry of Education (Monbusho) scholarship for postgraduate research in ceramics, in Japan, studying under the late Professor Yutaka Kondo at Kyoto City University of Fine Art. He then worked for three years in the Kyoto studio of Mr Satoshi Sato, a member of the 'Sodeisha' group of contemporary ceramic artists. In 1985 he completed his Master of Arts at the Royal College of Art, London. His work is held in public and private collections.

ACKNOWLEDGEMENTS

Brent Allpress, Robyn Barnacle, Lesley Duxbury and Elizabeth Grierson acknowledge the School of Architecture and Design, the School of Art, and School of Graduate Research at RMIT University, Melbourne, for fostering the practice-based approach to supervising practices for postgraduate research, and for their support of this project. They thank all the contributing writers for their insightful, scholarly and thoroughly readable contributions to this book and acknowledge the many research candidates whose work informs the supervisory experiences of these scholars. Thanks also to Michael Peters, Emeritus Professor, University of Illinois, USA, and Professor at University of Waikato, NZ, for his Foreword and for accepting this book into his series, Educational Futures: Rethinking Theory and Practice, and to Peter de Liefde of Sense Publishers, Rotterdam, for publishing this collection. Grateful thanks also to Pia Ednie-Brown for granting permission to publish the image of her artwork, *The Turn On* for the book cover, to Virginia Grierson for her copy editing and indexing, and to Rupa Ramanathan for layout and final manuscript collation.

BRENT ALLPRESS, ROBYN BARNACLE, LESLEY DUXBURY
AND ELIZABETH GRIERSON

1. SUPERVISING PRACTICE-LED RESEARCH BY PROJECT IN ART, CREATIVE WRITING, ARCHITECTURE AND DESIGN

SITUATING THE MODEL

This book offers insights into the supervisory practices of academics at RMIT University, in Melbourne, Australia, whose postgraduate candidates are undertaking research by project in art, creative writing, architecture and design. Over the past two decades there has been a decisive shift internationally in the focus of these disciplines towards an emphasis on applied practice-led research undertaken through project-based investigations. This model offers an effective means to conduct research on knowledge both embodied in, and discovered through discipline-specific art, architecture and design practices.

The shift can be contextualised as a response by the academy to global changes in knowledge generation. Today productive and creative forms of applied and situated knowledge are being validated for their contribution to innovation economies with universities and industry working in close partnership to forge a practice-focused research and innovation nexus. There is an increasing demand for research qualifications at master's and doctorate levels for exemplary art, architecture and design practitioners who are taking on professional leadership roles that bridge the academy and industry.

The modes of research supervision addressed in this collection can be understood in the context of broad socio-cultural changes in which creative and applied knowledge is defining and leading cultural, scientific, technological and creative economies. In this global condition of entrepreneurial knowledge enhancement and exchange there is a conspicuous emergence of new forms of knowledge and new ways of enacting, generating and communicating. To meet these demands the academy is adapting and reconfiguring its emphasis, approaches and applications, with research being positioned at the leading edge of economic enterprises. In this scenario research must adapt its formations to understand new physical and economic conditions and predict future patterns. Practice and project-based research is in a strong position to work with and understand knowledge as a practical action opening the way for creative research as a predictor and enabler of change. Activating this potential for critical speculation and effective responses to contemporary concerns calls for new methodologies and approaches to the

B. Allpress, R. Barnacle, L. Duxbury and E. Grierson (Eds.), Supervising Practices for Postgraduate Research in Art, Architecture and Design, 1–14.
©*2012 Sense Publishers. All rights reserved.*

research task at hand, with a focus on applied practice through the materials themselves.

Urban concentrations of intellectual capital are becoming significant drivers of economic productivity in the current phase of globalisation. Australian media theorist, Ned Rossiter has argued that Richard Florida's (2002) analysis of this shift emphasises quantitative measurements of economic activity, but does not adequately account for the qualitative value of this economic activity (Rossiter, 2006). The research by project models of supervision being employed in art, creative writing, architecture and design disciplines offer strategies for supporting the qualitative improvement in practices across diverse fields of creative production.

This innovative approach to supervision was inaugurated in 1987 at the level of masters in the architecture discipline at RMIT with the introduction of a research by project model of postgraduate candidacy. This was offered as an alternative to the orthodox model of research by written thesis. Subsequently the model has been adapted and adopted by all of the design disciplines across the university at both the master's and doctorate levels. Also it has been taken up selectively by other key international institutions such as the Bartlett School of Architecture at University College London in the UK, following the early involvement of academics from that institution as external examiners. There is a parallel lineage at RMIT of distinctive approaches to the supervision of postgraduate research by project in fine art and other creative fields such as creative writing. These diverse disciplinary approaches to supervision share common characteristics that can be contrasted with orthodox models of traditional thesis supervision.

Design researcher, Peter Downton argues that creative arts and design research by, and through projects involves methodologies and practices that are very different from more traditional postgraduate research models, which can be characterised as technical and scientific research for, and historical or critical research about art, architecture and design practice (Downton, 2003, 2009). Until recently, university regulations for the doctorate degree across Australasia have focused primarily on established science and humanities models of research. The shift to research by project supervision at RMIT recognises and reasserts the value of discipline-specific creative practices as distinct and effective modes of knowledge production. The strategies employed to supervise project-based methodologies and approaches support research outcomes relevant to these specific fields of practice that could not be achieved readily by other means.

In these models of Ph.D. supervision the research is undertaken primarily within and through a series of design projects or creative works. This embodied research is framed selectively through a written exegesis of around 40,000 words and relevant visual or other documentation and presented through a culminating exhibition and examination by a panel of experts in the field. Examinations in the design discipline also include an extended verbal defence by the candidate. This mode of research is of comparable scope to a traditional thesis and fulfils equivalent responsibilities to substantiate and make legible the candidate's contribution to knowledge. This outcome is achieved through discipline-specific practices relevant to the field.

AIMS AND LITERATURE

The aim of this book is to bring together supervisors from very different academic and disciplinary cultures of art, creative writing, architecture and design within the one institution to frame and open up dialogue and debate around these emerging modes of postgraduate research and supervisory practice. By so doing it is positioning forms of knowledge generation that have application in a wide range of fields and applied situations in global innovation economies.

Over the past two decades a collective body of institutional knowledge has accrued at RMIT around the implementation of a range of project-based research supervision models. This book seeks to capture, frame and make these approaches and insights available to broader academic communities that are undertaking or seeking to establish related models of such postgraduate research supervision.

While many supervisory concerns and responsibilities are shared across the different modes of postgraduate research by thesis and by project, this book seeks to foreground, frame and debate a number of particular issues, obstacles and opportunities raised through research by project supervision in the creative disciplines. Fostering and extending iterative cycles of production and reflection within a practice-led research context requires a clear sense of how project investigations may be framed and staged most effectively and what methodologies may be employed to achieve the best results in this process. Substantiating research primarily against qualitative criteria requires methodologies that are very different from many traditional science and humanities models of postgraduate investigation.

Increasingly, universities are requiring supervisors of doctoral degrees to demonstrate their suitability for the role by completing professional development programmes and courses. In the USA, Canada, New Zealand, Australia and UK, for example, postgraduate teaching and learning qualifications may include modules on supervisory practice. At present, however, there is surprisingly little in print on this topic. Numerous volumes exist on traditional thesis research methods and practice and there are also a number of books written specifically for these research degree candidates. There is little literature, however, that is written by supervisors about their supervision practice in the art, creative writing, architecture and design disciplines.

The Routledge doctoral supervisor's companion: Supporting effective research in education and the social sciences (Walker & Thompson, 2010) addresses supervisory practice but its disciplinary focus is restricted to education and social sciences. *Supervising doctorates downunder: Keys to effective supervision in Australia and New Zealand* (Denholm, Carey & Evans, 2007) provides a useful resource to supervisors by addressing a broad range of issues from candidate selection through to thesis examination. However, while some of the issues that it addresses are generic and of relevance to all supervisors, such as issues of care, its focus is the traditional written thesis doctorate. *Eleven practices of effective postgraduate research supervisors* (James & Baldwin, 2006), *The good supervisor: Supervising postgraduate and undergraduate research for doctoral theses and dissertations* (Wisker, 2004) and *Supervising the doctorate: A guide to success* (Delamont, Atkinson & Parry, 2004) are books that provide a useful general guide to effective supervisory practice of candidates undertaking a written thesis but do not address the unique issues facing supervisors of creative practice.

There is a range of articles on research supervision in journals such as *Studies in Higher Education* and *Higher Education Research & Development*, as well as specialist disciplinary journals. While there are some articles addressing supervisory practice in art and design, they are few and are scattered throughout a number of journals. The advantage of this book is that it brings together the collective wisdom of experienced creative practice supervisors within one collection.

In deciding to undertake this project, as editors we sought to position this book on postgraduate supervision, with its many faces and approaches, challenges and potentials, alongside existing literature in order to situate a point of difference and add to current dialogue and discourses. While there is a growing body of literature on creative and project-based research, we found little that specifically addressed supervision practice itself as a pedagogical process. Hence the focus of our approach in this collection became clear. The accounts provide a rich source of knowledge on specific supervisory practices that is complementary to other literature in the more general fields of creative and design research. For example it sits well alongside *Creative arts research: Narratives of methodologies and practices* (Grierson & Brearley, 2009), which presents a range of methodologies and approaches for research projects in creative fields. Through differing accounts of creative practice-led projects and the challenges presented by a range of methodologies, Grierson and Brearley shed new light on issues of research in the academy to bring designers, artists, performers, writers and philosophers into conversation with one another. The various accounts also raise important epistemological and ontological questions about doing research and being a creative practitioner researcher in these fields.

Other relevant books offering discourse on this emerging research field include, *Practice as research: Context, method, knowledge* (Barrett & Bolt, 2007), which provides supportive material for postgraduate students undertaking studio-based research in art, film and video, creative writing and dance. It gives an account of practice-led models of enquiry, the role of theory in creative research, and the relationship between processes of enquiry and modes of exegesis.

Design research (Downton, 2003) gives a thorough discussion of design as a model for knowledge production, drawing on Peter Downton's twenty years of experience as the coordinator of the RMIT School of Architecture and Design research methods course for postgraduate students. Downton is highly critical of the *design methods* approach that was dominant in the 1970s involving design science-based research *for* design rather than *through* design. This earlier reductive model imposed a linear and rule-based set of prescriptions on design practice and privileged quantitative and technical criteria. Downton's approach to design research methods focuses on qualitative, iterative and reflective practices. He gives a clear account of designerly knowing and discovery as a set of distinctive research practices. His chapter in this present book further extends these discussions by providing an account of his own supervisory practices across an interdisciplinary community of design researchers.

Leon van Schaik founded the design research by project model, with Downton, at RMIT in 1987. van Schaik continues to lead the supervision of a stream of candidates, who are exemplary and acclaimed practitioners in architecture and design. They are invited back into the academy to reflect on, and extend their embodied practices within a research by project degree framework. He places a strong emphasis on structures and practices that build innovative communities of practice and has documented and disseminated this model through a series of publications (van Schaik, 1993, 1995, 2000, 2003; van Schaik & Spooner, 2010), and related books that include *Mastering architecture: Becoming a creative innovator in practice* (van Schaik, 2004) and *Architecture and design, by practice by invitation, design practice research at RMIT* (van Schaik & Johnson, 2011).

Paul Carter and van Schaik have co-supervised a cohort of postgraduate architecture and design candidates whose research bridges between public and installation art, and architectural design practices. Carter's book, *Material thinking: The theory and practice of creative research* (Carter, 2004) outlines a model of interdisciplinary and collaborative research practice that forges productive relationships between critical writing, cultural inscription, and material and spatial production. *Studies in Material Thinking* is an academic journal for artists, designers and writers with an emphasis on the materiality and the poetics of creative research, informed in part by Carter's model (Rosenberg & Fairfax, 2008). The journal publishes discourse on invention, design, creative practice and research methodology, with a particular emphasis on innovations in curricula for research practice. Brent Allpress and Michael Ostwald founded and edited the initial three volumes of the first international, refereed, project-based, design research journal, *Architectural Design Research* (Allpress & Ostwald, 2005, 2007, 2008), which adapted the RMIT model of project-based research with accompanying exegesis as an alternative to the traditional written journal article format. Two further book series, *Design research,* through RMIT Publishing in Melbourne, and *Design research in architecture* through Ashgate in the UK, adopt aspects of this approach to the documentation of project-based, design research.

Other publications on Ph.D. by project supervision and practice-based education that include chapters by editors and writers in this present collection, are D. Boud and A. Lee, *Changing practices in doctoral education* (2009), with a chapter on project-based architectural design research by Brent Allpress and Robyn Barnacle, and Joy Higgs' edited collection, *Education for future practice* (2010), in which Allpress and Barnacle have a chapter addressing the educational practices of project-based, research-led teaching focusing a case study on the RMIT School of Architecture and Design. Another writer in this present collection, Lesley Duxbury has published on creative arts-based research in *ACCESS: Critical Perspectives on Communications, Cultural & Policy Studies* (Duxbury, 2011).

THEMES AND APPROACHES

For candidates re-entering the academy, often from well-established professional contexts, the process of becoming a beginner in research terms can be challenging. Enhanced research capabilities that extend and transform a candidate's practices can enable different models of professional leadership. This presents an opportunity to foster innovative communities of practice across the academy and industry that extend beyond any individual candidacy. Also creative practice and design-based modes of research can contribute potentially to the vibrancy of a practice community by enhancing collaborative ways of working.

For many candidates the possibilities of extending beyond the boundaries of solo practice can be challenging if not daunting, especially in a field such as fine art with its inherited lineage of artist as sole creative practitioner. Laurene Vaughan's chapter in this collection addresses this challenge by canvassing ways of overcoming the loneliness of being a solo researcher. In consideration is the overcoming of possible feelings of isolation that can arise in a sole supervisor-candidate relationship. Even if meetings occur at regular intervals both supervisor and candidate can feel divorced from the business of knowledge generation at the challenging interface of scholarly and creative ideas. These challenges and more are discussed in this book with pertinent examples and case studies of pedagogical innovations to overcome such isolating practices. Thus we start to see that supervisory practices involve far more than content knowledge. As we enter into the educational contract with candidates there is a responsibility to attend to ways of thinking, knowing, making, relating and being through the process of undertaking research.

Understanding or even recognising these sometimes subtle concerns or anxieties can be challenging when one is new to the business of being a supervisor. There needs to be recognition of the different ways people learn and discover through research, and a willingness to allow new ideas to take shape in their own way and time. Challenges can exist for beginning supervisors whose role it is to guide and advise the candidate, encourage new findings, recognise and share in the risk-taking and excitement of discovery as little by little they witness the mapping of new terrain and the creation and communication of new knowledge.

This book focuses primarily on the practices of supervisors who are working with fine art, creative writing, architecture and design candidates to support and open up the potential for thinking and enquiry through practice. It will be particularly relevant for academics seeking to improve their own supervisory practices informed by the experiences of colleagues in the same and similar fields. The collection is organised around the thematic focus on "practices of" supervision to illuminate key approaches to supervision while emphasising the practice-led focus of both the postgraduate research by project model and the contributors' supervisory insights. There is something very active here. As Elizabeth Grierson points out in her chapter, "*Practice* is identified as action, from Greek, *praktikē*, *practical work*, from *prattein, to do, to act*". Thus the focus of the book is on practical action with supervisory experiences presented as inventories or enactments of practice in the field of creative and design-based research.

The notion of "practices of" also implies that such practices are multiple, highlighting that experienced supervisors adopt a range of supervisory strategies and approaches in what they do. Moreover, by showcasing a range of supervisory practices the collection allows readers to benefit from multiple views and insights. To speak of fine art, creative writing, architecture and design practice is not to proscribe confined fields of scholarship. Each of these arenas of research is multifaceted and each comes with rich and varied histories and configurations that reveal their means of production as they materialise their new forms of knowledge.

THE CHAPTERS

Chapters have been organised to emphasise the range of stories that can be told about supervisory practices, from an integrative, whole of candidature perspective through to the ways in which supervisors address particular issues, such as writing, ethics approval processes, exhibitions, and activating theory and language as a creative practice. The contributors to this book are experienced supervisors of creative and practice-led research at RMIT who have engaged in scholarly reflection on selective aspects of their supervisory practices with the aim of providing insight to others regarding what they do, and how and why they do it. Specific fields of practice include contemporary art, architecture, creative writing and communication design. The writers document and discuss a range of different supervisory strategies, reflecting the diversity of disciplinary concerns and approaches that have been established through a sustained engagement with this emerging mode of postgraduate research pedagogy.

Following this chapter by the four editors situating the key aims, themes and approaches, chapters are arranged by sequences of thematic affinities. The first group of chapters from Lesley Duxbury, Brent Allpress, Catherine Cole and Philip Samartzis offers situating accounts of core supervisory practices in fine art, architecture, and creative writing, where the models of creative practice-led and project-based research elicit specific supervisory responses and engagements. The second sequence of chapters by Elizabeth Grierson, Robyn Barnacle, Linda Daley and Pia Ednie-Brown examines a number of selective thematic concerns involving project-based supervision. They acknowledge the challenges that can exist in these academic fields of research, such as activating language as a creative practice, bringing together theory and practice in generative ways, supervising experienced professionals who must negotiate the state of being beginners in research terms, supervising outside one's customary field of scholarship, and navigating requirements for ethics clearance and other institutional demands. The last four chapters by Peter Downton, Laurene Vaughan, David Thomas and Kevin White give accounts of their own particular embodied experiences of supervising creative and design research candidates as an integrative set of practices. This group includes narratives on particular supervisory histories and traits, communities of enquiry, supervision as a pedagogical practice, and supervising doctorates by distance in Asian locations. The rich cartography of practice presented by these twelve writers draws from decades of accumulated experiences of supervising postgraduate programmes in art, creative writing, architecture and design. Each of the writers speaks through the lived academic experiences of working in the academy while also being practitioner researchers themselves, as professional artists, writers, architects and designers.

The first group of chapters starts with Lesley Duxbury's 'Opening the door: Portals to good supervision of creative practice-led research'. Duxbury draws upon her personal experience of being supervised for her own practice-led Ph.D. during the early years of the introduction of doctoral degrees in Australia to determine what might constitute good supervision. Her first research supervision, a Master of Arts candidate, affords an entrée for her to tease out what was valuable and what was not as far as supervision is concerned, and an opportunity for reflection on processes of supervision and personal relationships to candidates. She acknowledges that there is not a one-size-fits-all approach to supervision and that often it falls somewhere between teaching and mentoring, between being 'hands-on' and 'hands-off' and constitutes a serious on-going relationship, during which it is essential that supervisor and candidate like and respect each other.

Brent Allpress, in Chapter Three, 'Pedagogical practices for supervising project-based research in architecture and design' takes a complementary approach to the first person accounts of individual supervision models outlined by many of the other contributors. Allpress situates the diversity of supervisory practices being employed within the RMIT School of Architecture and Design that have consolidated around particular research clusters with distinctive methodological practices and concerns. He outlines the infrastructural frameworks and supervisory procedures and practices that foster a dynamic and emergent research community. He addresses a range of obstacles and opportunities that are specific to the practice-based research by project model, particularly around strategies for framing, making legible and disseminating the research embodied within and across a series of project investigations. In presenting this account Allpress also canvasses the historical growth of this research supervision model and its trajectories into future practice with its presence in the European Union and Asia. In many ways, this chapter sets the scene for the model of design project-based research that other writers address and it provides a basis for understanding why design practice deserves, indeed demands, a model of supervision that is appropriate for its particular forms of knowledge generation.

In Chapter Four, 'Good supervision: The creative work in process. Effective and engaged postgraduate supervision in creative writing', Catherine Cole focuses on supervising postgraduate candidates in creative writing. She commences by positioning the emergence of creative writing programmes in Australia in the early 1970s and canvasses their growth and specific formations. She considers the often challenging relationship between a writer/student and writer/academic and examines the specific expectations for the supervisory relationship in postgraduate creative writing degrees, questioning the extent to which the supervisor and candidate may be able to enhance the creative experience of one another. She accounts for different perspectives and approaches to these relationships from a range of writers thus situating her discussion within a broader discourse. Through her writing she demonstrates that there may well be untapped potential for a more reflexive and reciprocal academic interchange in and through this specific form of creative practice-led research programme. She leaves the reader with a positive reflection on the academy's potential for enhancing creative communities and how such dialogues about creativity and research continue to reshape the academy's understanding of itself.

The final chapter in this group, Chapter Five, is by Philip Samartzis, 'Articulating sound in a synthesised material space', which places the exhibition of the doctorate research in a central role. Sound art comes with its own set of problems regarding the presentation of an exhibition in relation to candidates who undertake a Ph.D. in this discipline and who may articulate their projects through installations, performances or recordings. In this chapter, Samartzis considers the role of the supervisor regarding the examination process to create a compelling experience for the examiner and provide an encounter with new knowledge impossible to produce in any other way. Through an explication of the contemporary art gallery he outlines the positives and negatives for sound art researchers and the ways in which their projects need to take special account of the site for their examination.

The next group starts with Elizabeth Grierson in Chapter Six, 'A complex terrain: Putting theory and practice to work as a generative praxis'. Her stated philosophical project is to consider the relationship of theory and practice in the supervisory contract with candidates undertaking research degrees in art and design or other creative fields. Working through language as a creative practice she takes as her starting point the Greek identification of *praxis* as a generative way of acting or doing, from the Greek origin of *practice*, thus positioning the practical side of a field of study as the focus of attention. She makes a claim that within this practical knowledge language is a creative practice and art practice is a creative text. Thus she is interested in the way supervisors can activate the interrelations between theory and practice as a way of performing intertextually in a generative mode as the research seeks new pathways and discoveries. Arguing against a naturalistic and assumed or self-evident account of practice and creativity, she seeks to extend our understanding of what *praktikē* might mean when text and art come together in the candidate's project and how the supervisor might generate a creative interplay between the two. She draws from a range of philosophical writers to address how the candidate situates voice, questions of methodologies, critical pedagogies and the call for a political will, and applies these analyses to the task of supervision in the creative fields.

In Chapter Seven, Robyn Barnacle explores a set of predicaments unique to what she calls the "practitioner-researcher" coalescing around the problem of authority. Her chapter, 'Becoming a practitioner-researcher-writer' explores issues intrinsic to the situation of the practitioner-researcher straddling, as they do, the academy on the one hand and a professional practice context on the other. Barnacle argues that the problem of authorisation is particularly active in the context of scholarly or research writing where it can manifest, for example, in extreme responses to the literature or precedent, such as either deferring too much to external sources of validation or resisting them entirely. Another way that it can manifest is resistance to the risk involved in research by refusing to relinquish the role of expert professional and being a beginner in research terms. Barnacle also addresses the question of writing as a research practice with the positioning of writing as an embodied practice to be engaged from the very beginning of the candidature. Inhering within these issues, according to Barnacle, is the struggle to come to terms with what being a practitioner-researcher might mean, both individually and professionally. Her chapter sheds light on the nature of these issues and what supervisors can do to address them.

In Chapter Eight, 'Pedagogies of invention', Linda Daley explores the experience of supervising across paradigms that arise when supervising candidates outside one's own field, an expertise many supervisors acquire often by accident. For academics working in a constantly and rapidly changing sector where disciplinary mergers and institutional restructures occur with increasing frequency, such experiences are not uncommon and necessitate agility by academics toward supervision. By giving emphasis to this type of supervisory experience, Daley makes a claim for a certain kind of pedagogy within supervision, which treats supervision as a set of relations or a set of relays of knowing and unknowing held between supervisor and candidate of a research project. This process does not restrict itself to the idea of the skilled, master-practitioner in the role of supervising the practitioner-candidate. Moreover, it is an approach that foregrounds the relation between knowing and making in the candidature, with the implication that a supervisor without a practice-based background can offer highly productive and successful supervision.

Pia Ednie-Brown in Chapter Nine, 'Supervising emergence: Adapting ethics approval frameworks toward research by creative project', examines challenges of the ethics approval process for iterative cycles of speculative, project-based, design research activity. Her chapter offers three examples of candidates who have engaged with the ethics approval process using each story to highlight a different issue, or problem that has been faced. These stories provide a set of tangible examples through which to address what Ednie-Brown regards as the main problem in the tension between university ethics approval processes and research by creative project: that the mode of research enquiry in question pertains to a relatively new paradigm of emergent practices that can be understood in terms of broad socio-cultural changes, and valued in terms of an ethical framework demanded by those broad changes. Ethics approval processes assume that research methodologies are determined in advance of an investigation, whereas creative and speculative research often involves methodologies that emerge out of the practice of doing the research. Ednie-Brown argues that the paradigmatic shift towards emergent models of research practice has not yet been absorbed or adequately accommodated by ethics approval processes. Her chapter concludes by offering suggestions as to what both candidates and their supervisors can do to deal with this issue.

The final group of chapters begins with Peter Downton in Chapter Ten. 'Beside myself: Scrutinising decades of supervising designers' focuses on the processual nature of design research supervision, or what a supervisor does to assist in the production of design knowledge and to help shape the form and presentation of that knowledge. Downton argues that the process of design research supervision cannot be abstracted and bottled as a distilled essence, in that there is no single model for how supervisors should assist candidates in the production of knowledge. According to Downton, people undertaking doctorates have differing needs and, given the iterative and cyclical nature of design research undertaken through a series of projects, these may alter significantly and grow across the course of their candidature. Downton shows how patterns of need become more visible the longer one supervises, such that a supervisor's perception of, and responsive reaction to differing needs becomes a key factor in informing the nature of their supervisory practice.

David Thomas presents his experiences of supervising fine art projects in Chapter Eleven, 'How to work better: supervising for Ph.D. exhibition' by bringing into the supervisory relationship the model of the composite and duration, which has long held interest for him as a research and teaching approach. He discusses the doctoral project in fine art through its exhibition and supervision by relating these to the heterogeneous nature of a composite in the fine art context. To do this Thomas draws from the writings of Henri Bergson as an approach to understanding the temporal process of the conditions of art making, research practice, and supervision, all of which to one extent or another are ways of seeking meaning in the complicated realities and contingencies of life as a fluid state of existence. Working with the notion of the composite, the multiple, Thomas examines the work of filmmaker, Jacques Tati to consider timing and complexity relating these to supervision practice, and Henri Bergson on duration and the composite with application to supervisory and fine art practices. He then presents case studies of his own supervisor-candidate relationships and projects in fine art, practice-led research.

Laurene Vaughan in Chapter Twelve, 'Designing a practice and pedagogy of postgraduate supervision' offers an account of the foundation and context for supervision practices. The chapter starts with a discussion of her interest in the practices of walking as a framework of experiential knowing, and relates this to supervising a community of scholars as a pedagogical process. Thus Vaughan argues that supervision is a pedagogic practice and she gives an account of some of the systems and structures she uses to enact that practice. The discussion comes from the first person narrative approach to supervision and makes a case for communities of enquiry as a way of progressing the candidates' learning through their research discoveries. She covers areas such as how to overcome the loneliness or isolation of postgraduate research, working within frameworks of expertise, the challenges of institutional processes such as ethics clearance, and designing a practice for postgraduate learning and pedagogy. Throughout the discussion

Vaughan positions herself and her way of thinking as a design practitioner for whom transdisciplinary practices and design experiences foster a rich and fruitful dialogue for both supervisors and candidates.

Chapter Thirteen, the final chapter in the collection comes from Kevin White. 'The flying doctorate: Doctoral supervision by distance in Hong Kong' takes the reader on a journey both physical and metaphorical. He writes from his experiences of distance supervisory practice with fine art doctorate candidates in Asian locations. There are many challenges here. In presenting his experiences of distance education, White addresses what distance means within the context of a cross-cultural, educational experience, and how this distance is both navigated and negotiated by candidate and supervisor. Following his metaphor he considers the role of supervisor and candidate when packing for the journey; facing border controls and customs; the flight itself with in-flight entertainment; encountering 'turbulence' including translocation of meanings in working with complex theoretical and conceptual issues with candidates for whom English is a second language; arrival at the destination after a long-haul flight; and then the jetlag and the questions of what to do next. This chapter brings together the long experience of the writer in his field of postgraduate supervision in off-shore locations, and his understanding that postgraduate supervisors have a significant role and responsibility in issues that are often to do with identity and cultural change, as he leaves the reader with a hopeful message while looking up at the night sky at the end of a long journey.

This is a fitting end to the book. The chapters cover a rich terrain and offer a range of approaches to questions of supervision in the creative fields of postgraduate research, acknowledging the very real challenges, even problems that academics can face in this burgeoning field of knowledge generation. The twelve contributors to this book are senior academics with significant supervisory and research experience. They present through their writings a multi-faceted yet cohesive picture of the diverse models of pedagogy that can enhance creative ways of working, thinking and being. Together, they present a kind of academic community united by their dedication to the educational cause of creative, practice-led research by project.

CONCLUDING THOUGHTS

Supervising Practices for Postgraduate Research in Art, Architecture and Design is a book intended for readers seeking insight into supervisory practice within these fields of research. It meets this aim and more. Through considerations, investigations and analyses of the challenges posed by supervising in these specific fields of postgraduate research, there is a broadening and deepening of the concept of *practice*. Project-based research offers a framework for candidates to reflect on, situate, improve, and innovate their practices in order to make relevant and significant contributions to knowledge within their disciplinary community that can be of qualitative benefit to culture, society and the broader community.

As we undertake this work we can be reminded that the future is only as good as what we make of the present, and that our contributions to the stakes of knowledge are a very real legacy for future generations. At the end of her chapter in this collection, Linda Daley leaves us with a reflective yet challenging thought when she writes, "Practitioner research is not the only genre of knowledge production that has a stake in this matter, however, it is the very mode by which the stakes can be decisively shown and presented". It is here that our challenge really lies. We need to be decisive, to speak out and disseminate our experiences and ways of knowing; we need to enact leadership in this pedagogical field if *praktikē* is to be understood in the models and methodologies as presented here.

Practitioner researchers and those who supervise them to doctorate levels have an opportunity to mark and measure the terrain, to bring to the fore the matters that matter, to bear witness and not be silent when changes must be made and new ways of enacting may be found. This book ultimately sets out to capture reflections on supervisory practices through which affective, creative and practical knowledge can be enhanced and transformed, offering models for supporting the emergence of generative practices and of knowledge yet to come.

REFERENCES

Allpress, B., & Barnacle, R. (2009). Projecting the Ph.D.: Architectural design research by and through projects. In Boud, D., & Lee, A. (Eds.) *Changing practices in doctoral education* (pp. 157–170). London: Routledge.

Allpress, B., & Barnacle, R. (2010). Practice-based education: Engaging with emergent practices in architecture through research-led teaching by project. In Joy Higgs et al., (Eds.) *Education for future practice* (pp. 177–190). Rotterdam: Sense Publishers.

Allpress, B., & Ostwald, M. (Eds.) (2005). *Architectural design research: Project-based design research and discourse on design, 1*(1). Retrieved November 12, 2011, from http://issuu.com/brentallpress/docs/adr_vol1_1

Allpress, B., & Ostwald, M. (Eds.) (2007). *Architectural design research: Project-based design research and discourse on design, 2*(1). Retrieved November 12, 2011, from http://issuu.com/brentallpress/docs/adr_vol2_1

Allpress, B., & Ostwald, M. (Eds.) (2008). *Architectural design research: Project-based design research and discourse on design, 3*(1). Retrieved November 12, 2011, from http://issuu.com/brentallpress/docs/adr3_vol3_1

Barrett, E., & Bolt, B (Eds.) (2007). *Practice as research: Context, method, knowledge*. London: I. B. Tauris.

Carter, P. (2004). *Material thinking: The theory and practice of creative research*. Melbourne: Melbourne University Publishing.

Delamont, S., Atkinson, P., & Parry, O. (2004). *Supervising the doctorate: A guide to success*. New York: Open University Press.

Denholm, C., & Evans, T. (Eds.) (2007). *Supervising doctorates downunder: Keys to effective supervision in Australia and New Zealand*. Camberwell, Australia: ACER Press.

Downton, P. (2003). *Design research*. Melbourne: RMIT University Press.

Downton, P. (2009). Ways of constructing: Epistemic, temporal and productive aspects of design research. In E. M. Grierson, & L. Brearley et al., *Creative arts research: Narratives of methodologies and practices* (pp. 111–128). Rotterdam: Sense Publishers.

Duxbury, L. (2011). Picture this: Transforming artworks into exegetical texts to create new insights. *ACCESS: Critical Perspectives on Communication, Cultural & Policy Studies, 30*(2), 35–43.

Florida, R. (2002). *The rise of the creative class: And how it's transforming work, leisure, community, and everyday life*. New York: Basic Books.

Grierson, E. M., & Brearley, L. (2009). *Creative arts research: Narratives of methodologies and practices*. Rotterdam: Sense Publishers.

James, R., & Baldwin, G., (2006). *Eleven practices of effective postgraduate research supervisors*. Parkville, Melbourne: Centre for the Study of Higher Education and the School of Graduate Studies, University of Melbourne.

Rosenberg, T. E., & Fairfax, D. (Eds.) (2008). *Studies in Material Thinking, 1*(2). Retrieved March 6, 2012, from http://www.materialthinking.org/volumes/volume-012

Rossiter, N. (2006). *Organized networks: Media theory, creative labour, new institutions*. Rotterdam: NAi Publications.

van Schaik, L. (Ed.) (1993). *Fin de siècle and the twenty first century: Architectures of Melbourne*. Melbourne: RMIT School of Architecture and Design.

van Schaik, L. (Ed.) (1995). *Transfiguring the ordinary: RMIT Masters of Architecture by project*. Melbourne: 38 South Publications.

van Schaik, L. (Ed.) (2000). *Interstitial modernism*. Melbourne: RMIT Press.

van Schaik, L. (Ed.) (2003). *The practice of practice: Research in the medium of design*. Melbourne: RMIT Press.

van Schaik, L. (2004). *Mastering architecture: Becoming a creative innovator in practice*. London: Wiley.

van Schaik, L., & Johnson, A. (2011). *Architecture and design, by practice by invitation, design practice research at RMIT*. Melbourne: onepointsixone.

van Schaik, L., & Spooner, M. (Eds.) (2010). *The practice of practice 2: Research in the medium of design*. Melbourne: onepointsixone.

Walker, M., & Thompson, P. (2010). *The Routledge doctoral supervisor's companion: Supporting effective research in education and the social sciences*. Milton Park, UK & New York: Routledge.

Wisker, G. (2004). *The good supervisor: Supervising postgraduate and undergraduate research for doctoral theses and dissertations*. New York: Palgrave Macmillan.

LESLEY DUXBURY

2. OPENING THE DOOR

Portals to Good Supervision of Creative Practice-led Research

INTRODUCTION

In 1998 I successfully supervised my first research student to completion, a Master of Arts (Fine Art) through a creative project, and commenced a creative doctorate in the same department in which I was employed as a lecturer. Although practice-led masters had been offered for several years, Ph.Ds. through practice-led research were in their infancy in Australia at that time and there was limited experience of supervising them. Supervisors would be colleagues and few had qualifications commensurate with the programmes being undertaken by the candidates they supervised. These early experiences of supervising and observing the progress of the nascent practice-led Ph.D. programme have influenced and guided my role as a supervisor of practice-led research degrees.

TWO WAYS OF GETTING IT WRONG

I inherited my first practice-led research candidate from the lecturer I had replaced in the department where I had commenced employment. The candidate was more than half way through her Master of Arts (Fine Art) by creative project and was undertaking a topic I knew little about; in fact it could not have been further from my own evolving research interests although I was familiar with the artistic medium of her research, as it was my own specialisation. When I completed a Master of Arts through practice-led research five years previously, not only had I expanded the ways I intellectualised my subject, but also I had developed the ways of utilising my mediums. This led to some extraordinary and innovative results. However it appeared to me that my MA candidate, who was illustrating particular feminist theories, was sticking with her well-established ways of producing images. To my way of thinking, her images and theory did not sit easily together although her previous supervisor had allowed her to progress thus far in this manner. In my meetings with her over the ensuing months I tried to encourage her to think in different ways about articulating her ideas and to avoid direct illustration. However, as her examination loomed I was concerned firstly about her progress and then became more directive by suggesting possible resolutions to ideas and images. She strove hard to complete her research project and presented for examination an experimental exhibition of work, which included installation and performance, and she successfully achieved her MA degree. However soon

B. Allpress, R. Barnacle, L. Duxbury and E. Grierson (Eds.), Supervising Practices for Postgraduate Research in Art, Architecture and Design, 15–24.
©2012 Sense Publishers. All rights reserved.

after receiving her award she reverted to her pre-MA practices. Even today when occasionally I see her work I notice that it has changed little since she commenced her degree. During our short period together she appeared to follow my suggestions obediently, but ultimately these recommendations were not useful in her subsequent professional role as an exhibiting artist. On reflection, my supervision of her had been too didactic and directional, and did not take into account her future needs.

In the early years of the introduction of creative practice-led Ph.Ds., during the late 1990s in Australia, there were situations where supervisors failed to share the research interests of their candidates, provided little input, and thus exacerbated the isolation of those candidates. At this time it was not the norm for artist-academics in universities to hold a doctorate although their art history colleagues in the same departments were often doctorate qualified. In these early years at RMIT University the role of senior supervisor fell predominantly to the Ph.D. qualified art history lecturer who had little expertise in the practical focus of their candidate. A senior staff member of the same department, who was an artist, usually supported the senior supervisor, although often the artistic concerns of the second supervisor did not correspond with that of their candidate. Likeminded artist-academics undertaking a Ph.D. tended to form loose, support groups to celebrate research discoveries and share information, however this was no substitute for a good supervisor. Early artist-academics as research candidates often missed out on critical feedback and potentially inspirational conversations, which should have been central to their experience as a research candidate. My own experience of being supervised for a practice-led Ph.D. was as the one described above and, although I successfully completed my doctorate, this model of supervision was not the one I wished to emulate when I subsequently became a supervisor of doctoral candidates.

Since 1998, I have supervised 15 MA (Fine Art) and eight doctoral (both Ph.D. and professional doctorate) research students to completion. They have come from a wide variety of backgrounds and experiences: some directly from undergraduate studies with no experience other than that of a student, and others from the art profession as extremely successful local and international artists, and also colleagues and lecturers from other universities. Happily, since graduating with their research degrees the majority of them have become successful in their careers as practitioners and/or academics.

Neither of the accounts I have described above provide a good example for the supervision of creative doctorates. However each presents an opportunity for reflection and reassessment of the needs and requirements of both the supervisor and the research candidate of creative, practice-led projects.

WHAT TO DO, WHAT TO DO

...supervision is a complex process that requires both situational awareness and a flexible posture... (Grant, 1999, p. 1).

While there may be many models of research supervision that are adopted or that change over time in differing circumstances, the personality traits of any given supervisor are constants in all interactions with research candidates. The characteristics of the supervisor may affect "the essentially rational and transparent engagement between autonomous individuals" (Delany, 2005, p. 5) that research supervision is generally understood to be. In retrospect, the expectations I had of my first Master of Arts candidate were based solely on my own experience of undertaking this degree, and I wanted her to exhibit similar enthusiasm and attain extraordinary achievements through rigorous practice and experimentation. However my candidate, who had acquired a certain amount of success as an exhibiting artist prior to embarking on a Master of Arts, appeared to me to be afraid of changing her style and work practices, perhaps fearing rejection from galleries and her buying public. Becoming her supervisor late into her programme meant that these issues had not been addressed earlier and I could deal only with my concern for her seeming lack of progress by prescribing ways of working that related to my own experiences and work practices. This was certainly an example of a mismatch between the expectations of candidate and those of the supervisor.

According to Joram ten Brink, "You're not there to teach them how to do the research other than critically look at their research and offer them positions to consider" (2008, n.p.n). Brink recommends that the supervisor's main role is to give the candidate confidence to own her research, lead it, ask the questions and look for the answers from people other than the supervisor. He advises that the supervisor is there to encourage the candidate to go out and present their research as papers and exhibitions, the approach being that the candidate drives the process. While this appears to be the course for a number of candidates, especially those with a little more independence, the majority of research candidates expect a great deal more from their supervisors, and usually considerably more than the instilling of confidence and a hands-off approach.

Of the research candidates I have supervised to completion, the majority have been those who have progressed from undergraduate bachelor degrees to masters and doctoral studies, followed by artists returning to study for a variety of reasons. Within these two diverse groups of candidates there are requirements for quite different approaches to supervision. If I add to this the students who are academics from other tertiary institutions upgrading their qualifications for professional reasons, local colleagues doing the same, and a scattering of international academics and artists, it is obvious that a one-size-fits-all approach to supervision is out of the question. In my interactions with such a diverse range of personalities, abilities and dispositions I may find myself in one or more of a number of roles, such as a director, facilitator, advisor, teacher, critic, supporter, collaborator, friend or mentor, who may be approachable and friendly, supportive with a positive attitude, open-minded, organised and stimulating; the list of desirable features is a long one (Delany, 2005, pp. 6–7). If variables such as workload demands, conflicting individual needs, new modes of communication and the challenges faced by those in the newer academic disciplines such as the creative arts are thrown into the mix, then the supervisor-candidate relationship becomes a bespoke challenge (Brien & Williamson, 2009, p. 1).

In a contradictory way my experience of working more-or-less alone on my own creative, project-based Ph.D. provides a useful model for being a supervisor of doctoral practice-led projects. It required me to be resourceful, less reliant on others than I might normally have been in seeking information and answers, and it gave me the confidence so desired by ten Brink. Even the experience of "aloneness" was useful in retrospect as, according to ten Brink, this is crucial:

> It [research], like the marathon runner, is absolutely lonely. Here is a marathon runner on his or her own, absolutely lonely and difficult and it is why, like marathon runners a lot of them do stop half way through. Because it is a singular occupation, there are no mates, there are no other people who do the same thing, you're not in a classroom situation, you're not at work and you don't have colleagues (2008, Afternoon Discussion, para. 14).

Humility or "the ability to understand one's strengths and weaknesses, willingness to learn from others and to exceed one's usual limits [to] forge a connection to a larger perspective" are considered to be key characteristics of good leadership (Morris, Brotheridge & Urbanski, 2005, p. 1330), and yet could be applied equally to the leadership role of the research supervisor in her interactions with research candidates. Leadership abilities that are imperative in research and relevant to supervision such as inspiring someone to do or think something differently are aligned also to the three distinct dimensions of humility, which according to Morris et al. are, self-awareness (knowing one's strengths and weaknesses), openness (open to new ideas and ways of knowing) and transcendence (exceeding one's usual limits to forge connections to a larger perspective) (2005, p. 1331). These qualities are apt for the research supervisor of practice-led research, given that the traditional conception of artists representing the constituency of the majority of research candidates under discussion here is of the creative and independent individual. It is a humble supervisor who can engage with and guide the research candidate to think and act as a researcher while retaining the spirit and independence of an artist.

Over the past thirteen years or so supervisory arrangements have improved considerably for current research candidates. Because of the changing research environment in the overall university environment and more rigorous selection procedures today it would be rare for a candidate to be assigned a supervisor who is not fully cognisant of the proposed field of research. At RMIT University, for example, there are now groupings of academic staff in research clusters of common themes and ideas, and research candidates are aligned with supervisors who have similar research interests. From the rather disparate group of artist-academics of thirteen years ago and supervisory arrangements that aligned candidates to supervisors in the same practical artistic field, the situation now is one that is specialised and particular. In accordance with university-wide processes, applications for places in postgraduate research in the School of Art are scrutinised for compliance with the basic requirements, such as having the right qualifications and exceptional grades, and applicants cannot be considered unless appropriate supervision can be provided and the proposed research project aligns with the research foci of the school, which are ultimately the research priorities of the university. This means that research supervisors have had to clarify and make public their own research interests and need to be able to field enquiries from prospective students, which has made academic staff more aware of what is involved in supervision and the needs of the candidates. Now it is not good enough simply to be available to take on a new candidate; research supervisors must prove their abilities as artists, thinkers, theorisers and mentors.

At present I am senior supervisor to nine research candidates undertaking creative projects predominantly through Ph.D. and professional doctorates, and second supervisor to two Ph.D. candidates. All of these research candidates are engaged in practice-led projects ranging from overt environmental concerns to artistic cartography and curatorship. They engage in specific media in which I have an intrinsic interest, such as photography and printmaking. Each project is idiosyncratically different and yet I am able to contribute to each investigation through theory and history, and most importantly through my personal experiences of on-going research and explorations as an artist and writer. It is vital to practice and exhibit as an artist, to write and publish, and to ensure that both these strands of research are up-to-date and current, as a way of setting an example and publicly demonstrating one's own research strengths and abilities.

WHOSE DREAM IS THIS ANYWAY?

I have taught a research strategies course to all new research candidates for a number of years now, the aim of which is to impart ways and methods of going about research. There is also a requirement to develop the proposal by contextualising the research project in terms of the fundamental questions: What? Why? How? Through this process, all candidates apply for a postgraduate research programme through the presentation of a proposal for a research project based in their own arts-based practice. However the project needs, as does all research, a firm theoretical base, a context through a review of current literature and art practice, research questions and an appropriate methodology. This fundamental necessity tends to induce considerable anxiety in candidates. I have noticed during the first few research strategies classes of each year that students undergo a form of crisis and a period of self-doubt when they realise that their proposed project must be converted from one grounded in professional practice to one that meets the requirements of research. The candidate is required to articulate how the project will add to the field and create new knowledge and also there must be a rationale for doing it, one that is centred on relevance to the community. During these early and fluid stages all aspects of the project are up for negotiation and require "a very creative and positive approach on both sides" (Biggs & Buechler, 2009, p. 10). The role of the supervisor is to reassure the candidate that the project can be reconfigured to address real-world research questions, through valid aims and objectives that will produce outcomes not only meaningful to the candidate, but also accessible and relevant to the community. Quality supervision ensures the candidate will be confident that the articulation of ideas through her practice as an artist *is* the research and has the potential to result in new knowledge.

Figure 1. Studio of Ph.D. candidate, School of Art, RMIT University. Photo by the author.

The first and vitally important stage of the research programme is to sort out and clarify the project, not only for the supervisor and candidate to ensure they are both travelling in the same direction, but also for the examiner or the audience for the project, to know at the outset what is being aimed for and why. As a seasoned supervisor I spend many sessions with my candidates in the early days of the project talking about and around the subject and concepts of the proposed research. We meet most frequently in the candidate's studio with her work surrounding us. I encourage my candidates to display their work, to live with it and to allow the work to have a 'voice'.

Together the candidate and I have intense discussions as I attempt to draw out the thinking that underpins the work while posing hypothetical scenarios. Often I play devil's advocate, tossing in possibilities and sometimes, outrageous alternatives with the aim of nudging the candidate to articulate what the project is not, with the object of arriving at the nub of the question. I encourage my candidates to investigate their topic widely, beyond their own medium and familiar references, stretching to other genres such as film, text and yet beyond to science and history – where practitioners have investigated similar themes. Often I become intensely interested in the potential of the project and envisage outcomes of which the candidate is not yet aware. Sometimes, because of our common interests and the situation by which candidates are assigned to supervisors with similar research interests, the candidate's project can start to feel like my project and I have to resist the temptation of taking it on as such. My aim is to instil in my candidate a curiosity and a means to make discoveries for herself. As one of my candidates emailed to me recently: "…and I was telling her [a friend] what a good supervisor you are because I know that you know what I need to write/do but instead of telling me the way you make sure I discover it myself. It's exactly what good mothers do. I also figure I'm extremely lucky to have a supervisor who is just as excited by my topics as I am!" (24 March, 2011). Informed by my training and my own work practices I set out to be challenging and curious, and acknowledge the inspiration and intuition that give rise to the research processes and form the conceptual framework. In the end, however, I am not the expert, so as supervisor I must accept that my candidate will become the expert of her particular project and will know more about the topic than I do.

DOWN THE ROAD TOGETHER

After the initial, very intense period of defining the research for approval of the project and confirmation of candidature, candidates normally require a period of time alone just to get on with the practical work without the 'distractions' of writing the research proposal, and I support this as a practice-led process. The making of art is a reflective activity that takes time – time to make mistakes, time to experiment with unfamiliar media perhaps, and time to engage in creative play. It is an important period for the candidate to regain her independence, collect her thoughts and test out ideas without someone overseeing her or regularly checking in for meetings. This middle period of the programme is when most of the creativity in the form of trial works and experimentation takes place. I encourage my candidates to exhibit their work as this form of publication is the essence of the research and in fact the work cannot be considered research unless it is made public. During this seemingly more relaxed period I hold regular reviews of work; we complete progress reports together and agree on plans for the forthcoming months. There are times, however, when it is obvious that the work is not progressing and it is necessary to intervene. Quite often candidates become side-tracked; the processes of research through art practice can be exciting and open up possibilities and directions that were not part of the original plan and these must be taken into consideration. What happens if a candidate does not follow advice or do as requested? How does the supervisor get the candidate back on track? According to Mark Sinclair, 'hands off' supervisors who are reluctant to intervene or redirect are the least successful; they expect their candidates to function too independently without a great deal of guidance (Sinclair, 2004, pp. vi–vii), and although this may work for some, even the most experienced artists or mature-age candidates do need the regular input of supervisors. The 'hands on' supervisor is more successful because she tends to structure the candidate's journey and establish a peer relationship with the candidate using her 'superior' position to mentor and encourage trust (2004, p. vii). I usually find that by refocussing the candidate on the original plan, providing appropriate direction and structure, and acknowledging the good work already created, the candidate can get back on track with renewed enthusiasm. It is also important that I support my candidate by visiting her exhibitions, attending and taking part in opening celebrations, and by providing critical feedback.

In the final stages of the programme candidates again seem to require more intensive supervision. Unlike conventional doctoral candidates who produce a thesis, the majority of my candidates are examined through an exhibition of resolved artwork accompanied by a durable record of the project in a visual format and an extensive text or exegesis, which contextualises the research project. Each element of these requirements for examination needs a particular form of supervision and this is where a more directive approach may be justified, as certain criteria must be adhered to and fulfilled. The exegesis inevitably takes up the most time, often because candidates whose art practice is their primary activity are neither used to, nor confident about writing such texts. Working on the exegesis as supervisor and candidate does produce a different relationship from the peer relationship that we have as artists. As the supervisor who has guided several candidates successfully through this process, I do take on a more authoritarian role and state clearly what needs to be done, and how, which is quite different from a conversation about the artwork where there is more opportunity for negotiation.

Having examined nationally more than 15 doctoral projects, from my point of view the exegesis is the most difficult and unresolved aspect of practice-led research. When advising my own candidates I draw on what I have read as an examiner to impart to my candidate what not to do and to discuss the ways it can be done better. As a supervisor of the exegesis I am both content and copy editor, setting particular tasks for chapters, and requiring compliance regarding referencing, legibility and relevance. Often I am tempted to write sections for the candidate, but keep a check on this, although I do confess to extensive copy-editing. I encourage exegesis writing as an ongoing activity for the candidate, ideally right through the three or so years of the research although it takes place invariably during the final year. Other aspects, such as the visual durable record mentioned above, have to be routinely kept up-to-date with sound and appropriate data. When it comes to selecting work for the examination I make this a joint activity and together we carefully choose the work that best represents the intentions of the research project along with the ways in which it will be presented. Sometimes even the most experienced of artists loses confidence at this final stage and needs help and support to present the exhibition for examination.

CURIOUSER AND CURIOUSER

To sum up my role as a supervisor of candidates undertaking practice-led research projects, as for supervisors of all research projects, I need to be interested in the potential research project, which has to sustain me along with the candidate throughout the years of the degree. I find that I need to like my candidates as people, in fact this is a very important aspect, so that we can carry out a peer relationship, agree to respect our individual differences and maintain civility towards each other.

As the mentor, guide and leader I need to be a good listener yet know when to interject and offer advice and support; try to be humble yet challenging and curious about all aspects of the candidate's project and findings; know when to be 'hands-on' and when to leave the candidates alone, and calling upon my seniority to be authoritative when necessary, while being aware that my candidate will surge ahead in a particular field, which may be partially mine. At the end of our first year together the same candidate who sent the earlier email sent another one and it encapsulates much of what I have been writing here:

I was thinking about that approach the other night whilst watching bits of *The Matrix*. There's a part where Morpheus says to Neo, 'I can only show you the door. You are the one who must walk through it'. All very Zen-like and like good therapy too. Supervision is a lot like psychological therapy. Good therapists get you to look at a problem from a different angle, to make the discovery yourself. Bad therapists tell you what to do (16 May 2011).

REFERENCES

Biggs, M., & Buechler, D. (2009). Supervision in an alternative paradigm. In D. L. Brien, & R. Williamson (Eds.) Supervising the creative arts research higher degree: Towards best practice. *TEXT* Special Issue Website Series, *6*. Oct. 2009. Retrieved May 9, 2011, from http://www.textjournal.com.au/speciss/issue6/content.htm

Brien, D. L., & Williamson, R. (Eds.) (2009). Supervising the creative arts research higher degree: Towards best practice. *TEXT* Special Issue Website Series, *6*. Oct. 2009. Retrieved January 24, 2010, from http://www.textjournal.com.au/speciss/issue6/content.htm

Brink, J. ten. (2008, May 8–9*). 6 Month scoping project: Practice-based Ph.D. supervision. State of play.* Project Arts Centre, Dublin. Retrieved March 12, 2011, from http://ualscopingPh.D.wordpress.com/literature-review/conference-transcripts

Delany, D. (2005). *A review of the literature on effective research supervision.* Dublin: Centre for Academic Practice and Student Learning.

Grant, B. (1999, July 12–15). *Walking on a rackety bridge: Mapping supervision.* Paper presented at the HERDSA Annual International Conference. Retrieved May 9, 2011, from http://www.herdsa.org.au/branches/vic/Cornerstones/pdf/grant.pdf

Morris, A. J., Brotheridge, C., & Urbanski, J. C. (2005). Bringing humility to leadership: Antecedents and consequences of leader humility. *Human Relations 2005. 58*(10), 1323–1350. Retrieved May 16, 2011, from http://hum.sagepub.com/content/58/10/1323

Sinclair, M. (2004). The pedagogy of 'good' Ph.D. supervision: A national cross-disciplinary investigation of Ph.D. supervision. Canberra: Department of Education and Training. Retrieved May 16, 2011, from http://www.dest.gov.au/sectors/higher_education/publications_resources/profiles/pedagogy_of_good_Ph.D._supervision.htm

BRENT ALLPRESS

3. PEDAGOGICAL PRACTICES FOR SUPERVISING RESEARCH BY PROJECT IN ARCHITECTURE AND DESIGN

INTRODUCTION

This chapter takes a complementary approach to the first person accounts of individual supervision models outlined elsewhere in this book. It situates the diversity of individual and collective supervisory practices employed within a common framework of research by project within the School of Architecture and Design at RMIT University,[1] and discusses approaches to supervision that have consolidated around key research clusters involving cohorts of postgraduates undertaking design research with specific methodologies. It presents a range of infrastructural frameworks and supervisory procedures and practices that support and foster a dynamic and innovative research community in this particular school. Further, it addresses a range of supervisory obstacles and opportunities specific to the practice-based design research by project model, concerning in particular how research embodied within and across projects is framed and made legible, and the extension of the supervisory role to support candidates in the subsequent dissemination of their research within the relatively new and emerging economies of practice-based, design research.

DESIGN RESEARCH BY PROJECT

In the late 1980s the School of Architecture and Design at RMIT University pioneered the introduction of a supervisory model for postgraduate research by project in Australia. The first candidates were based in the architecture discipline[2] undertaking postgraduate research at the master's level. The model subsequently expanded across the other design disciplines in the school including landscape architecture, interior design, industrial design and fashion. Over the past ten years the Ph.D. by project has become the primary focus of supervision with the majority of candidates enrolled in this practice-based degree. There are currently around 180 research postgraduates in the school, mostly active professionals and/or academics who are enrolled part-time, with about 50% of these being architects.

While there is a diversity of approaches to research by project across RMIT, as this book documents, there is a particular set of common supervisory practices within the School of Architecture and Design fostering the emergence of a distinctive research community. Postgraduate research within the school is undertaken primarily within and through a series of design project investigations.

B. Allpress, R. Barnacle, L. Duxbury and E. Grierson (Eds.), Supervising Practices for Postgraduate Research in Art, Architecture and Design, 25–40.
©2012 Sense Publishers. All rights reserved.

This embodied research is framed selectively through a written exegesis of around 40,000 words and relevant visual or other documentation, which is bound as a Durable Visual Record (DVR). Candidates are examined through a culminating exhibition with a verbal defence to a panel of three external examiners. All examinations are recorded by video. The DVR and documentation of the exhibition and examination are archived subsequently in the university library and together they comprise the equivalent of a traditional, written, doctorate thesis.

An important characteristic distinguishing this model from the traditional Ph.D. thesis is that the research is not located solely within the written document but is enacted through the project work itself, with written materials and documents playing a framing and situating role. This structure can raise issues of scope. Some candidates need to be cautioned not to attempt to undertake the equivalent of two Ph.Ds., by project and by written thesis rather than exegesis. Careful advice is required from supervisors on how to balance the focus of attention on the different yet related components and cycles of research and documentation.

The exegesis is not simply a write up of the research that occurs at the end of the candidature. Supervisors generally encourage candidates to undertake concurrent project-based investigations and discursive written reflections and documentation at every stage of the candidacy, in order to forge and provoke a productive dialogue between these complementary modes of enquiry.

The inclusion of an extended verbal defence is particular to the School of Architecture and Design and is not a requirement in other disciplines at RMIT such as fine art. The examination viva extends the model of verbal presentation and critique common to the design disciplines at the undergraduate and professional degree level. The role of the examiners at the postgraduate level is to raise questions and elicit further exposition of the thesis rather than engaging in a direct critique of the work, although it is common for examiners to make positive comments about the research.

The Practice Research Symposium (PRS), formerly known as the Graduate Research Conference (GRC), is held twice a year and gives all candidates an opportunity to trial the verbal presentation of their provisional research to a panel that includes their supervisors, other supervisory staff and invited external critics. These events provide opportunities to test the exhibition and visual or spatial communication of the research. In the weeks prior to examination most supervisors also set up a rehearsal of the verbal presentation in camera to fine tune the candidate's delivery and alleviate the inevitable performance anxieties arising from this high-pressure assessment process.

DESIGN RESEARCH PRACTICES

Design scholar, Peter Downton has categorised the common traditional research models in architecture as technical and scientific research *for,* and historical or critical research *about* design practice (Downton, 2003). Design research *by* and *through* projects involves very different methodologies and practices. It is a form of speculative and applied research, with a greater emphasis placed on qualitative rather than quantitative criteria for assessing the value and contribution of research outcomes.

Design research is projective and integrative. It seeks a qualitative improvement in practices, in response to key criteria nominated through framing research questions. It is an iterative activity undertaken through a cycle of project-based investigations. The research question is often redefined through the act of doing the research, and it is a primary responsibility of the supervisor to review and negotiate any redefinition of the primary research question through the duration of the candidacy.

Another key characteristic of this model of research by project is the emphasis on research practices and methodologies specific and relevant to the design disciplines. This includes various modes and technologies of design representation, drawing, diagramming, modelling and making, prototyping and building. Modes of communication take on multiple roles in design research. They are the means and medium through which the primary design investigations are undertaken. Visual representations such as generative or analytical diagramming can also play an exegetical role, along with written discourses, in framing and making legible the embodied research. This is a responsibility that is different from conventional, professional, communication practices employed to document and promote design work. Candidates are encouraged to be critical about the role that various modes of communication play at the different projective and reflective stages and cycles of their research investigations.

PRACTICE-BASED RESEARCH ECONOMIES

The common model for research in architecture over the past century has been research *about* architecture employing art historical methodologies, or research *for* architecture employing empirical, building science methodologies. It is no coincidence that there have been disproportionate numbers of architecture academics with building science or art history backgrounds employed across Australasian universities. The traditional Ph.D. model has skewed the focus of qualified academics and precluded the advancement of design as an area of research despite the obvious priority this should have for design disciplines. This is a common situation for universities internationally. It has remained a self-perpetuating situation in many Australasian schools because there has been limited supervisory expertise in practice-based design research.

The RMIT School of Architecture and Design has addressed this issue by employing new academic staff with innovative design practice and master's level research experience and then mentoring and supervising them internally to the completion of project-based design research Ph.Ds. This has gradually given the school a distinctive staff profile. Over the past 15 years the founding, supervisory academics, although small in number, have mentored a new generation of supervisors who have gained a distinctive grounding in design research methodologies and practices.

The Ph.D. by project model allows design practice-focused candidates to extend their professional expertise and mastery within a research framework. They gain relevant postgraduate qualifications that provide a pathway to more senior design-focused teaching and research positions within the academy, and they take on leadership positions within the profession through innovative research-led practices. Within practice specialisations such as urban design and key areas of practice innovation such as the application of digital communication and fabrication technologies there is a range of industry roles with a research focus. The Ph.D. by project degree is being undertaken increasingly by candidates seeking professional positions that bridge between the academy and industry. Many applicants are already academics who are sustaining a parallel external design or consultancy practice. For academics engaged in speculative research by project there is a range of avenues for the validation and dissemination of their work, such as international exhibitions and biennales that are now recognised by the Excellence in Research in Australia (ERA), national, research quality, auditing process, or equivalent research metrics in New Zealand, Hong Kong and the UK.

Supervisors confer with candidates at the outset to clarify their primary motivations and goals for undertaking a research degree. Provisional research questions and methodologies can be focused usefully by considering which particular communities of practice the candidate seeks to participate in and make an on-going contribution to. The Ph.D. research by project offers a vehicle for trialling new practices and establishing pathways to emergent roles.

The traditional and customary pathway for a Ph.D. student in the arts and sciences is to progress directly from an honours degree to full-time postgraduate study. However, the majority of postgraduate candidates in the RMIT School of Architecture and Design are well established and experienced in their professional roles and have not been students for many years. They generally have active and demanding practices and are studying part-time. This presents some issues for supervisors as such candidates are effectively learning to learn again, to extend their well-established mastery and transform their practices; and the re-acculturation to academic discourses and concerns can be challenging initially for some candidates.

If professional practice projects within industry are vehicles for research then supervisors establish with candidates what selective aspects of those projects they will focus on within a research context. Candidates can struggle with distinguishing and framing the contribution to knowledge embodied within and across built works that necessarily also address a range of other contingencies and broader professional responsibilities. For many practitioners the primary benefit of supervisory dialogue is the opportunity to be exposed to, and engage in reflective discussion and debate within a research community traversing a longer arc of practices across a body of work.

Having exemplary design practitioners involved in a Ph.D. programme enhances the relevance and currency of the applied research focus of the academy, and fosters an innovative community of practice across industry and the academy.

These are relationships that have the potential to extend well beyond any individual candidacy.

PRACTICE RESEARCH SYMPOSIUM (PRS)

In addition to regular one on one or studio-based meetings with candidates, the supervision of candidates and processes of progress review are staged and structured around the Practice Research Symposium (PRS) held twice a year. This collegiate event, formerly known as the Graduate Research Conference, provides a key supervisory framework to support a broader collective network of relationships between supervisors, candidates, international researchers and practitioners in which candidates formally present work in progress to their supervisor and a panel of two or more critics in one-hour sessions.[3] A series of parallel streams occur concurrently over two days organised according to thematic research clusters and disciplinary groupings. Presentation panels consist of supervisory staff and invited external, national and international critics who are experts in the field. Time is reserved at the end of each presentation for supervisors and external panel members to confer and have frank conversations about candidates' research questions, methodologies and progress, and the particular supervisory strategies being employed.

These presentations are aligned with the different stages of candidacy from initial approval of research question and research methodology and mode, through interim stages, to a penultimate presentation where recommendations are made on a candidate's readiness for examination, and their specific mode and medium of examination and accompanying exhibition. Candidates have opportunities to trial strategies for framing, communicating and presenting their research. They gain exposure to the work and practices of other candidates within their own area of research and across adjacent fields. They are better able to envisage the future progress of their research through presentations by other candidates who are at later stages of their candidacy and closer to completion.

Examinations are held over the prior three days and all enrolled candidates benefit from being able to attend examinations and accompanying exhibitions and see a range of approaches to framing a body of design research. Examiners serve as critics for interim candidates over the PRS weekend. If the examiners are new to the school they usually offer a public lecture, which serves to ground the dialogue that supervisors and candidates have with external contributors. Lectures and workshops extend the internal discourse and debate around the research by project model. Exposure to external views and alternative frameworks challenges the potential insularity of the shared supervisory model. A plenary session at the end of the PRS has been a crucial vehicle for external examiners and critics to offer their insights on project-based, design research models, and give constructive critical feedback on the practices and conduct of supervisors and candidates. Postgraduate coordinators and supervisors have an opportunity to share their reflections on the PRS structures and processes, and postgraduate candidates have a forum to articulate their experiences of the model and raise general requests or concerns.

During the PRS supervisory training workshops are held for new supervisors, drawing on the expertise of experienced senior supervisors and visiting experts. These events supplement the centrally resourced supervisory staff development programme. They ensure that academics are provided with a forum for sharing discipline-specific institutional knowledge and experience around the Ph.D. by project model of supervision.

SUPERVISORY STRUCTURES FOR OFFSHORE CANDIDATES

There are still few programmes internationally that offer Ph.D. by project in design research. The school has experienced a significant international demand for places in the RMIT programme and increasing numbers of postgraduate enrolments are from candidates who remain offshore in Europe and Asia during their candidature. This presents a range of logistical and communication issues for supervisors who need to be vigilant in managing any issues of isolation and discontinuity of contact that such students may face. Increasingly supervisors are using Skype as a more direct form of virtual face-to-face contact supplemented by other broadband technologies to facilitate the sharing of higher resolution documentation of design research. Most offshore candidates also travel regularly to attend the PRS events. This is an important mechanism for distance students to maintain intensive and direct contact with their supervisors, and it assists in acculturating students to the postgraduate community and the models of research being undertaken.

The PRS process has been franchised with the PRS EU being held twice a year in the city of Ghent, Belgium, in partnership with the Sint-Lucas School of Architecture. This event acts as a new regional anchor for offshore, postgraduate candidates, who are coming together from across the UK, Europe and the USA, with Melbourne-based RMIT supervisors now travelling regularly to Europe and holding smaller supervisory meetings and events. A cohort of Sint-Lucas academic staff formed the foundational group of candidates, along with a diverse mix of other design practitioners and researchers from across the EU who have an affinity with the RMIT research by project model. Building international networks for RMIT supervisors and candidates, this partnership situates the model of design research by project within an international economy where applied practice-based research is gaining increasing prominence and priority. This European hub also provides an opportunity to resource the participation of a wider range of invited external critics, examiners and co-supervisors who are based in the EU and USA. A similar venture is also under development in Asia, with RMIT Architecture and Design postgraduate events to be hosted at the RMIT campus in Ho Chi Minh City in Vietnam. It is assumed that candidates based across Asia will alternate between travelling to this new hub in Vietnam and attending the Melbourne PRS events.

The research by project model has attracted a diverse range of local and international candidates. The sections that follow outline the collective structures that have been adopted and adapted by the school for organising divergent supervisory groupings and practices.

TRI-POLAR POSTGRADUATE RESEARCH SUPERVISION

Postgraduate supervision within the RMIT School of Architecture and Design is not conceived as a series of isolated supervisory relationships between individual candidates and senior academic staff. Over the past ten years the research culture of the school has consolidated and gained critical mass through a curatorial tri-polar framework, with supervisors and candidates from a range of disciplinary backgrounds forming groups and clusters around particular methodological affinities and shared concerns. This aids in the mentoring of postgraduate students through dialogue with other co-located candidates. It also provides opportunities for resourcing alternative models of group supervision and co-supervisory collaborations.

There is a range of discipline-specific group names and designations that have been in use across the school to describe the tri-polar model. The meta-account that I would argue best characterises this grouping of research within and across disciplines in the school, is that supervisors and candidates are predominantly engaging in *situated*, *emergent* and *synthetic* design research practices.

The *situated* pole can be defined as design research situated against economic, contextual and urban constraints, historical and precedent practices, and discursive and theoretical frameworks. The school identifies this stream under the general title 'Urban Environments'.

The *emergent* pole involves design research engaging with emergent technologies and practices, with a current key but not exclusive emphasis on digital design and fabrication technologies. This includes design research into generative properties of emergent bottom-up systems of composition and organisation. The school describes this area as 'Advanced Technologies'.

The *synthetic* pole includes design research undertaken through trans-disciplinary and collaborative practices, usually between architecture and other design industry disciplines and spatial art practices such as installation and public art. It contends with knowledge gained from the transfer of practices across disciplinary boundaries. The cluster is characterised by an engagement with diverse modes of cultural and creative production, often involving community-based design projects and consultancies. The umbrella name for this stream across the school is the 'Expanded Field' borrowing Rosalind Krauss's terminology for describing the intersection of different, disciplinary, spatial design and art practices (Krauss, 1979).

The aspiration for this tri-polar pedagogical model has been to sustain a range of contested areas of scholarship and research. The situation of holding multiple, articulated positions serves to foster a productively dynamic research environment. The poles act as clusters of intensity within a constellation rather than as fixed positions. Any design research activity or project may involve some combination of these approaches. The tri-polar identification does not imply some exclusivity of concerns, but rather that there is a degree of priority given to a particular set of practices that characterises these provisional groupings of supervisors and research candidates.

The tri-polar model gives flexible structure to the diversity of supervisory groups shaping the consolidation of research activities within and across disciplines while maintaining a productive tension between numbers of complementary adjacent models. Further, the supervision of these cohorts of candidates is resourced and organised through the establishment of design research laboratories co-locating postgraduate students, supervisors and other related research staff in dedicated spaces with a semi-autonomous identity.

URBAN ARCHITECTURE LABORATORY (UAL)

In the architecture discipline the postgraduates in the Urban Environments stream are based at the RMIT Urban Architecture Laboratory (UAL), which is a dedicated studio space and consultancy office. The focus of this grouping is not on urban design in the traditional planning sense, but more on the urban implications of architectural design strategies and interventions situated within metropolitan contexts and constraints, with Melbourne as a primary test-bed (Murray & Bertram, 2005).

An innovative model of studio-based group supervision of postgraduates at the research master's degree level was established by the UAL in the mid-1990s. Groups of around eight candidates have joint supervisory sessions with two primary co-supervisors. The students initially work collaboratively on a series of urban design research project vehicles. Usually these have been live consultancies run by the UAL supervisors in partnership with local government authorities and regional municipal councils.

Students make a selective contribution to the research underpinning the consultancy and gain exposure to a rich set of urban constraints and challenging contexts. Candidates trial the application of a set of urban strategies and design research methodologies through these vehicle projects with supervisory dialogue focusing less on the specific design values of any particular project and more on generalisable strategies that can be tested through these collaborative projects as case studies.

Candidates then identify and refine their own research questions, and implement their individual design research strategies in a culminating urban project responding to selective contextual and programmatic conditions that they have nominated. This supervisory structure provides a flexible balance between collaborative practices, precedent methodologies, situated constraints and individual research interests.

Following the shift of the professional architecture and landscape architecture degrees to a three year undergraduate and two year professional master's degree in line with the EU Bologna protocol, the school is founding a new, post-professional, urban, master's by coursework degree, while individual candidates will continue to undertake urban, master's degrees by research. There is also a small grouping of

Ph.D. students focusing on this field. The master's degree by coursework offers the opportunity to further resource more specialised aspects of urban research supervision for these candidates through elective coursework modules in urban design and planning. Ph.D. candidates in the UAL benefit from the critical mass of consultancy and supervisory activities and also, where appropriate, have opportunities to contribute selectively to the shared projects being undertaken by the master's students.

Ph.D. candidates in the UAL have been resourced through Australian Research Council grant-funded scholarships to undertake research into generalisable, affordable, housing strategies embodied within a range of exemplary, architect-designed, housing precedents (Murray, Ramirez-Lovering, & Whibley, 2008). There can be a tension between the student researchers' responsibilities to service the grant-funded research and their desire to define their own particular contribution to the field with a potential danger that the postgraduate supervision becomes more instrumentalised. This can be avoided by treating the grant research as a vehicle for a selective aspect of the Ph.D. without fully conflating the two research tasks.

SPATIAL INFORMATION ARCHITECTURE LABORATORY (SIAL)

The Advanced Technologies pole in the school is focused around the interdisciplinary activities of the Spatial Information Architecture Laboratory (SIAL).[4] Professor Mark Burry, the Director of SIAL, leads a team of researchers working on a range of projects that include the design development and construction for the completion of Antoni Gaudi's unfinished *Temple Sagrada Familia*, in Barcelona. This grant-funded research focuses on the role of parametric modelling technologies and digitally controlled fabrication systems. Related consultancy projects and collaborations with leading contemporary practices such as dECOi, Gehry Partners Architects and Arup situate the work of SIAL researchers within an international practice network.

Specialist SIAL researchers are also investigating diverse digital applications such as collaborative communications platforms, the spatial configuration of virtual environments and spatial sound design practices. All these areas involve applied research into emerging, digital design, technologies and techniques (Allpress, 2011). This focus was extended through the ARC, grant-funded, SIAL research project, 'Technology transfer through embedded research within architectural practice: the creation of an Australian practice-based architectural research and development network'. This incorporated an innovative, embedded, practice model of supervision for the postgraduate Ph.D. research by project. Candidates were situated within four Australian architecture and engineering practices of differing scales to explore and capture how their design practice processes could be mapped onto, and transformed by new digitally-supported ways of working.[5]

Academic supervision was supplemented by close dialogue with the directors of each linkage partner firm. This included the small architectural practice *BKK*, a larger practice *MGS*, both in Melbourne, the distributed practice *Terroir* based in Hobart and Sydney, and the engineering firm *Arup*. Embedded candidates were resourced to undertake a unique form of practice research that sought to "capture 'tacit' or inexplicit disciplinary knowledge" on the design role of digital technologies generated through collaborative project work that is often not retained within individual firms.[6] The SIAL model represents a hybrid position within the school combining research by project through design with highly specialised and technically grounded research for design.

REFLECTIVE PRACTICE

The founding model for architectural research by project at RMIT is the Reflective Practice Invitational stream directed by Professor Leon van Schaik. Exemplary practitioners who have demonstrated professional mastery in their design practice and have received peer reviewed acclaim are invited back into the academy to reflect on their body of work and the implicit research embodied within their practice. Candidates then extend this mastery in a research context through new projects undertaken during their candidacy, in dialogue with the community of supervisors and other candidates within the programme (van Schaik & Johnson, 2011). The supervisory emphasis of this approach is on the study of practice as an activity, a set of design practices rather than designed outcomes. Glanville and van Schaik write:

> We are convinced that studies of practice as an object miss the point. Design is an activity, and designers, in order to study the activity, need less to study the outcome of the activity (the process, design-as-verb) and more to study the activity itself. Designers always knew this, but Donald Schön (Schön, 1983) made the view respectable in the wider community. Nor does the activity need to be studied from outside: the point of studying, if you are a designer, is not to marvel at what goes on in designing, but to do it better. We are interested in assisting designers to study (their) practice in order to improve it, which we believe is achieved through growth in the type of knowledge appropriate to design, i.e. 'design knowledge' This means the (research) question to be asked necessarily concerns 'how?' more than the more traditional scientific question, 'what?' and will be both found and founded in the designer's practice (Glanville & van Schaik, 2003).

One of the most common reasons given anecdotally by practitioners for re-entering the academy is the opportunity to participate in dialogue with a supportive critical community to deepen design thinking and develop innovative and effective practices.

A key theoretical framework informing this supervisory approach is second order cybernetics and circular causality, with a focus on the practice of practice (van Schaik, 2003). The role of theory in relation to practice is also given particular attention, with an emphasis on developing theoretical frameworks that are based in the practice of designing: "We do not study practice exclusively. We study how, studying practice, we can develop theory that informs practice as practice informs theory" (Glanville & van Schaik, 2003).

A supervisory innovation in the Reflective Practice Invitational stream has been to employ group supervision of candidates who are also co-directors of architectural practices. This reflects the necessarily co-authored nature of design practice. It also initiates a discourse within a practice about the nature of particular contributions to knowledge by the individuals within the group and the nature of shared knowledge generated through their collective collaborations.

The Invitational stream began as a research Master of Architecture by project, and has been extended and developed more recently as a Ph.D. by project stream. This in part recognises the potential change of status of the Master of Architecture by research with the shift across Australia to a variant of the EU Bologna Protocol model, with five year undergraduate professional architecture degrees being replaced by three year undergraduate pre-professional degrees followed by two year professional master's by coursework degrees.

The move towards the Ph.D. in Architecture (research by project) as the primary postgraduate qualification also acknowledges the demand latent within existing architecture schools internationally from academics who are active practitioners. These candidates, often with a master's degree, would hit a glass ceiling of promotion and professional advancement, and now they are seeking to undertake a Ph.D. to develop and capture the original contribution to knowledge they are making through their practice-based research.

The Ph.D. (by project) Invitational stream initially employed an approach that extended the scope of research undertaken through master's supervision, with candidates aiming to "produce new knowledge from existing practices by deriving propositions from that practice, comparing these to those that can be aligned elsewhere, and surfacing the processes of design practice" (van Schaik, 2011, p. 29). Informed by the reflective analysis of their body of work, candidates have undertaken a series of projects during the candidacy exploring the potential future development of their practices that might result from these investigations.

A further recent development in the Invitational stream has been to offer supervision through the framework of the Ph.D. (by publication) model where the publications are "built (or designed) projects that have received the admiration of peers and other critical attention, locally and internationally" (van Schaik, 2011, p. 30). Candidates document their seminal projects to an archival standard, assemble a biography of the critical attention the work has received, and reflect on that critique. A further peer interview is conducted with an informed critic that is edited as a scholarly document. This then informs a reflective essay and examination exhibition (van Schaik, 2011, p. 30–32). The advantage of this model is that it maintains a primary emphasis on the medium of design practice in the research, rather than extended exegetical writing about practice.

EXPANDED FIELDS OF PRACTICE

A further supervisory grouping of candidates was established within the Reflective Practice Invitational stream consisting of candidates who were undertaking interdisciplinary design research in various combinations of architecture, landscape architecture, interior design, land art, public art and spatial installation practices. They all shared an interest in ephemeral spatial and experiential conditions and thus were dubbed the 'Ephemeral group'. This effectively became a founding postgraduate cohort in the Expanded Field stream. They were co-supervised by Leon van Schaik with visiting professor, Paul Carter, then based at the University of Melbourne. Joint supervision occurred primarily in a group context, which gave this stream an immediate critical mass and coherence.

The candidates shared an interest in collaborative practices. Professor van Schaik was commissioned by the Melbourne Arts Festival in 2002 to curate a series of urban installation and event-based, public art projects staged by these candidates in city laneways. These project installations became key case-study vehicles in the early stages of degree candidacy through which the candidates could trial a range of design-research methodologies and practices. This group had a more explicit investment in exhibition and installation practices, and their culminating examination exhibitions contributed significantly to the exploration of the role of the exhibition as a performative enactment of the research as well as providing framing documentation of the investigations.

RESEARCH DISSEMINATION

In traditional models of Ph.D. research it is common for supervisors to encourage their candidates in the latter stages of their candidacy to prepare an article for submission to an academic journal. This helps establish a research track record, and is a useful focusing task for a student to engage in formal processes of external academic refereeing and validation of their work. It requires the candidate to consider the audience of their research, and the community and field to which they are making a contribution. It also encourages a clarity and concision of communication of a selective aspect of the research.

These issues all hold equally for Ph.D. by project candidates. However, due to the emergent nature of the model, there are as yet few publishing venues for design research. In order to address this, a colleague and I co-founded the first dedicated journal of refereed, design research by project entitled, *Architectural Design Research (ADR)* (Allpress & Ostwald, 2005, 2007, 2008). This journal was funded by the Association of Architecture Schools of Australasia (AASA) and replaced a previous model of refereed design exhibitions that proved to be logistically unworkable.

Precedent for this design-research publishing model can be found with Leon van Schaik's series of documents of record through which he has edited the publication of candidate research projects he supervised in the Reflective Practice Invitational stream (van Schaik, 1993, 1995, 2000, 2003; van Schaik & Spooner, 2010). Subsequently he has published a number of related books through Wiley and other publishers that document his approach to the research by project supervision model (van Schaik, 2004; van Schaik & Johnson, 2011).

I took the postgraduate research by project model and supervisory framework employed at RMIT and translated it into a refereed journal format. Instead of publishing conventional articles, the *ADR* journal published project-based design research, with framing exegesis. An extended article in each issue provided scholarly discourse on design research. Contributors to the *ADR* journal have addressed many of the issues faced by candidates who are being examined. My role as editor involved the mentoring of contributors to enhance their communication of the design research embodied within and through a series of projects.

The innovative graphic design practice, *Studio Anybody* set up a flexible series of publication formatting templates. Each volume consisted of around six projects plus an extended essay. Each project had an internal cover page and operated as its own mini-journal with distinctive formatting that reflected the genre of project research. This approach was labour intensive, but resulted in a series of journal volumes that were unique design artefacts in their own right. This clarified for me the role of the design of communication and representation of design research in framing and making legible the embodied research undertaken by candidates of the Ph.D. by project. Attention needs to be given to the exploration of effective ways to frame the research in the DVR documents and examination exhibition, and in subsequent dissemination through publication and exhibition.

The role of the written exegesis is an area in which, as a supervisor, I have a particular interest. Many candidates have anxieties about writing and initially default to a position where philosophical or cultural theory is referred to as an external authorisation of practice. Practice cannot flourish as a mere illustrative application of theory. The rationalist desire for instrumental and universal theory that precedes and governs action prescribes outcomes. It is not adequate to account for emergent architectural conditions and possibilities. Tussling with the complex, contested and mutually informing relationship between discourse and design is an activity that all candidates need to undertake if they are to find their voice to better articulate and theorise their own practices, and to situate them critically against the field to which they are contributing.

The first three volumes of the *ADR* journal were conceived as a proof of concept and have seeded two related publication series. The submission guidelines for the journal were directly adapted for the new *Design Research* book series published through RMIT Press. UK academics with whom I conferred while promoting the *Architectural Design Research* journal model subsequently grouped together to found a related book series through Ashgate in the UK entitled, *Design Research in Architecture*. These publishing ventures all respond to the recent shift in the UK, Australia and New Zealand towards a qualitative model of assessing academic research that encompasses project-based research and creative works. Venues for disseminating design research will consolidate as more academics who have undertaken the equivalent of a Ph.D. by project seek exhibition and publication outlets. Supervisors have a key role to play in supporting candidates in the cultivation of ongoing design research and dissemination practices beyond the candidacy to extend and transform professional and disciplinary knowledge.

NOTES

1   RMIT School of Architecture and Design. Retrieved November 12, 2011, from http://www .rmit.edu.au/architecturedesign
2   RMIT Architecture. Retrieved November 12, 2011, from http://www.architecture.rmit.edu.au
3   RMIT School of Architecture and Design Graduate Research Conference. Retrieved November 12, 2011, from http://www.rmit.edu.au/architecturedesign/grc
4   RMIT Spatial Information Architecture Laboratory. Retrieved November 12, 2011, from http://www.sial.rmit.edu.au
5   RMIT Spatial Information Architecture ARC Linkage grant funded project: Technology transfer through embedded research within architectural practice: the creation of an Australian practice-based architectural research and development network. Retrieved November 12, 2011 from http://www.sial.rmit.edu.au/Projects/Embedded_Research_within_Architectural_Practice.php
6   RMIT Spatial Information Architecture ARC Linkage grant funded project: Technology transfer through embedded research within architectural practice: the creation of an Australian practice-based architectural research and development network. Retrieved November 12, 2011 from http://www.sial.rmit.edu.au/Projects/Embedded_Research_within_Architectural_Practice.php

REFERENCES

Allpress, B., & Ostwald, M. (Eds.) (2005). *Architectural Design Research, 1*(1). Retrieved November 12, 2011, from http://issuu.com/brentallpress/docs/adr_vol1_1
Allpress, B., & Ostwald, M. (Eds.) (2007). *Architectural Design Research, 2*(1). Retrieved November 12, 2011, from http://issuu.com/brentallpress/docs/adr_vol2_no1
Allpress, B., & Ostwald, M. (Eds.) (2008). *Architectural Design Research, 3*(1). Retrieved November 12, 2011, from http://issuu.com/brentallpress/docs/adr3_vol3_1
Allpress, B. (2011). Pedagogical frameworks for emergent digital practices in architecture. In Kocatürk, T., & Medjdoub, B. (Eds.), *Distributed intelligence in design* (pp. 51–70). London: Wiley.
Downton, P. (2003). *Design research*. Melbourne: RMIT University Press.
Glanville, R., & van Schaik, L. (2003). Designing reflections, reflections on design. In D. Durling, & K. Sugiyama (Eds.), *Doctoral Education in Design* (pp. 35–42). Tsukuba International Congress Center, Japan, 14–17 October 2003, University of Tsukuba.
Krauss, R. (1979). Sculpture in the expanded field. *October, 8*(Spring), 30–44.
Murray, S., & Bertram, N. (Eds.) (2005). *38South: Urban architecture laboratory 2002–2004*. Melbourne: RMIT University Press.
Murray, S., Ramirez-Lovering, D., & Whibley, S. (Eds.) (2008). *Re: Housing*. Melbourne: RMIT Press.
Schön, D. (1983). *The reflective practitioner: How professions think in action*. London: Basic Books.
van Schaik, L. (Ed.) (1993). *Fin de siècle and the twenty first century: Architectures of Melbourne*. Melbourne: RMIT School of Architecture and Design.
van Schaik, L. (Ed.) (1995). *Transfiguring the ordinary: RMIT Masters of Architecture by project*. Melbourne: 38South Publications.
van Schaik, L. (Ed.) (2000). *Interstitial modernism*. Melbourne: RMIT Press.
van Schaik, L. (Ed.) (2003). *The practice of practice: Research in the medium of design*. Melbourne: RMIT Press.
van Schaik, L. (2004). *Mastering architecture: Becoming a creative innovator in practice*. London: Wiley.
van Schaik, L., & Spooner, M. (Eds.) (2010). *The practice of practice 2: Research in the medium of design*. Melbourne: onepointsixone.

van Schaik, L. (2011). The evolution of the invitational program in design practice research. In van Schaik, L., & Johnson, A. *Architecture and design by Practice, by Invitation Design practice research at RMIT* (pp. 14–37). Melbourne: onepointsixon.

van Schaik, L., & Johnson, A. (2011). *Architecture and design by Practice, by Invitation Design practice research at RMIT.* Melbourne: onepointsixone.

CATHERINE COLE

4. GOOD SUPERVISION: THE CREATIVE WORK IN PROCESS

Effective and Engaged Postgraduate Supervision in Creative Writing

INTRODUCTION

In this chapter I examine the manner in which postgraduate degrees in creative writing offer a unique and often challenging relationship between a writer/student and writer/academic. I focus on the extent to which the supervisory relationship should be viewed in traditional terms or whether a modified analysis is required given the nature of the subject matter and processes of enquiry/research. I explore an additional consideration on this point, questioning the extent to which the supervisor and candidate may be able to enhance the creative experience of one another. I reflect on whether there is, as yet, an untapped potential for a more reflexive and reciprocal academic interchange.

BACKGROUND TO CREATIVE WRITING PROGRAMMES AND THE SUPERVISORY RELATIONSHIP

An overview of the historical factors shaping the development of creative writing postgraduate degrees is helpful in understanding the supervisory relationship, particularly when establishing appropriate supervisory protocols with students and responding to their expectations of the relationship. Creative writing programmes emerged in Australian universities in the early 1970s, with doctoral programmes developing in the late 1980s. This was not simply a new development for universities but marked a significant shift in the professionalisation of creative writing. Although visual artists, craftspeople, musicians and performers had benefited from tuition in special schools of excellence for centuries, writers had a much shorter tradition of such government or university support.

Typically, pedagogical tools of creative writing in universities highlight workshops or studios, the constitution of learning communities aligned to the notion of "communities of practice", i.e. situated, experiential and collective learning by practitioners with a shared interest (Lave & Wenger, 1991; Wenger, 2001). In the case of creative writing higher degrees, there exists a more academically traditional supervisory relationship between a creative writer/candidate and their creative writer/supervisor. In addition to this, most university writing programmes have strong, informal partnerships and synergies with well-established, literary, community activities or have spawned their own literary journals with communities-of-practice functions. These dynamic

B. Allpress, R. Barnacle, L. Duxbury and E. Grierson (Eds.), Supervising Practices for Postgraduate Research in Art, Architecture and Design, 41–50.
©*2012 Sense Publishers. All rights reserved.*

relationships between university creative writing programmes and broader literary communities are key elements in any writing programme and a key reason for writers seeking engagement with the academy.

Since the late 1980s, postgraduate degrees in creative writing have offered established writers, who have a major body of work, an opportunity to claim prior learning and educational research equivalence for entry into a doctoral programme, usually a Doctor of Creative Arts, while less established writers with educational qualifications such as honours or masters by research degrees, but with limited publications, have entered a traditional Ph.D. with a view to completing a critical/creative exegesis within the parameters of that degree. While postgraduate degrees in creative writing offer a range of benefits to their candidates, they also elicit questions about why successful, established writers seek a higher degree. Respondents usually argue that creative higher degrees provide an opportunity for writers, including those already lauded in their fields, to develop and explore their ideas through a mix of creative and critical projects, offering an opportunity to reflect upon their own and other practitioners' writing approaches. Higher degrees also allow writers to work closely with experienced academic supervisors with a creative practice of their own, who guide and support them through their research and writing. The programmes link writers with a creative academic community of like-minded writers with whom to discuss and share ideas and writing processes – a community which, it could be argued, has grown as much from changes in the wider literary world, including a loss of editing, publishing and writer support in publishing houses, as from a need for academic conversations and qualifications.

Since the 1980s, university writing programmes have expanded as creative activities have become more highly valued for their economic, cultural and social benefits (Smith, 2009). Other significant impacts on creative writing higher degrees that have reconfigured notions of creative practice and research include the Australian Research Council's recognition of creative outputs via the research quality audit scheme, Excellence in Research for Australia (ERA), and new paradigms for examining and ranking these outputs. In future, whole-of-government arts policies seem set to embody inclusive transversal approaches as well (Madden, 2009, pp. 32, 34). Advocates for writing programmes have long stressed the importance of the academic/creative relationship as a form of tertiary study, a view that these developments support and reinforce.

That creative writing higher degrees have increased in popularity since their inception has been remarked upon by various commentators, some lamenting creative writing's ascendency at the expense of more traditional arts degrees. However it is just this expectation of a community of practice that has attracted applicants away from traditional arts areas as they seek an opportunity to work with, and be supervised by a practitioner who has creative experience and understands the complex relationship between creativity and creator. In general, higher degree candidates in creative writing are seeking someone who knows all about the creative pain through a community of practice in which supervisor and student are familiar with, and actively engaged in creative acts.

As literary communities such as those in Bloomsbury, Greenwich Village and Paris have attested historically, writers have sought the support and collegiality of other writers. Like their forebears, contemporary writers continue to rely on self-initiated and self-managing networks, which focus on peer review and support for their professional development. When this model shifted into the academy, writers were able to take advantage of new communities of practice. Their candidacy as higher degrees students also extended the inter-relationship between writers in active communities of practice and the working environment of the academy. The latter offered wider industry, government and academic relationships whose activities supported significant literary production, thus providing a unique link between ideas and exegetical exploration coupled with creative production.

Given the lure of these extended communities, what other issues affect the supervisory relationship in the creative writing higher degree and to what extent, and in what distinctive ways do writers learn from their supervisors and the other writers with whom they may engage in the academic community? In relation specifically to creative writing higher degrees, how do these learning activities differentially benefit writers at different stages, and in different forms and genres, to produce notable work? Are writers drawn to the academy for the increased value of their work?

EXPECTATIONS OF THE SUPERVISORY RELATIONSHIP

If a creative writing higher degree offers an established writer an open door through which to undertake a project to completion, what kind of relationship is expected during a candidature, and what pitfalls might be identified and avoided? How, for example, might established writers baulk at the theoretical component of their degrees or resist the reflective analysis of their own and others' work? What are the implications of various research approaches for writing pedagogies, especially if we support the belief that writing must be an intellectual discipline in its own right? Surely writing should be a creative conversation with the history of its genres and a theoretical exploration of the ideas embedded in a creative project; it must be supported by a scholarly, theoretical exegesis or dissertation that is rigorously supervised and supported. But do creative writing candidates support this view, and if they do not, how might divergent views be accommodated, explored or explicated through supervision?

The role of the postgraduate supervisor is pivotal in this and has been examined by scholars in Australia and in those countries where creative writing is a discipline in the academy, most notably the UK, USA and Canada. *Text*, the journal of the Australian Association of Writing Programmes, has dedicated a number of issues to this concern, and academics in the discipline have written at length about the complex relationship between student and academic, though few have differentiated the relationship between the aspiring or newly published writer/student and the well known writer/student of considerable reputation or fame.

Dominique Hecq, for one, has offered an interesting Lacanian overview of the manner in which the student/supervisor relationship mirrors that of the therapist/client, especially in the way transference manifests itself between the two (Hecq, 2009). Jeri Kroll sees the role as one of practice-led coach and trainer, preferring the sports analogy to the psychotherapeutic (Kroll, 2009, p. 1). Kroll also highlights the need for supervisors to be aware of their own disciplinary limitations. Creative writing teachers may need to teach themselves as their student progresses or develop panels of experts from other disciplines to guide the student in those areas of expertise (scientists, historians, cultural theorists and so on) where this is not possible (Kroll, 2009, p. 10).

Understanding the student's desire to pursue a higher degree is critical to any discussion about supervision. A wise supervisor understands fully why the writer has entered the academy for their next writing project. Why have they not just completed their next novel on their own? The writer's answers are likely to be diverse, reflecting social and economic trends in literary production. The candidate may, for example, express the desire:

- for an academic qualification, especially to enhance their future access to primary or secondary employment to support their writing life;
- to mix with and engage in conversations with other scholars;
- to gain a postgraduate grant or award – an essential income when literary grants or government support are not available;
- to connect with and share their supervisor's own creative practices;
- for mentorship and access to their supervisor's or the university's literary community;
- to gain a greater structure for their project, for a discipline imposed by the time and reporting expectations of the degree;
- have access to research resources and specialist knowledge such as historical, philosophical or cultural academics as primary or secondary supervisors.

The student may not articulate these concerns in advance of the degree, or may shift their expectations and needs as the degree progresses, thus necessitating a constant re-shifting of focus and research intent. These shifts will require a vigilant reassessment of approach by the supervisor with changes to their role, and the complex student/supervisor relationship may have a major impact on the student's creative process and their academic progress.

GROUND RULES AND RELATIONSHIPS

In supervisory management setting 'ground rules' based on these expectations is an important practice. As well as accessing the university's support services and protocols for higher degrees students, postgraduate writers need a clear understanding of the role they will share with their supervisor. Expectations of meetings and feedback mechanisms, reporting relationships and progress reports, deadlines, student presentations and research management, all need to be clearly articulated and managed.

This approach can often run counter to a writer's established ways of working. For many, the early years of a fiction writing project are spent in ideas' generation and research, in character development and scene setting. For these writers the structured, formal protocols of university reporting and expectations of progress can seem restrictive at best. How then should writers be accommodated and how best should they align their artistic approaches with their academic aspirations?

Kroll, who sees the creative writing supervisor as a "manager, coach and trainer all in one" has argued also that the supervisory relationship in creative writing can take some lessons from the "successful collaborative hard science supervisory model" (Kroll, 2009, p. 1). She believes that 'hands on' supervisors not only work effectively with students individually:

> [They] also set up external structures such as creative mentorships and, most importantly, exploit the power of the group. Scheduling practice-led research seminars that unpack the methods of creative writing research can be particularly useful. They demonstrate this type of research in action and allow refinement of research questions. Supervisors can also manage regular creative writing postgraduate support groups (Kroll, 2009, p. 1).

COMMUNICATION AND RESPECT

Protocols about behaviour are central to the need for clear supervisory rules and relationships. This is especially important in the latter stages of the candidature when a student's focus is shifting towards the exegetical component of the degree. Often supervisors are alarmed when a student demonstrates hostility in a projected rage about the work for which the supervisor becomes the focus of creative or theoretical frustrations. Hecq outlines such cases in her essay on transference. In these circumstances the student may challenge the supervisor, questioning their skills as a writer, noting better writers or more skilled supervisors. Detailed note taking and end of meeting reports, student emails after each meeting setting out understandings about the matters discussed can assist in defusing such moments.

Supervisors should expect demonstrations of 'writerly' resentment. Writers of fiction, for example, are not always good writers in other fields or in the formal and disciplined writing of the academy. In resisting the formalities of the exegesis, especially the reflective and theoretical exploration of their own work, writers may be voicing their anxiety about essay writing and critical analysis. It is important that throughout their candidature, writers are supported in essay writing skills, and theory and research techniques including citing. Leading writers may be particularly problematic in this regard, feeling that they are exposing a side of themselves or laying themselves open for harsher criticism than their unpublished colleagues.

While some students may prefer their supervisor to leave them to their own creative devices, in circumstances such as these Sinclair has cautioned against being too "hands off, noting that supervisors who do not actively intervene or direct, may fail to note that their students are not equipped to function independently" (Sinclair, 2004, in Kroll, 2009, p. 5).

SOLE AUTHORSHIP OR NEW PARADIGMS

The creative writing degree highlights the shifting nature of the multiple-authored text. Students and supervisors may differ in creative approach and students can resent the supervisor's suggestions in relation to character and plot. Remaining hands-off in offering suggestions especially in the early stages of the writing project is often the best course, but this can reduce the supervisor to the role of editor rather than a supervisor of a complex and challenging academic text.

The freedom to create is especially important in these first stages of the degree and the supervisor and student need to confer, agree upon, and document their discussions in this regard. Time management may seem to run counter to notions of freedom and creativity, but the time constraints and completion expectations of the degree are ever-present elements of creative discourse, however much the student would prefer they were not.

SOLE RESISTANCE TO THEORY AND THEORETICAL REFLECTION

There are two schools of thought about the need for creative writers to expand theoretically on their creative projects. Psychologists, such as Mihaly Csikszentmihalyi and Ernst Kris have argued that every creative act is a search for truth. Writers live sensed moments which offer the imagination the possibilities of projection – the ways in which a writer re-imagines so acutely that which they have not seen or heard in real life because they have lived intensely in other ways. Acts of creativity, Kris also has argued, "are in themselves a necessary part of artistic creation" (Kris, 1946, p. 15). Kris sees creativity as a type of problem-solving behaviour through which emotions are transferred to aesthetic activity. By giving these emotions life or letting them 'take thought' they become complex patterns, and, in the case of fiction writing, for example, are narrated and understood. From this perspective creativity is analytical in itself. Why then do creative writing candidates need to complete a further theoretical work?

Then there is the view that creative practitioners need to think (and research) more widely than their creative production. The American academic, David Radavich (1999) suggested writing programmes needed to review their over-emphasis on self-expression. He saw creative writing degrees, particularly those in the USA, "as developing from a kind of updated version of the 1960s *Me Generation*". "This is understandable and desirable so far as it goes," he claimed, "but writing instructors must take the next step and encourage toward a broad range of people in a rapidly changing world" (Radavich, 1999, n.p.n).

Radavich's concerns, it could be argued, have been addressed largely by the manner in which writing programmes are located in their wider schools or faculties, be they in arts, communication or creative arts. Through these disciplinary inter-relationships, universities offer candidates, who are focused on a specific creative project, ideas that engage them in on-going connections with the wider world of ideas, such as cultural studies, sociology, history, literature, new media and film. One presumes higher degree candidates are drawn to postgraduate study because of the cross-disciplinary, cross-fertilisation offered by this mix or because, as Dorritt Cohn has argued, "writing is not a mere game, a histrionic, ventriloquist use of serious discourse; it is a highly serious endeavour, having a unique mission to portray the operation of other minds in their very otherness" (Cohn, 1978, p. 7). In understanding the world through characters of other's or our own creation, we also understand ourselves. Radavich also has views on the ways in which creative writing and the wider academy should meet, believing that "if creative writing is to have meaning in the academy of the future, it needs to partake of those very qualities and purposes best representative of true scholarship: namely, broad, informed, intensive reading, thinking, and writing, and a commitment to a social betterment of a troubled world" (Radavich, 1999, n.p.n).

AND AFTER THE DEGREE?

In addition to the creative projects undertaken by writers during their postgraduate candidature there is the expectation of vocational enhancement from the conferred degree. Other than the writing and publication of their creative and critical theses, creative writing postgraduates may aim for employment in the academy or in literary and publishing agencies such as publishing houses, PR agency and advocacy services.

Creative writing has become an important sector of employment. Australian Bureau of Statistics (ABS, 2007, p. 13) data show that during the last five years over 800,000 Australians (15 years and older) worked in writing and publishing, almost 350,000 of them were in paid work. It is of particular significance to supervisors of creative writing higher degrees how they fill conspicuous gaps in the daily practices of writers, how they lead writers to develop skills in collective settings, and how such insights can inform arts policy-making and creative writing teaching and supervision. Today new definitions of 'creativity' stress the economic benefits of artistic activity (Throsby, 2008; Jones, 2009, pp. 54–60; Wu, 2005, pp. 8–9, 25; Oakley, 2007, pp. 5–7). While traditionally benefits have acknowledged literary, publishing, printing, designing and illustrating activities, creativity now encompasses the connections between writers, the sharing of professional knowledge and skills development, and the promotion of their work.

For a supervisor, awareness of these opportunities as well as the realities of the publishing sector is of key importance. While established writers may have a high expectation of publishing their degree, less established writers will have no such guarantee. A supervisor may find themselves caught between the limitations of the publishing world – especially with student work that is experimental or different from the popular norm – and their student's aspirations. Being honest while encouraging may be the best approach, but this may lead supervisors to encourage the student to write for the market. A common criticism of creative writing programmes is that they have a 'house' style, one that either leans towards conservative or market driven approaches, or one where students write experimentally without any thought of the publishability of their work.

THE ATTRIBUTES OF A SUCCESSFUL SUPERVISORY RELATIONSHIP

Effective postgraduate supervision in any discipline requires thoughtful and measured communication between candidate and supervisor. The role of the supervisor in a creative writing, postgraduate degree also requires a unique blend of the formal characteristics of more traditional research while allowing full play to the student's creative project. The background, creative experience, creative philosophy and approaches of the candidate are uniquely connected to those of their supervisor who may work in an area similar to their own or may offer something completely different – a paradoxical relationship where their creative 'disconnect' provides the potential for new ideas and new approaches. There are a number of ways these different characteristics can be managed, ranging from university protocols to jointly exploring new research paradigms:

– as noted above being clear about the reasons a writer wants to engage with the academy for their next creative project;
– understand what they want/need and expect from you as their supervisor. Are you their supervisor, editor, sounding board, mentor or all of these? Being clear about your role and establishing protocols about the supervisor/student exchange is particularly helpful if concerns arise about research and writing quality or progress. Being specific about your role as required by university governance is very important here;
– ensure that students set a research and creative writing plan even when, and especially if, there is resistance to the idea of meeting Faculty progress requirements;
– anticipate anxiety about the exegesis. Expect concerns about essay and exegetical writing and ensure students attend and are supported through their theoretical writing and research from the earliest stages of their candidacy.

For example:

– encourage students to stop telling themselves that the creative part is the exciting bit and the exegesis is 'boring', 'too hard', and 'dull', 'to be endured/resisted'. This negativity acts like molten lead on top of the writing;
– students should see the exegesis as a kind of story telling about their work;
– right from the beginning, suggest students collect quotes and fully cite them under headings or the questions they want to explore;
– they should keep a journal of questions/observations that will inform the exegetical text;
– read other theses and wider non-fiction work noting what interests or captures their attention about the writer's ideas;
– collect good opening sentences. Students often need 'springboard' sentences as a means of getting started. Assist them with this;
– creative writing students sometimes feel anxiety about the 'voice' of the exegesis. Encourage them to say things like: "at this point I'll digress a little" or "was I right in assuming this?" Questions allow a series of perspectives on an idea;

- examine good academic writing that uses traditional language and use the best of this: "While Smith argues ... and Jones says ....the argument that Hawkings puts is strong..." but subvert these by taking the ideas somewhere else: "Well, that may be the case, but as I sat on St Kilda beach that Sunday afternoon, I couldn't help but see in the sky and the water a wider meaning than that. An artistic one. A challenge to science....";
- suggest they play with sentence structure, sub-headings, and pose questions to the theorists: "I'd like to ask Duchamp a question: where did you get the saddle? Because it seems to me ...";
- establish protocols about sharing the writing with editors and publishers where the expectations of the writing may be different from those of the academy. Publishers may be anxious about what might happen to a writer's work when it faces the critical scrutiny of the academy. One Melbourne publisher expressed concerns about "the smell of the academy" on one of his client's work. Students may feel torn about these conflicting relationships. This needs to be identified and clarified early in the candidacy;
- develop and communicate a clear understanding of university rules and protocols as well as the wide support and creative opportunities the degree offers. Develop creative conversations and shared ideas. Offer good advice about editing and research, but carefully manage the needed distance from the student's own, specific, creative approaches, and your own.

CONCLUSION

Postgraduate degrees in creative writing offer a unique and often challenging relationship between a writer/student and writer/academic. They also provide an opportunity for creative writers to write within the community of the academy, its support and guidance, resources and research potential. By engaging in this way, the creative writer challenges the role of supervision, questioning through their creative research approaches the nature of research and its traditional definitions. It is a necessary, binary relationship between the creative and critical: a conversation about practice, creativity and ideas.

The role of the postgraduate supervisor is pivotal to this. As well as supporting and mentoring the process they often become the focus of their students' frustrations and their resistance to the constraints of the academy. Students may fear that the creative will be contaminated by the critical or that their experience of the critical will expose a dearth of ideas.

Yet the supervisor/student relationship in the creative arts has demonstrated also an untapped potential for a more reflexive and reciprocal academic interchange. As more and more writers engage with the academy, their experiences – especially those on-going dialogues about creativity and research – continue to reshape the academy's understanding of itself and the manner in which creative arts will continue to develop through a wide range of communities.

In the meantime, the effective management of postgraduate degrees remains an essential element to the success of these programmes. By supporting established protocols while developing new paradigms for the relationship, reviewing notions of authorship and collective creative processes, allowing full play to creative development while assisting creators to engage with the critical, the academy is developing new literary and creative conversations, and new communities.

REFERENCES

ABS (2007). *Work in Selected Cultural/Leisure Activities, Australia* (Cat. No. 6281.0) Australian Bureau of Statistics. Retrieved May 10, 2011, from http://www.abs.gov.au/

Cohn, D. (1978). *Transparent minds: Narrative modes for presenting consciousness in fiction.* Princeton, New Jersey: Princeton University Press.

Hecq, D. (2009. To know or not to know: the uses of transference in Ph.D. supervision. *Text, 6,* October 2009. Retrieved May 22, 2011, from http://www.textjournal.com.au/speciss/issue6/Hecq.pdf

Jones, K (2009). *Culture and creative learning: A literature review.* London: Creativity, Culture and Education. Retrieved October 1, 2009, from http://www.creativitycultureeducation .org/literaturereviews

Kris, E., & Pappenheim, E. (1946). The function of drawings and the meaning of the 'creative spell' in a schizophrenic artist. *Psychoanalytic Quarterly, 15,* 6–31.

Kroll, J. (2009). The supervisor as practice-led coach and trainer: Getting creative writing doctoral candidates across the finish line. *Text, 6,* October 2009. Retrieved May 22, 2011, from http://www.textjournal.com.au/speciss/issue6/Kroll.pdf

Lave, J., & Wenger, E. (1991). *Situated learning: Legitimate peripheral participation.* Cambridge: Cambridge University Press.

Madden, C. (2009). *The Independence of Arts Funding: A Review.* IFACCA D'Art Report No. 9. Sydney: International Federation of Arts Councils and Cultural Agencies. Retrieved May 2, 2011, from http://www.ifacca.org

Oakley, K. (2007). *Educating for the creative workforce: Rethinking arts and education.* ARC Centre of Excellence for Creative Industries and Innovation with Australia Council for the Arts. Retrieved May 4, 2011, from CCI website http://www.cci.edu.au

Radavich, D. (1999) Creative writing in the academy. Retrieved December 31, 2011, from http://www.davidradavich.org/creative.html

Sinclair, M. (2004). The pedagogy of 'good' Ph.D. supervision: A national cross–disciplinary investigation of Ph.D. supervision. Canberra: Department of Education and Training. In Kroll, J. (2009). The Supervisor as practice–led coach and trainer: Getting creative writing doctoral candidates across the finish line. *Text, 6,* October 2009, Retrieved May 22, 2011, from http://www.textjournal.com.au/speciss/issue6/Kroll.pdf

Smith, A. (2009). Peter Garrett, Federal Arts Minister [Interview], *Artworks* [Radio Braodcast], ABC Radio National 4 October. Retrieved May 9, 2011, from http://www.abc.net.au/rn/artworks/

Throsby, D. (2008). *Creative Australia: The arts and culture in Australian work and leisure.* Occasional Paper 3/2008 Census Series 1. Canberra: Academy of the Social Sciences in Australia.

Wenger, E. (2001). Communities of practice. In Neil J. Smelser & Paul B. Baltes (Ed.) *International encyclopedia of the social and behavioural sciences* (pp. 2339–42). Kidlington, Oxford, UK: Pergamon/Elsevier Science.

Wu, W. (2005). *Dynamic cities and creative clusters.* World Bank Policy Research Working Paper 3509. Retrieved September 1, 2009, from World Bank website http://www.worldbank.org/

PHILIP SAMARTZIS

5. ARTICULATING SOUND IN A SYNTHESISED MATERIAL SPACE

INTRODUCTION

This chapter draws on my experience as a postgraduate research supervisor to discuss the way creative-based research into sound and music uses the agency of exhibition as a means of dissemination. It begins by defining exhibition, how it relates to sound and music, and the ways in which exhibition can lead to innovation. It then proceeds to discuss the methods of presentation and their associated risks and benefits. Audience engagement and interaction in relation to the practice of exhibition is also considered, as are the role of the supervisor and examiner, and the process of examination. A reflection on the dissemination of creative research through exhibition concludes the chapter.

WHAT IS AN EXHIBITION?

An exhibition is usually understood to be a public display of works of art held in an art gallery or museum. While this definition describes the way some forms of art are presented, the demands of contemporary art require a more expansive definition to account for the range of presentation strategies often sitting in parallel sites or outside conventional sites of exhibition. These may include sites designed for the performing and screen-based arts, or ones located in the virtual realm. While the art gallery or museum provides particular conditions suitable for some visual, sonic, and object-based art, these very conditions can have the effect of undermining artworks that rely on a different set of operational conditions. The art gallery or museum, for instance, is comprised usually of large volumes of empty space informed by hard surfaces and reverberant acoustics that combine to create a functional yet austere site for articulation and engagement (Samartzis, 2007).

While these highly reflective and diffuse environments are designed to promote contemplation and reverie, the material conditions that have been outlined are more suited to silent and static art. On the other hand, artworks of a temporal nature are often constrained by these very acoustic, spatial and material conditions. This has led to a move away from the gallery or museum as the preferred site of exhibition for artists working in sound and video in favor of more mutable locales (Samartzis, 2009). While the art gallery and museum still play an integral role in the dissemination of ideas and experiences, they provide one option of many that artists now use to display their ideas and methods. Therefore one can argue for a definition of an exhibition that is inclusive of all practices in all possible sites. This

B. Allpress, R. Barnacle, L. Duxbury and E. Grierson (Eds.), Supervising Practices for Postgraduate Research in Art, Architecture and Design, 51–64.
©*2012 Sense Publishers. All rights reserved.*

definition takes into account the vast range of virtual and physical sites that artists now use as an adjunct to the gallery or museum including the online gallery or museum, music and performing arts venues, public sites and screens, the cinematic environment, audio and visual recordings such as CD and DVD, as well as other forms of publication.

WHAT IS SOUND ART?

While 'exhibition' can now be described as something that involves all manner of sites, materials and processes, the concept of an adaptive and mutable set of strategies underpinning contemporary notions of exhibition also aptly describes the protean quality of sound. Sound is, by its very nature, hybrid and interdisciplinary. It is the building block of music, the aural fabric of cinema, the immaterial murmur of installation art, and the often awkward stammer of performance art. It is everywhere and nowhere and usually goes unnoticed until explicitly expressed.

Sound art emerged from the combination of the technical innovation of the late nineteenth century and the lateral thinking of the early twentieth century. It drew on opportunities proffered first by the phonograph, then by cinema and radio, to integrate non-musical sound into the realm of composition and performance. It benefited from musical and artistic mavericks including Luigi Russolo, Edgard Varese, and Walter Ruttmann, who each argued for the importance of environmental sound as a means of forwarding contemporary music. By integrating the general chaos of everyday life into their projects through specially constructed noise machines by Russolo, and with un-pitched musical instruments by Varese, and field recordings of various objects by Ruttmann, their aim was to capture and celebrate the dynamism of progress within the industrial age.

The experiments that emerged from the early part of the twentieth century provided a reference for artists from various disciplines to consider the nature of sound outside the constraints of musical convention to articulate new and innovative practices. Nowhere is this more clearly evidenced than in the immediate aftermath of World War Two when the microphone, tape recorder, loudspeaker, and oscillator provided new methods of sonic exploration completely separated from the dissonant tonalities of serialism, and the balance and restraint of neo-classicism that had dominated the avant-garde up to that point. In addition, concepts of chance and methods of improvisation drawn from jazz, abstract expressionist painting and Eastern philosophy suggested new forms of organisation and instrumental articulation, to promote new understandings of the musical and material properties of sound. What emerged were radically new concepts of production, presentation and distribution, which drew on traditional venues such as the museum and concert hall and were complimented by specially conceived events in unusual locations; or purpose-built environments and installations were designed to maximise the aural and spatial aspects of sound art and experimental music. The radio and record also provided additional opportunities for the creation and presentation of new works for distributed listening. The ease with which contemporary sound art now occupies multiple sites of experience can be traced to this fertile period of experimentation in which the boundaries between music, art and performance collapsed. Recommended publications that document this history include Chadabe (1997), Nyman (1999) and Young (2002).

Figure 1. Towards a Cinema of Pure Means by Bruce Russell. Shown at The Physics Room, Christchurch (2010). Photo by The Physics Room. Copyright The Physics Room Trust.

EXHIBITING SOUND ART

So what are the similarities and differences between exhibiting sound art and visual art? Superficially at least, both share some clear benefits of exhibiting in an art gallery or museum. A specially designed and constructed environment that attempts to establish the ideal conditions for deep engagement and contemplation of artworks should be a positive development. Nevertheless it is a site full of contradictions. As the architectural design of the modern art gallery can be traced to Sir John Soane's purpose built, Dulwhich Picture Gallery of 1817, it seems at times only capable of benefiting art of a bygone era with its emphasis on interconnected rooms of compacted white walls, hard floors, diffuse lighting and sharp acoustics, yet it does provide an opportunity for experimentation and reflection for all art forms. The space, at its best, acts as a conduit between artist and audience that often transcends the perceived limitations of the site itself, while at its worst can severely compromise the exchange through ostentatious interior spaces, poor acoustics and extraneous noise.

Visual art continues to rely heavily on conventional sites of exhibition; however, sound art and music can draw on a range of spaces, mediums and technologies for expressive affects. In order to test and disseminate a supposition, though, an artist undertaking a formal programme of research must determine the best form of publication, accounting for its spatial, temporal, and material attributes to promote the research agenda as effectively as possible. Some researchers may decide to use only one key method of representation, others will draw on a broader range of presentation methods to communicate their key findings. In the realm of creative research, how one presents the work is a major consideration, as the exhibition is often a culmination of many years of rigorous experimentation. How an audience experiences the artwork is integral to the way significance and innovation is measured, therefore strategies of exhibition are often as important as the artwork itself (Samartzis, 2010).

As discussed previously, exhibition is a more versatile process than it once was when one considers the range of options now available to creative researchers. While an exhibition can include a presentation in a gallery or museum, this tendency only accounts for artwork favouring a particular design and arrangement of space, and the isolated and isolating experiences that sites such as these offer. However, this type of rarefied presentation is being complimented or contrasted more frequently by other types of production and presentation strategies, such as those artworks produced in situ that seek to engage with social and environmental issues within a public site. Whereas one provides a controlled and controlling environment, the other privileges a level of uncertainty that may lead to unexpected encounters between audience and artwork at any given time. Regardless of which form of exhibition is used, the fundamental role of the creative researcher is to understand the way each venue and/or space operates, and how each can be deployed to articulate significance and innovation most effectively through specially devised encounters (Samartzis, 2007).

The gallery or museum provides an homogenous environment, yet, nevertheless it can undergo a certain level of modification to heighten encounters between audience and artwork. A researcher working in sound or music will often modify a space using sound absorbing materials to mitigate reverb and extraneous noise. Once poor acoustics are addressed, researchers may install their own sound system to provide an auditory experience best suited for their creative aspirations. Researchers may also customise their composition by mixing and mastering in situ to account for the way sound propagates and disperses within the space of presentation. These types of interventions are designed to maximise the experience of the artwork yet they are undertaken within a history and tradition of exhibition. This enables the artwork to embody a series of questions within a continuum of practice-based research that speaks from within, and to, that tradition of exhibition and its attendant assumptions.

Whereas live art and performance demand different forms of exhibition, the spatial conventions that shape a music venue or concert hall are not dissimilar to those found in the gallery or museum. Live art and performance often occur in a specially designed and constructed environment built around a proscenium as the focus of the space. Usually, sound absorbing materials are employed to reduce reflected sound in order to provide a sympathetic acoustic environment isolated from intrusive background noise. The scale of the building may vary depending on the type of performance that it specialises in, but the venue is usually designed to provide a good line of sight between audience and performer through a rigid and stepped seating arrangement. The venue may be designed specifically for acoustic or amplified music but rarely can it support both equally. This is due to the specific technical demands that each requires. Regardless of the advantages that the live music venue offers, performing artists are often drawn to other less formal sites in order to play in a more relaxed environment, or to respond to a particular set of social and environmental stimuli that they may encounter in the public realm. Rather than operate in a vacuum these artists are inspired by the spontaneous and unexpected, and they construct responses accordingly (Samartzis, 2009).

Figure 2. Towards a Cinema of Pure Means by Bruce Russell. Shown at The Physics Room, Christchurch (2010). Photo by The Physics Room. Copyright The Physics Room Trust.

Recordings provide a different form of exhibition: one that is fixed and distributive. Recordings can act as a form of documentation for site-specific work, or they can embody original artwork designed specifically for dissemination through CD or DVD, and/or radio and Internet broadcast. Recordings may comprise audio-only stereo compositions or performances, or include more elaborate spatial works using surround-sound formats, which may be accompanied by visual or textual documentation. Recordings provide an audience with the opportunity to encounter artworks in their own time and space using their own technology and methods of audition independent of the prescribed conditions encountered in the art gallery, museum, or live music venue.

Recordings also provide the opportunity for listeners to revisit artworks multiple times for closer scrutiny, which is distinctly different from the ephemeral quality informing much contemporary artwork. The fact that recordings can be manufactured into objects and distributed through retail outlets, or experienced immaterially through pervasive computing and radio broadcasting, extends the range of possibilities as to how one publishes research and the manner in which it is encountered and absorbed.

THE PROCESS OF DISCOVERY

Creative research uses technology, material, and process to produce artworks that articulate new experiences of a particular problem. It affords the opportunity to consider information experientially to deepen understanding while providing a system for the extrapolation of ideas that can lead to discovery and innovation. The significance of creative research is that it opens up research to processes of knowledge generation constructed from a continuum of self-reflexive experimentation in order to arrive at new forms of articulation and engagement through public discourse. It also provides a mechanism that builds upon the history of exhibition using methods of production, fabrication, and installation to posit the artist and artwork within a broader cultural context, which may operate well beyond the limits of the research itself to generate additional associations and readings.

Sound artist, Bruce Mowson's research into existence as a state of immanence, aimed to produce new understandings of immanence through audio/visual installation art.[1] Immanence describes a subjective state that emphasises an embodied sense in time and space. It is explored in Bruce's artworks through the use of materials and techniques that heighten one's sense of being a receptor, of seeing and hearing, rather than being an identity formed in language. The research is conducted using non-linear, audio/visual technologies to create installation artworks that elude narrative sequencing through generative techniques. Typically this involves a computer-generated image and sound, projected into space in ways that seek to heighten the audience's sense of embodiment. These works are non-repetitive, and close attention to the materials reveals a structure of non-hierarchical variation and of continual change. Philosophically, this emphasises immanent notions of the self as being in a state of becoming, of being simultaneously complete in the present moment yet continually in change. Mowson made a number of presentations of the works during his candidature, as installation spaces, documenting the tension between the framed format of video, and the immersive and surrounding embodiment, which is activated in installation practice.[2]

Figure 3. Zippered by Bruce Mowson. Shown at RMIT School of Art Gallery, Melbourne (2006). Photo by Bruce Mowson. Copyright Bruce Mowson.

Artists draw on a range of strategies to solve problems, some of which may be haphazard while others may be methodical. The shift from concept to implementation often involves a certain amount of intuition, spontaneity, and play, where materials are manipulated to provide new readings. The process of play is important in creative research as it enables the artist to improvise with ideas to arrive at forms and structures that provide enough gravity to facilitate rigorous investigation. The artwork that is produced from this process may be one of a series of works that examine a specific problem, or one that is a culmination of all the findings produced during candidature. The way audiences are implicated within the notion of play is also an important consideration, in the formulation of an exhibition and the methods of interaction deployed to augment the experience of the artwork.

Figure 4. Abe Sada performing Abe Sada: Corridor, Western Australian Academy of Performing Arts, Edith Cowan University, Mt Lawley (2009). Photo by Andrew Ewing. Copyright Andrew Ewing.

Performance provides a significant component of Cat Hope's doctoral research into the musical possibility of infrasound, which is a frequency band that operates below the threshold of human hearing.[3] Using an ensemble of bass players to improvise within the sub-audible frequency range, Hope organised a series of public performances under the moniker of Abe Sada in places that included an underground car park and shop front window, in which the resonant frequency of the building materials comprising each space, including glass and metal, were activated as part of the performance. These performances provided the audience with an immersive and tactile sonic experience that was as much physical as aural, while the arrangement of musicians throughout the site of each performance provided a certain amount of spectacle within each event. As these performances occurred in public spaces, they operated quite differently from those based in a proscenium, as the musicians were distributed in different parts of the location to activate and respond to the architecture and materials of site. The audience, therefore, had to move in and around the musicians to experience the specific relationships being explored between direct and reflected sound, and localised and collective ensemble playing.[4]

Collaboration between artists and artists, artists and curators, and artists and theorists provides further opportunity to incorporate disparate fields of knowledge to the process of creation. Collaboration provides a mechanism for an artist to bring knowledge and skill to a project, thus expanding the parameters of investigation to arrive at outcomes born from collective effort. This can lead to outcomes dense with ideas and references, and hybrid in materials and methods, while modes of presentation and engagement may vary from the extremely focused to the wildly eclectic. Creative research thus benefits from the wide range of strategies derived from conceptual, theoretical, and practice-based processes that together help facilitate a method for discovery.

SUPERVISING PRACTICES OF EXHIBITION

Creative research is predicated on the interrogation of a series of questions through praxis. Exhibition is a strategic mechanism that embodies the research methods used to extrapolate significant new knowledge through sustained and rigorous enquiry. The role of the supervisor is to question the methods of research in order to ensure efficient transference of knowledge from artist to audience. The exhibition is central to this transaction as it provides a space and mechanism for an artist to situate their work in the best possible light. The supervisor usually assists the artist in selecting the most appropriate form of exhibition and the venues particularly suited to supporting the specific characteristics of the artwork. The supervisor may also help select the artwork or series of artworks that best demonstrate the objectives of the researcher while offering ideas as to how the exhibition could be staged and the resources required to support it in the most effective way. These conversations infer a close working relationship between researcher and supervisor built over the period of candidature.

James Hullick's research into recursion in sonic art generated an enormous amount of material during his candidature including recordings, performances, musical scores, and exhibitions. One of the more difficult tasks for supervisor and candidate, in this instance, was deciding the best balance of material to demonstrate innovation in the most direct and focused manner without compromising the integrity of the artwork. The exact type of presentation was another issue that needed to be resolved given the range and eclectic nature of the artworks. During the last six months of candidature, Hullick and I worked closely to select a group of artworks that most effectively addressed the set of research questions, which then led to strategic planning sessions around exhibition and examination. In Hullick's case no single presentation strategy was deemed adequate, so multiple sites were selected for their specific acoustic, spatial, and architectural qualities to demonstrate different facets of his research. The range of public outcomes Hullick produced during his candidature to test his research for critical feedback and reflection influenced these strategies, as he had already accrued considerable experience around the most effective forms of articulation and engagement for his various projects. Therefore, providing the best conditions for engagement of each key work became the focus of our planning, which led into examination.

The manner in which audiences navigate the space and interact with the artwork is also a crucial consideration for researcher and supervisor. The general audience that attends an exhibition is a surrogate for the external examiner and, therefore, it is implicated in the research process. How well the concept of new and original knowledge is articulated by the researcher through their art practice, and the manner it is received by the audience is therefore crucial to the way an exhibition is evaluated by artist and supervisor. To achieve a successful outcome when designing an exhibition there must be consideration of who the audience is and what their expectations are. An audience cognisant of the field will bring a deeper level of engagement and appreciation to the work than will one unfamiliar with the key tenets underpinning the research. A naïve audience, however, will bring with it a certain open-mindedness that can be useful in determining how effectively the researcher is communicating their findings. Each audience makes a useful contribution towards the framing of research, and the ways structures and methods tested in public can be applied to the process of examination.

EXAMINATION

The examination is the culmination of all the research undertaken by the candidate embodied in an exhibition of key artworks. The exhibition acts as a survey by including only the most salient artworks that combine to exemplify the overall research agenda. Sometimes an examination may involve only one artwork in which the key research objectives coalesce into the one cohesive form. Mostly, however, it is an exhibition of many disparate works with each artwork investigating one or two key questions. Together these artworks produce a narrative that describes the trajectory of research, what was learnt and how it impacted on subsequent projects.

The external examiners are usually peers of the research candidate, and familiar with the field of research and the methods of articulation. Their role is to evaluate the significance of the artwork comprising the exhibition and whether it has provided new knowledge to the field. They are guided by an exegesis, which is a contextual body of writing by the candidate, outlining the research agenda and the process of discovery through reflective critical discourse and supported by an appropriate durable record of audio or visual works. While the exegesis is used to guide the examiners as to the aspirations of the research candidate, the exhibition is the site where new knowledge must be articulated. Its role in creative research is therefore critical to the way artwork is appraised for innovation and significance.

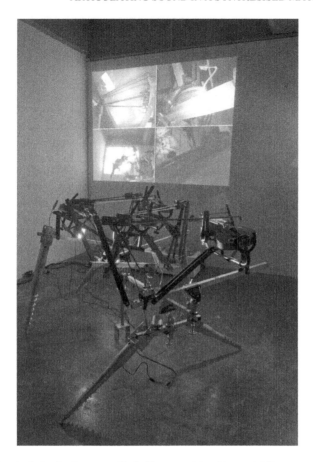

Figure 5. The Gotholin by James Hullick. Shown at West Space, Melbourne in Sonic Body (2008). Photo by Tim McNeilage. Copyright James Hullick.

The examiners sift through all the evidence presented by the candidate through exhibition, exegesis, and supporting documentation to determine how well the artworks have addressed the key questions underpinning the research. The researcher usually posits the work in a frame of reference using particular artists or artworks to highlight a problem or opportunity. The originality of the artwork is usually measured within this context while the body of knowledge that has been generated to answer the research questions determines the level of innovation. It is then incumbent on the examiners to make a determination as to how well the researcher has addressed their research questions, and whether the research itself has provided new information towards the field of investigation. The choice of examiners and their knowledge of the field are therefore critical to the way in which innovation and significance is measured within a structure that can verge at times on the oblique, and where poetics and aesthetics are equally at home as are the rational and coherent approaches.

RISKS AND BENEFITS

An exhibition can incorporate many types of presentation strategies for different types of artworks; however, the exhibition itself can be a fraught and difficult form of publication. The creation of any type of exhibition is in itself quite a difficult task when one takes into consideration the range of jobs necessary to achieve a successful outcome. These jobs include booking an appropriate space, securing financial support, acquiring technical infrastructure, liaison with gallery staff, designing and installing the exhibition, assisting with marketing and promotion, preparing didactic panels, maintaining exhibits, gallery supervision, site security, and documentation. An exhibition at its most basic form is already a very complicated enterprise made even more complex with the addition of a research agenda that must emphasise innovation and significance within a public forum. The stress and anxiety that this can place on a research candidate cannot be underestimated; therefore it is necessary for the supervisor to establish clear and attainable targets to mitigate potential problems.

The benefits of an exhibition, however, can far outweigh the risks when all aspects of a presentation are accounted for in planning and implementation. An exhibition provides an opportunity for a research candidate to customise an environment in order to provide the most effective form of encounter and experience of the research. The artwork materialises the theoretical concepts informing the researcher's agenda within a tactile and immersive environment designed to facilitate a direct exchange between artwork and audience. Exhibition provides an opportunity to create a controlled spatial-temporal and material experience that extrapolates the research through the unique prism of an artist's vision. While the exegesis enriches the exhibition, it is the first hand encounter with the artwork that often demonstrates the ability of creative research to interrogate ideas and processes in distinctive and compelling ways.

REFLECTION

So how does exhibition provide agency for the promulgation of new and significant ideas? An exhibition provides:

- an avenue for the expression of ideas through various sites and media;
- a space for exploration and encounter;
- the conditions for intellectual exchange;
- the capacity for the embodiment of research;
- an opportunity to communicate to a broad audience.

An exhibition is multi-faceted in the sense that it can serve many different forms of articulation and experience. It provides creative researchers the opportunity to design an experience of their work that is extremely personal to emphasise the unique attributes of their field of investigation. It allows them to posit their work within a continuum of intellectual discourse and creative practice while developing new propositions that enrich the field. An exhibition also speaks to a broad constituency comprising an audience that is often as invested in the idea of new and significant knowledge and practices as is the creative researcher. It is a complex mechanism for the dissemination of research yet provides numerous possibilities for how one can encounter and experience innovation within a synthesised material space.

The supervisor plays an important role in assisting the researcher to frame and elucidate their research in a manner that is compelling to the examiner. While the researcher is responsible ultimately for the way in which their findings are presented, the supervisor can help organise a set of priorities to afford the most convincing demonstration of the strengths and originality of the research. Although the examiner provides external expertise to the process of evaluation, effective communication can extend the evaluation well beyond the subjective parameters of the research to incorporate a broader narrative of material and immaterial experience.

Neither the gallery nor the museum can be considered neutral spaces as they are sites loaded with history and tradition, yet these very aspects enable the creative researcher the opportunity to posit their artwork within a richer cultural discourse. The researcher and supervisor, therefore, use the mechanism of exhibition and its assorted associations to advance original knowledge, a distinct form of dissemination when juxtaposed with conventional modes of publication such as a thesis, yet comparable in that each method of publication provides a particular means of expressing innovation. Practices of exhibition are no less rigorous or demanding than their written counterpart, yet they can provide a first-hand encounter with knowledge that really is impossible to reproduce in any other form. In that regard, exhibition will continue to play a distinct and vital role in creative research.

NOTES

[1] I was senior supervisor on Dr Bruce Mowson's doctoral research titled, *Sound and video installation art: Existence as a state of immanence* (2008), RMIT University.

[2] This summary references the abstract accompanying Bruce Mowson's Ph.D. exegesis. For further information refer to http://www.brucemowson.com

[3] I was senior supervisor on Dr Cat Hope's doctoral research titled, *The possibility of infrasonic music* (2010), RMIT University.

[4] For further information on Cat Hope's research refer to http://www.cathope.com

REFERENCES

Chadabe, J. (1997). *Electric sound: The past and promise of electronic music.* New Jersey: Princeton Hall.

Nyman, M. (1999). *Experimental music: Cage and beyond (music in the twentieth century).* Cambridge: Cambridge University Press.

Samartzis, P. (2010). Sound, art and curation. In David Forrest (Ed), *The curator in the academy* (pp. 100–112). Melbourne: Australian Scholarly Publishing.

Samartzis, P. (2009). Why do electronic birds sing?. In *Laneways commissions 09 artist book* (pp. 26–31). City of Melbourne.

Samartzis, P. (2007). The space of sound. In Lesley Duxbury, Elizabeth Grierson & Diane Waite (Eds), *Thinking through practice: Art as research in the academy* (pp. 42–53). Melbourne: RMIT Press.
Young, R. (2002). *Undercurrents: The hidden wiring of modern music.* New York and London: Continuum.

ELIZABETH GRIERSON

6. A COMPLEX TERRAIN

Putting Theory and Practice to Work as a Generative Praxis[1]

INTRODUCTION: QUESTIONS AND DEFINITIONS

My heart in hiding

Stirred for a bird, – the achieve of, the mastery of the thing!

(Gerard Manley Hopkins, *The Windhover*)

The philosophical project of this chapter is to consider the relationship of theory and practice in the supervisory contract with candidates who are undertaking research degrees in art and design or other creative fields. The approach works towards a generative form of praxis. The Greek origin identifies *praxis* as a generative "doing, acting, action, practice" from Greek, *prassein (prattein), to pass through, experience, practice.* This refers to the practice or practical side of a field of study. Generative, from Latin, *gererāre, to beget,* from *genus, kind,* is used here in the sense of producing something new, creating, or bringing something into being.

In this chapter creative research is identified as *art-based* with exhibitions or performances, and accompanying exegetical texts, the combination of which comprise the project to be examined; and creative research can be *text-based* in which language is itself a creative practice. They are both forms of practice for the identification of research questions and generation of ideas for the adoption of a new body of work. *Practice* is identified as action, from Greek, *praktikē, practical work,* from *prattein, to do, to act.* By seeking an approach that activates the web of language in *text* as a form of practice as much as it activates the aesthetic action in *art* as a form of practice, this discussion is extending our understanding of what *praktikē* might mean when text and art come together. It is seeking to dismantle the separated and normative categories of theory and practice by putting them to work in a relationship of practical action. This practice, in its broadest sense, carries the economies of newly created ideas, objects, technologies, and cultures into a world of action, thus achieving the aim of a postgraduate research degree, which is to create something new and add to the body of knowledge in the field.

The relations of theory and practice are complex and inherently creative, but by no means naturalistic; their categorisations are not to be assumed as normal or natural. The act of supervising calls for a few fundamental questions about theory and practice to be kept in mind. For a start, what kind of practice are we talking about when we refer to practice-based research? Is practice positioned as an engine

B. Allpress, R. Barnacle, L. Duxbury and E. Grierson (Eds.), Supervising Practices for Postgraduate Research in Art, Architecture and Design, 65–80.
©2012 Sense Publishers. All rights reserved.

that drives the adoption of theory, or is it the other way around? Or can they operate inter-textually in easy relationship one with the other? How do we define theory and what happens if it is displaced or inherently slipped from cognition by the practitioner? Similarly what happens when practice is cast aside by the theoretician? What is at work here?

It would seem unreasonable to expect new knowledge to be created in a philosophical, theoretical, or practical vacuum. So perhaps the crucial question is: How to activate theory in a critical space of practical reflection, and likewise how to activate practice in a critical space of theoretical reflection? Significantly, how to turn both forms of creative practice (art and text) into *praxis*, action?

LITERATURE AND APPROACHES

There are a number of writers whose work can inform a pedagogical approach to these questions in postgraduate supervision. Writings from Martin Heidegger, Jacques Derrida, Gilles Deleuze and Félix Guattari aid a critical approach to understanding flux, complexity and dynamism in the relations of theory and practice as generative sites of enquiry. Hannah Arendt activates a theory of action in her use of the term *praxis*, in that she seeks to go beyond the reflective or contemplative life (*vita contemplativa*) and into the active life (*vita activa*), affirming one's capacity to struggle with ideas and engage in practical action (Arendt, 1958).

Writings by Henri Giroux (1983) and Paolo Freire (1996) show how to seek a transformative pedagogy through enhancing critical awareness of the learner's life conditions in order to transform them through *praxis*. Implied here is the potential for transformation of a learner's specific subjectivity. Useful also is Michel Foucault's approach to genealogy, as a replacement for ontology, in considering subjectivity. For Foucault, as for Nietzsche, there are no *essences* of human beings, as Besley and Peters so aptly remind us in *Subjectivity and truth: Foucault, education, and the culture of self*, when they write, "For Foucault as for Nietzsche genealogy replaces ontology ... Genealogy challenges the humanist idea that the self is unified and fully transparent to itself ... It also challenges the progressivist agendas of the Enlightenment by emphasising dispersion, disparity and difference, taken-for-granted universal 'truths' about life" (2007, p. 25).

Foucault understands the workings of power in the productive sites of *praxis* in the institutions of society with their regulatory mechanisms and practices of surveillance, which produce dominant and marginalised discourses. Within such discourses the candidate's research takes place and seeks legitimation. With regard to legitimation, Jean-François Lyotard (1984) wrote about systems of legitimation in the narratives of society, and the need for small stories (*petits récits*) to speak their actions. This is in light of the dominance of knowledge that makes explicit appeal to metanarrative certainties. Lyotard showed how the prioritisation of "truth statements", which are premised in modern metanarratives of progressive historicism, will no longer give a legitimate account for different genres of discourse in the postmodern condition of knowledge (Grierson, 2000, pp. 153–154). Each of these writers has a bearing on understanding the procedures of knowledge formation through creative-led research supervision.

The approach discussed here is grappling with the perils of servitude to naturalism and aesthetic constancy, as it considers the potential for difference in creative scholarship. This approach also calls on Jacques Derrida (1978a, 1978b) and his process of activating *difference* in the web of language. A generative form of *praxis* implies a working relationship at the interface of difference or between opposing ideas that a candidate may bring to, or find in the research project. Chantal Mouffe (2005, 2007) assists the understanding of what it means to struggle with opposing or conflicting ideas in different lineages of knowledge, such as theory and practice. Working with radical democracy, as a condition of difference, Mouffe acknowledges *agonism* at the interface of ideas, people, opinions and actions, a procedure that can be found in the working relations of theory and practice in the research contract. 'Agonism' characterises a form of dispute that acknowledges difference and allows difference its space of existence. This enacts a process different from the customary modes of political thought of setting up opposing forces and antagonisms, through which one person's ideas and practices can win only at the expense of another's, or through which art practice as a condition of knowledge can win only by rendering theory to a negative position.

DISCOURSES AND CONDITIONS OF KNOWLEDGE

Both art and textual practice as research have the capacity to bring something new into existence when they are driven by the impetus to create. As I have written elsewhere, this impetus is "manifested through ideas, imagination, materiality, thinking through practice, coupled with risk-taking, making unlikely connections, accepting failure and success, and transferring this knowledge to others via a range of aesthetic practices" (Grierson, 2011, p. 349). The *making new* is a foreign terrain of discovery, an essence of creativity, and sometimes it is quite inexplicable where the drive comes from. A similar impetus drives us into advanced research and supervision. There is always the potential for entering new discourses and opening knowledge to the "more". As Michel Foucault said, "discourses are composed of signs; but they do more than use these signs to designate things. ... It is this 'more' that we must reveal and describe" (Foucault, 1994, p. 49, in Grierson, 2003, p. 111). However, "before one can reveal, describe and analyse 'modes of existence' one must have the political will to do so" (Grierson, 2003, p. 111). Here I am questioning the postulations of creativity as a self-evident condition known best (and only) to the artist or creative practitioner-researcher. The will to enter the challenge, the will to think in a questioning way, and the will to know that you do not know, is crucial if one is to sustain research as a candidate or supervisor.

The condition of creativity as a way of forming new knowledge through practice calls for a more critical awareness of the discourses in which we create or make new, and of the power and politics of knowledge itself. This way of working involves the recognition and exploration of aesthetic, epistemological, ontological, and genealogical questions. These are multifaceted discourses, so we need to understand what Foucault calls, "the modes of existence of this discourse", asking along with Foucault, "Where does it comes from, how is it circulated, who controls it?" (Foucault, 1977, p. 138).

I have argued elsewhere that as one undertakes creative arts practice and research, one *becomes* a creative subject (Grierson, 2009a). There is at work a condition of being, as in the words of Deleuze and Guattari, we are in process, always in the middle of things, in a state of becoming; we are particular beings, historised rather than universalised. To that extent the researcher is implicated in the process of creative arts-based research, which is genealogical and rhizomic.[2] Creative practice as research is a structuring way of finding a particular voice and position within this circuitous process, a way of speculating, speaking, constructing, struggling, revealing, testing, discovering, questioning, creating new knowledge, and paving the way for new and further questions or speculations for another time.

TESTIMONY, VOICE, METHODOLOGY

But how did you make your presence felt (which I saw as a kind of honesty) while keeping that self subsidiary to the work under discussion? (Stead, 2008, p. 13).

The question of voice deserves consideration here. How does the researcher claim a particular speaking space in the research field under examination? Critical pedagogy (Giroux, 1983, 1995) is an approach that enables a candidate to be part of the knowledge systems under construction, and to enable political discernment of officially inscribed constructions of knowledge. It is a way of empowering candidates in their academic quest through critical awareness of how their knowledge is formed, framed, and legitimated. In these research systems, the researcher is seeking to legitimate his or her voice in the research findings. Adopting the first person narrative genre to provide a testimony can be a methodological decision available to postgraduate candidates, particularly in the creative fields. However, it is my experience that often research candidates feel the need to prioritise objective language in their writing, as though they themselves do not have an authentic voice, thus effectively writing themselves out of the research. One's experience in the field can be cited as evidence of authenticity, or can be tapped as a way of addressing questions, but as New Zealand writer and literary critic, C. K. Stead asks: How do we make our presence felt?

The question of how voice is used is not a new concern. Feminist, post-colonial and postmodern epistemologies have, for several decades, interrogated the place of power relations in research. This is consistent with revisionism in the disciplines of humanities and social sciences, with reconsiderations of dominant voices and ways of knowing, and questioning practices that advantage certain groups, cultures, experiences, or knowledge fields over others. One can be marginalised, too easily, through denial of voice, place, and position. The denial of epistemic voice or authority is a serious issue and one for the research candidate to grapple with, in coming to decisions of methodology.

Methodology is not neutral, neither is one's speaking position. Methodological decisions demand early discussion and disclosure of an epistemological, social, and cultural standpoint.[3] It can be said that at the start of any project, one of the supervisor's responsibilities is to ensure the candidate is aware of the politics of voice and exclusion through methodological decisions. They need to be aware of the way methodology frames and forms the research itself, and the consequences of this framing for the body of knowledge and for themselves as scholars.

I am quite ready to declare that my writing in this chapter takes the standpoint of situated knower in that I am not impartial.[4] The positioning of voice is implicit here in that I am drawing on over 25 years of first-hand experience as an academic in tertiary education, and also from my doctorate research on the politics of knowledge in education.

The experience of supervising doctorate and master's projects extends over 16 years to date, with 26 successful completions,[5] and examiner for over 20 doctorate and master's degree projects. These supervisions and examinations come from a range of disciplinary fields of fine art, design, music, philosophy of education, literature and art education. They include practices, philosophies and theories. This experience has taught me that there are many and various ways to approach the postgraduate research project, and as many ways of approaching supervision. It is a complex terrain, often demanding. In approaching this complexity, I have drawn from my formalised learning in English language and literature, performing arts, fine art, art history and theory, and philosophy of education, and teaching in these subjects. This experience brings me to the supervisory field conditioned to work with diverse disciplines in relational ways.

As supervisors, we also bring with us the experiences of being supervised. Elsewhere I have written about the process of selecting a supervisor, and how crucial this is for a successful project (Grierson, 2010, pp. 120–123). For my part I sought a Ph.D. supervisor who was a specialist in the scholarship and philosophies of education in which my research was grounded. Researching the political dynamics of the constructed object of art, I was investigating issues of production and legitimisation, through poststructuralist philosophies and approaches, to activate a critical history of present politics and practices in education. The research positioned art as a site of knowledge, but more than that I was interested in the politics of knowledge, and the political processes and dynamics of power that such positioning of art gives rise to. This project tested assumptions, and uncovered identifiable grounds of dispute in the archives of educational practices, and it became "clear to me that the methodology is the political framing device to ensure a critical outcome" (Grierson, 2010, p. 123). My research and practice shows that the supervisory relationship is itself a pedagogical space requiring a methodological clarity.

NEGOTIATING THEORY AND PRACTICE

Thinking about methodology calls for a grappling approach to relations of theory and practice, and a supervisory confidence in such an approach. It is not always an easy relationship. I have defined theory as "critically interpretative procedures, which engage with aspects of ideology, history and culture, in a generic sense rather than through specific adherence to the Frankfurt School of Critical Theory" (Grierson, 2000, p. 387). To be propositional about it, theory does not situate knowledge on a lofty perch, nor is it "defined exhaustively by the principles of verification and empiricism" (Giroux, 1995, p. 27). Working through creative projects soon reveals that both theory and practice are active in the political acts of knowledge generation through art and design, and in Giroux's words, "both exist within a constant and shifting terrain of negotiation" (p. 27). This is the critical terrain that one must activate as a supervisor, and encourage in one's candidates as they grapple with the exigencies of practice and seeming intrusions of theoretical concepts. It is all about negotiation, as they recognise, investigate and tentatively work with, and activate their projects.

Through centuries of Western enlightenment the categorising practices of institutional thought positioned theory and practice as different discourses, with art theory and art history finding their home in the humanities, quite separate from the home of fine art or design practice. Undeniably each has different historical trajectories, and it is particularly in Western knowledge systems that theory has been construed in a way that can separate it from practice *per se*. Much is to do with the genealogy of practice as being naturalistic, or in other words some sort of God-given gift or insight confirmed by the patriarchal discourses of creativity as a natural condition, rather than a skill that can be gained via rigorous learning and application.

Problems of the naturalistic discourse in liberal traditions of education and political subjectivity have been well rehearsed for several decades of critical writing, yet we can witness how the hour glass of privileging practice has been upturned in some institutional settings to the detriment of critical rigour. The subsequent outcome of privileging practice over critical interrogation, and overlooking robust theoretical and philosophical debate, inevitably renders theory to somewhere else at the bottom of the hour glass, as though artists and designers do not need the intrusions of such thoughts, concepts, and writings into the 'purity' of practice – a problematic position indeed, and one arising from a post-critical turn in the academy in context of the pragmatics of market-driven demands of globalised economies.

GENERATIVE RELATIONS

What is being advocated here is a generative state, no less rigorous for its generativity, through which something is revealed that may not have been available previously to the senses or cognition. The German philosopher, Martin Heidegger (1977a, p. 9) speaks about the process of "presencing" in his argument that "technology is a mode of revealing" (1977a, p. 13). He speaks of the starting of something in order to "set it free" and "start it on its way… into its complete arrival" (p. 9). These philosophical ideas are very accessible for a practitioner-researcher in that they cohere with the practitioner's way of working as a creative process.

Following Heidegger, I would argue that the "starting of something" occurs through working in a questioning and open way with indeterminacy as a crucial condition of the relations of theory and practice. Further to this, if supervisors work with candidates toward this sense of generativity as a "bringing-forth" of something new, the research project can benefit. It needs to be said that disembodied theory serves little useful purpose; it must have a transitive element, something able to be activated in practice, as practical action. The silent insensate condition of theory, as a mode of philosophical practice speaking primarily to itself, serves little purpose in the generation of new knowledge, particularly in any sort of creative enterprise. Similarly, it could be said that practice serves little purpose as a primarily expressive element if it has no room for critical reflection and rigorous scrutiny.

My doctorate research grappled with the assumed relations between theory and practice, through pedagogies of art history and studio-based practice, in university art education. Research of a number of art-based projects showed that an active approach to generative relations on the part of supervisor and candidate can be found in the practical and theoretical discourses under investigation. Theoretical, practical, historical, and philosophical questions about image and object, and their epistemological frames, can be prised open for further investigation, when the activation of skills, knowledge, and understanding of the research field situates a form of practice. Then, the agent of construction (the artist, designer, or performer) can dialogue in a relational way within the object of investigation (the artwork) and its context (the life world) through the interventions of other discourses (Grierson, 2000, p. 370).[6]

THEORISING THIS DOMAIN: A NEW FORM OF PRAXIS

There is a process of praxis being advocated here, which rests in ground rules of *indeterminacy*, or *paralogy*. For instance, in the equation $y = x + 1$, the inclusion of two unknown variables y *and* x disallows a determinate solution. Language, art, and thought speak in indeterminacy with variable rules of reason proliferating.[7] Knowledge is not something value-free, neither is it independent from the researcher. Knowledge and the knower are implicated with each other through the process of discovery, and by collapsing binary formations. "Our subjectivities are implicated as positivism's faith in value-free enquiry is repudiated. … [as we] work with indeterminacy and paralogy as a generative form of praxis" (Grierson, 2000, pp. 172–3).

Lyotard (1984, p. 61) defines *paralogy* (*para*: beside, beyond, amiss, irregular) as "a move (the importance of which is often not recognised until later) played in the pragmatics of knowledge". In his introduction to Lyotard's book on postmodern knowledge, Fredric Jameson (1984, p. xix) describes this process as, "a search, not for consensus, but very precisely for 'instabilities,' a practice of *paralogism*, in which the point is not to reach agreement but to undermine from within the very framework in which the previous 'normal science' had been conducted". He acknowledges the site of "struggle, conflict, the agonic [in] the rhetoric in which all this is conveyed" (p. xix). Thus *paralogy* is to be welcomed as a condition of knowledge (in theory and practice) throughout the research process, as it problematises forms of knowledge that exude dominance and exclude other ways of thinking.

A brief genealogy of the domains of theory and practice takes us to the ancient Greek philosopher and logician, Aristotle[8] and his school, the *Lyceum*, where he developed a theoretical and pragmatic approach to political theory, natural phenomena, ethics, education and science. Basing his philosophies on phenomena that are the product of natural design, and the gaining of irrefutable facts through an ordered process of theory and practice, logic and reason, Aristotle had divided sciences into three main categories: *theoria*, theoretical, with truth as end goal; *poiesis*, productive, with production as end goal; and *praxis*, practical, with action as end goal. Practical knowledge, divided into ethics, economics and politics, sought empirical data for its legitimating principles. This process was aimed at knowledge and action situated through *praxis*, the practical, with the quest for knowledge as an objective domain of truth being undertaken by theories of deductive reasoning as in science. The propositional logic is based in *kinesis*, the action of the human being coming into actuality by achieving its rational *telos*, its end goal.

If we fast forward from Aristotle to the twentieth century, there is a shift in the understanding of *praxis* via Jacques Derrida's project of deconstruction. Derrida displaces the centrality of propositional logic, and the prioritisation of reason as a progressive force in liberal thought and political design. His deconstructive approaches are brought to bear upon the classical opposition between the projects of literature as style and fiction, and philosophy as the domain of truth objectively presented (see Howells, 1999). Similarly, a deconstructive approach to art, and/or design, would dismantle binary oppositions of art as practice (compare literature), and art as aesthetic theory (compare philosophy). It would soon be shown that if philosophy (theory), as a process of propositional logic, claims to find or present 'truth' in a way that is independent of the language used in that finding and presentation, then it deludes itself and its followers. Thus, theory and approach become as one. It could be argued that accessing artworks or art practice via universal principles of 'natural insight' or 'creative intuition', or grounding art history or theory in metaphysical assumptions of ontological presence or objective rationality, might engage similar delusions. Furthermore, as "literature is not primarily fictional representation, clothed in a pleasing style" (Howells, 1999, p. 72), so art as practice is not primarily concerned with pleasing (aesthetic) style. As Howells points out, Derrida's procedure conceptualises literature and philosophy as 'texts', a methodology enabling philosophical writings, as texts, to be subject to the same kind of analysis as literary texts. Thus the writer as critic can be at work in his or her own texts, just as the artist as critical researcher can bring heightened rigour to his or her own artworks. By the same procedure, both theory and arts practice, and the languages through which they are represented, are easily subject to methodological questioning and deconstructing for closer examination (Grierson, 2000, p. 377).

THE FORMATION OF A POLITICAL WILL[9]

The aim is, therefore, to activate and decentre the rational orders of presence as pre-conditions of knowledge, in both theoretical and practical procedures of 'coming to know' through arts-based research. The pedagogical aim is to allow a state of indeterminacy to exist, and to invest the supervisory site with relational possibilities as a new form of *praxis*.

When a deconstructive procedure is brought to bear upon those pre-conditions in this way, then theory and practice will come forth from opposing corners, reject the antagonisms forced upon them, not by further antagonism and finding flaws in the other, but by performative intervention and relationality. There is something here of Chantal Mouffe's discursive subject of radical democracy. The approach goes beyond the authorial intention of a proposition. It suggests a way of grappling with ideas through practice, and rigorously positioning them or debating them through theoretical discourses. Foucault had talked about the kind of intellectual that does not seek replication or representation via authorial intention of propositional logic, but to "question over and over again what is postulated as self-evident ... to dissipate what is familiar and accepted ... to participate in the formation of a political will" (Foucault in Kritzman, 1990, p. xvi).

The pedagogical aim suggested here is to inscribe theory and practice with something of this political will, to enable an agonistic spirit to promote creativity and the determinations of new thought in practice. This process will activate a form of *difference*, coined by Derrida (1981, 1982) as *différance,* which is deferral of the centre, whereby sameness and difference are both possible at one and the same time. Difference may be then understood, examined, and activated, for the enabling of speaking positions as an epistemic right – the right to speak from the perspective of one's own world-view. An episteme is the body of ideas that determines acceptable or agreed knowledge at any given time and place, which is determined, according to Michel Foucault, by the strategic apparatus of society. Inevitably through the workings of power in the institutions of society, there are formations of dominant and marginalised practices. The supervisory relationship needs to take account of this.

As a way forward, working with potentially different world-views, Derrida shows through a process of differing from, and deferring to, that the generation of knowledge need not be determined dualistically through antagonistic separations. As with practice and theory, the knowing subject and epistemic object may intertwine, each turning to the other in *deferral*, as the Möbius strip (see Grosz, 1994).[10] Such entailment and entitlement can be confirmed through the supervisory process, as one works with research practice as a theoretical and practical research with its own kind of praxis. As discussed elsewhere (Grierson, 2009b) there is a critical attitude here, a way of deconstructing dominant discourses and instrumental thinking, as an approach to the task of supervision.

SOME PRAGMATICS ALONG THE WAY

Once the projects have been formulated and the relationships established in the supervisory site, then the years of research begin, as time and risk-taking mark the landscapes of supervisory meetings and discoveries, the lapses and critiques, with the inevitable Mouffe-style agonistic struggles, the rejections and disappointments, the analysis and soul-searching, the ah-ha! moments, the terrible doubts and wanders down paths that go nowhere, the determined labours to bring it all back home, the creative energies to activate the way of it, the excitement of renewal, consolidation and resolution, and always the risk of projecting onto others the self-doubts and non-resolvement.

At this point it is timely to make some pragmatic observations. Firstly, that the supervisor-candidate relationship develops as a kind of contract, each party with a responsibility to the other, a promise or agreement with common obligations, not to be entered into lightly. At the outset, it is wise to discuss these obligations, and set parameters to establish sound working relationships and patterns, ensuring regular meetings occur even if, apparently, there is little to discuss; and trusting that nothing to discuss can easily turn into something and, if nothing else, it can provide a sense of stability and care for the contract.

Then there is the challenge of what to do if either party finds the contract breaking down. Pragmatically speaking, it is better to acknowledge this rather than continuing with unsatisfactory dialogue or no dialogue at all. Changing supervisors is not such an onerous task, yet candidates can be reluctant to articulate their concerns, and supervisors need to be alert to this. I recall in my own doctorate process, I had a second supervisor who was rarely present and, I felt, was not connected to the project, so I requested the name be removed from my candidature records. It was a straightforward matter and an entirely appropriate action. The candidate must be happy with the arrangements and feel that he or she is well matched with the supervisor, otherwise no one will be happy and research cannot advance; likewise the supervisor must be well matched to the candidate and project.

Research questions, challenges and issues need to be discussed, debated and disseminated, throughout the project. Constructing opportunities for this to occur while the candidate is in the safety zone of the institution is a worthwhile way to build confidence and test ideas. During my time as a Visiting Research Fellow at the University of Brighton, in England, there were regular doctorate group meetings over coffee, with sharing of projects, raising questions and issues, discussing methodology or literature reviews, structures or formulations, field work or analysis, or whatever was at hand. In a relaxed and unpressured atmosphere of conversation one did not feel so alone. Over the years as a supervisor I have initiated opportunities for symposia, seminars, articles for journal and book publications, with the aim of ensuring candidates will have opportunities to speak in public, and publish findings during the process of candidature, rather than waiting until afterwards. It takes courage and resilience to speak as an expert in the field, and I have always deemed it better for the candidate to be party to rigorous critique in the relative safety of the supervisory relationship, rather than waiting to hear it and experience it for the first time in the public domain, where judgement and criticism can be harsh and difficult to contest as a lone scholar. One must learn to wear that invisible suit of armour through knowing your material so well you are indestructible (see further in Grierson, 2010, p. 135). Activating the candidate's power of speaking with authority and disseminating findings in a range of different scenarios and audiences would seem to be a valuable component of the supervisory process.

PROJECTS AND THE ART OF PRACTICE

As one works towards a new kind of *praxis*, there is always the need for moving aside from the position of 'knowing subject' as supervisor, or adducing endless explanations and justifications from the candidate. An overabundance of didactic and dialectical reasoning, with its privileging of epistemological presence, may not provide the landscape for the generation of new practice. It takes time and steady patience on the part of the supervisor to allow the candidate to find the way, own the struggle, and articulate the questions. It is not a 'show and tell' of how clever he or she is; or how clever the supervisor is; rather it is about exposing new ideas in a safe environment of practice, and having the confidence to hand ideas over at every turn of the discourse.

The research projects that I have supervised, and those I am supervising currently, involve the crafting of substantial 'texts' of art practice plus exegesis, or of solely text-based practices. Both art and language are conveying the research findings. Thus art as practice, and theory as practice, are working as co-existing texts that can be read and experienced through their activations of epistemological and methodological difference. Over the years, many projects have given evidence of this way of working. One was a master's project on "perpetual mutability" through discourses of image and text. The examination presentation consisted of a hand-crafted book combining an acute poetic sensibility and the interrelations of subjective experience, coupled with a refined form of visual semiotics via projected video images and installation emptied of any excess.[11] Another worked overtly with a Derridean process of *différance* as a deferring to, and differing from, at one and the same time. It showed an understanding of how such an approach and methodology could be the subject and substance of research practice.[12] Another doctorate project, practice-led, on sound and video installation, worked with the intervention of a Heideggerian sensibility to activate sound art as a potential for immanence in the praxis of living.[13] And notable was an art-based project premised on inclusive exchange addressing matters of identity politics, at the heart of what has become known as Aboriginal and non-Aboriginal knowledge systems. This doctorate project on visual practices as cultural translations contributed new findings to the perspectives of knowledge itself as an epistemological and genealogical process of translation, in specific cultural settings, and it was there that a generative *praxis* was in evidence.[14]

Some projects work principally through theory to produce language as an artefact or material form of practice. Crucial in such an approach is to keep the creative sense of language alive in the candidate, just as one keeps the art practice alive in a creative arts-based project. Examples in my archive of supervision practices include one that examined art-writing as a Marxist critique of contemporary idealism bringing theory and practice together in its foundational approach;[15] and another performed a philosophical investigation of gendered ontology through a process of writing that could only be described as exquisitely poetic and theoretical at one and the same time. This candidate enhanced the theory of practice, and the practice of theory, through theory *as* practice.[16]

A DISCURSIVE AND OPEN SYSTEM

We come to know what it means to think when we ourselves are thinking (Heidegger, 1977b, p. 369).

These brief descriptions give a sense of the indeterminate and even risky spaces one enters at the outset of a postgraduate research programme in the creative fields. Between the supervisor and candidate, there are explorations in spaces of potential with the infinite variations, connections and possibilities of a rhizome, de-territorialising and re-territorialising in constant flow and flux, to use the explanations of Gilles Deleuze and Félix Guattari in *A Thousand Plateaus* (1993, p. 7). A willing suspension of judgement, coupled with a well-articulated rigour and scrutiny is required, as a fundamental pedagogical principle.

Such projects are accomplished through discursive processes by identifying a continuous and recursive self-informing process of enquiry. This is not achieved through any kind of self-referential or pre-ordained certainty as an instrumental equation. Remembering Heidegger's idea of "the question", the discursive terrain may be opened via the enactment of a Heideggerian sensibility or way of thinking. As Heidegger reminds us, "Questioning builds a way. We would be advised, therefore, above all to pay heed to the way, and not to fix our attention on isolated sentences and topics. The way is a way of thinking" (1977a, p. 3).[17]

In this way of thinking there is not only a way of questioning, but also a legitimating principle at work. One set of legitimating principles cannot be used to judge the other's value, and "one side's legitimacy does not imply the other's lack of legitimacy" (Lyotard, 1988, p. xi). Working through the unknowable and indeterminate is a risky venture, yet one to be welcomed in the creative research process, as theory and practice oscillate in the struggle of negotiating meaning. It is an open system allowing for active participation by all parties and in the creation of new game rules, new knowledge then becomes apparent.

CONCLUDING COMMENTS

This investigation extends the understanding of what *praktikē* might mean when text and art, as languages in *différance*, work together to dismantle separated and normative categories. With pedagogical concerns uppermost, the discussion has sought an understanding of the complex relations between theory and practice, and the ways supervisors may navigate and utilise these relations with candidates in the creative fields. With an economy of language, at the start of the chapter, Gerard

Manley Hopkins observed the magnificence of a falcon finding its mastery through catching "underneath him steady air". The poet could only gaze in awe. In much the same way, through allowing conditions of dispersion, disparity and difference to breathe within *praxis*, the supervisor may look in awe at the candidate's ultimate mastery of research practice.

Throughout this discussion the crucial issues lie in the question: What means do we have at our disposal to put theory and practice to work in the indeterminacies and possibilities that comprise the research process? We cannot be over concerned by protean and unrehearsed possibilities. Generative practice elevates the acute need for a vital awareness that the supervisory relationship is, itself, a pedagogical space requiring a methodological clarity and self-imposed discipline keeping up with ever-changing contexts.

This discussion has shown, by explicit examples, how forms of hegemonic domination can be averted via the activation of new rules of practice. In the open work of the supervisor-candidate contract there are constant negotiations as each acknowledges an obligation to the other. Writing this chapter may have been a way of working through a complex terrain in a generative relationship of *praxis*, practical research action; and perhaps it is possible that here the transformative potential of creative research may find and legitimate its enterprise.

NOTES

[1] I acknowledge the review of this paper from Nicholas Gresson, with his recommendations of rigour in the explication of *praxis*, and suggested application of this model to psychotherapeutic practice. I also acknowledge the many postgraduate candidates past and present for giving me the privilege of working with them in their research endeavours. From them, and with them, I have learned so much.

[2] The use of rhizomic here is making explicit reference to the way Deleuze and Guattari use "rhizome" as a non-linear, non-teleological way of thinking and being.

[3] For a wide range of approaches to methodologies in creative research see Grierson and Brearley (2009a).

[4] For further discussion of positioning the researcher's voice see Grierson (2005); and Grierson and Brearley (2009b), particularly pp. 168–171.

[5] Supervisions include Doctor of Philosophy, Doctor of Fine Art, Doctor of Education, and Master of Arts (Art & Design) candidates from Auckland University of Technology NZ, The University of Auckland NZ, and RMIT University Melbourne, Australia.

[6] In my Ph.D. I wrote through an active relationship of theory and practice deconstructing the privileging of language as a propositional affair, and contesting the privileging of practice as a natural path to insight about ourselves and our world.

[7] I addressed indeterminacy and *paralogy* in my doctorate, and also in an article in ACCESS journal (Grierson, 1999).

[8] Aristotle, b. 384 – d. 322 BCE.

[9] See Grierson (2007). for further discussions of the concept of political will in creative practice and research.

[10] Möbius strip is named after German mathematician, August F. Möbius (1790–1868). The Möbius strip is "a surface with one continuous side formed by joining the ends of a rectangle after twisting one end through 180°" (*OED*). Elizabeth Grosz (1994) advocates a disruption to the bifurcated dichotomised terms of otherness, whereby the knowing subject and the knowable epistemic object are totally separated. Through reference to the Möbius strip, Grosz gives an account of the inscription of binary epistemological formations.

[11] Katy Yakimis, *A discourse through image and text: Identity in perpetual mutability*, MA (Art & Design), Auckland University of Technology, 2002.

[12] Moata McNamara, *Translating Derrida, a question of style: An exposition of processes of translation*, MA (Art & Design), Auckland University of Technology, 2005.

[13] Dr Bruce Mowson, *Sound and video installation: Existence as a state of immanence*, Doctor of Philosophy, RMIT University, 2008.

[14] Dr Emma Barrow, *Visual practices – cultural translations. A meeting of Indigenous and non-Indigenous perspectives*, Doctor of Philosophy, RMIT University, 2008.

[15] Vaughan Gunson, *The object of art writing: A Marxist critique of contemporary idealism*, MA (Art & Design), Auckland University of Technology, 2000.

[16] Dr Maria O'Connor, *ASHES without reserve: Her pro-nominal tracings of the strictures of sexual difference*, Doctor of Philosophy, Auckland University of Technology, 2010.

[17] For further discussion of this approach through Heidegger, see Duxbury and Grierson (2008).

REFERENCES

Arendt, H. (1958). *The human condition*. Chicago: University of Chicago Press.

Besley, T. & Peters, M. A. (2007). Subjectivity and truth: Foucault, education and the culture of self. New York: Peter Lang.

Deleuze, G. & Guattari, F. (1993). *A thousand plateaus: Capitalism and schizophrenia* (Brian Massumi, Trans.). Minneapolis: University of Minnesota Press.

Derrida, J. (1978a). *Writing and difference* (Alan Bass, Trans.). Chicago: University of Chicago Press.

Derrida, J. (1978b). Structure, sign, and play in the discourse of the human sciences. In Joyce Appleby, Elizabeth Covington, David Hoyt, Michael Latham and Allison Seider (Eds.) *Knowledge and postmodernism in historical perspective* (pp. 437–54). New York: Routledge.

Derrida, J. (1981). *Positions* (A. Bass, Trans.). Chicago, IL: University of Chicago Press.

Derrida, J. (1982). Différance. In *Margins of philosophy* (Alan Bass, Trans.) (pp. 1–27). Sussex: The Harvester Press.

Duxbury, L. & Grierson, E. M. (2008). Thinking in a creative Field. In L. Duxbury, E.M. Grierson, D. Waite (Eds.) *Thinking through practice: Art as research in the academy* (pp. 7–17). Melbourne: RMIT School of Art.

Foucault, M. (1977). What is an author?. In D. F. Bouchard (Ed.) *Michel Foucault: Language, counter-memory, practice. Selected essays and interviews* (pp. 113–138). Ithaca, NY: Cornell University Press.

Foucault, M. (1990). *Michel Foucault: Politics, philosophy, culture. Interviews and other writings 1977–1984* (L. D. Kritzman, Ed., and A. Sheridan Smith, Trans.). New York: Routledge.

Foucault, M. (1994/1963). *The archaeology of knowledge* (A. Sheridan Smith, Trans.). London: Tavistock Publications.

Freire, P. (1996). *Pedagogy of the oppressed* (Myra Bergman Ramos, Trans.). London: Penguin.

Giroux, H. A. (1983). *Critical theory and educational practice*. Victoria: Deakin University Press.

Giroux, H.A. (1995). Language, difference, and curriculum theory: Beyond the politics of clarity. In P. L. McLaren & J. M. Giarelli (Eds.) *Critical theory and educational research* (pp. 23–38). Albany: State University of New York Press.

Grierson, E. M. (1999). Spaces of indeterminacy: Towards a theory of praxis in visual arts pedagogy. Special Issue, Divarifications: Aesthetics, art education and culture. *ACCESS Critical Perspectives on Cultural & Policy Studies in Education, 18*(1), 1–15.

Grierson, E. M. (2000). The politics of knowledge: A poststructuralist approach to visual arts in tertiary sites. Unpublished Doctor of Philosophy thesis, The University of Auckland, New Zealand.

Grierson, E. M. (2003). Framing the arts in education: What is really at stake? In E. M. Grierson & J. E. Mansfield (Eds.), *The arts in education: Critical perspectives from Aotearoa New Zealand* (pp. 93–117). Palmerston North: Dunmore Press.

Grierson, E. M. (2005). An art educator's narrative: 'Where am I in the text?'. *Te Whakatere: Navigating through the arts in the Pacific*, ANZAAE Aotearoa New Zealand Association of Art Educators Refereed Conference Proceedings Vol 2. Palmerston North: ANZAAE.

Grierson, E. M. (2007). Creativity and the return of a political will: Art, language and the creative subject. In *Creativity, Enterprise, Policy – New Directions in Education*, PESA Philosophy of Education Society of Australasia 36th Annual PESA Conference Refereed Proceedings, Te Papa Museum of New Zealand, 5–9 December. http://www.pesa.org.au

Grierson, E. M. (2009a). Ways of knowing and being. In E. M. Grierson & L. Brearley, *Creative arts research: Narratives of methodologies and practices* (pp. 17–31). Rotterdam: Sense Publishers.

Grierson, E. M. (2009b). Ways of deconstructing: Risks, imagination and reflexivity. In E. M. Grierson & L. Brearley, *Creative arts research: Narratives of methodologies and practices* (pp. 149–163). Rotterdam: Sense Publishers.

Grierson, E. M. (2010). Thoughts on a Doctorate: Another mountain to climb. In D. Forrest & E. Grierson (Eds.) *The doctoral journey in art education: Reflections on doctoral studies by Australian and New Zealand art educators* (pp. 116–140). Melbourne: Australian Scholarly Publishing.

Grierson, E. M. (2011). Art and creativity in the global economies of education. *Educational Philosophy and Theory, 43*(4), June, 336–350.

Grierson, E. M. & Brearley, L. (2009a). *Creative arts research: Narratives of methodologies and practices*. Rotterdam: Sense Publishers.

Grierson, E. M. & Brearley, L. (2009b). Ways of learning from creative research. In E. M. Grierson & L. Brearley, *Creative arts research: Narratives of methodologies and practices* (pp. 165–173). Rotterdam: Sense Publishers.

Grosz, E. (1994). *Volatile bodies: Towards a corporeal feminism*. Bloomington: Indiana University Press.

Heidegger, M. (1977a). The question concerning technology. In *The question concerning technology and other essays* (W. Lovitt, Trans.) (pp. 3–35). New York: Harper and Row.

Heidegger, M. (1977b). What calls for thinking. In D.F. Krell (Ed.) (1999), *Basic writings, Martin Heidegger* (pp. 365–391). London: Routledge.

Howells, C. (1999). *Derrida: Deconstruction from phenomenology to ethics*. Oxford: Polity Press.

Jameson, F. (1984/1979). Foreword. In J-F. Lyotard, *The postmodern condition: A report on knowledge* (G. Bennington & B. Massumi, Trans.) (pp. vii–xxi). Minneapolis: University of Minnesota Press.

Lyotard, J-F. (1984/1979). *The postmodern condition: A report on knowledge* (G. Bennington & B. Massumi, Trans.). Minneapolis: University of Minnesota Press.

Mouffe, C. (2005). *On the political*. Oxford: Routledge.

Mouffe, C. (2007). Artistic activism and the agonistic struggle. *Art and Research, 1*(2), 1–5.

Stead, C. K. (2008). *Book self: The Reader as writer and the writer as critic*. Auckland: Auckland University Press.

ROBYN BARNACLE

7. BECOMING A PRACTITIONER-RESEARCHER-WRITER

INTRODUCTION

This chapter takes as its topic the "practitioner-researcher", a species of doctoral candidate common within the art, architecture and design fields, for whom a doctorate accompanies what is often a thriving, professional practice. For this group, professional practice and research have the potential to be mutually informing and transforming. The research degree offers both an opportunity to extend and reflect upon professional practice from a distance, and therefore to do things that are often not possible in the office, so to speak. In my experience, these candidates are very rewarding to supervise and have much to offer as researchers, for a host of reasons, but they can also struggle with a set of issues intrinsic to their situation, or perhaps predicament is more apt a term, straddling, as they do, the academy on the one hand and a professional practice context on the other. For the purposes of this chapter, I am going to treat these issues as coalescing around the problem of authority. One issue is its development; that of becoming authoritative as a researcher and the other is in terms of its development as a researcher: practices of authorisation. The problem of authorisation is particularly active in the context of scholarly or research writing where it can manifest, for example, in extreme responses to the literature or precedent, such as either deferring too much to external sources of validation or resisting them entirely. Another way that this can manifest is resistance to the risk involved in research by refusing to relinquish the role of expert professional and be a beginner – in research terms. Inhering within this issue is the struggle to come to terms with what being a practitioner-researcher might mean, both individually and professionally.

I am coming to this as a researcher whose primary mode of 'thinking' is writing. My research literacies, if you like, are limited to a single domain. My background is philosophy and I am interested, philosophically, in meaning-making or research practices themselves, in how meaning gets made, for want of a better description. Most researchers are more interested in the 'what' than the 'how' of meaning-making, i.e. in what they are trying to propose, claim, communicate, discover etc. This is how it should be; the how part is implicit and rarely needs to be made explicit. Where it might be useful or interesting to make it explicit is for pedagogical purposes. To let research candidates see, that is, how their adopted meaning-making practices are working (or not). My professional practice over the last ten years is in the area of research education and I work with higher degree by research supervisors and candidates from a range of disciplinary backgrounds. In

B. Allpress, R. Barnacle, L. Duxbury and E. Grierson (Eds.), Supervising Practices for Postgraduate
Research in Art, Architecture and Design, 81–90.
©2012 Sense Publishers. All rights reserved.

this chapter I explore some of the thinking and practices that inform what I do in the hope that this may be useful for other supervisors working in this area.

BECOMING PRACTITIONER–RESEARCHER

Some of the challenges faced by practitioner-researchers have to do with being a pioneer. The practitioner-researcher from art, architecture or design can be seen as a subset of a larger wave of professionals who have come in increasing numbers from many fields, such as education, health and business, to undertake research degrees, particularly doctorates. This trend is evident in the last decade or so, not just in Australia but across Europe, the UK and North America. These people tend to be mid-career, aged in their 30s, 40s and 50s, undertaking their degree in part-time mode (Evans, 2002; Barnacle & Usher, 2003). Their mutual presence has led to transformations in the ways the purpose of the doctorate is conceived. To borrow from Bourner et al. (2001), if the doctorate was intended traditionally to develop *professional researchers*, in the hands of the practitioner-researcher its purpose becomes instead to develop *researching professionals*. The subtlety of this formulation perhaps belies its full import for the implications are considerable. Not least of all is a shift in the purpose of the doctorate from advancing knowledge *per se* to advancing knowledge of, and indeed the practice of, ones' own professional practice and the practices of the profession more broadly. While the latter need not and should not preclude the former, this in itself can be a challenge to achieve in practice, in all senses of the term.

The purpose of the doctorate is conceived traditionally as the production of new knowledge as embodied in a thesis and/or body of works. Usually the research outcomes are couched in these terms, such as a significant contribution to knowledge that meets the standards of academic publication. This focus on knowledge production and dissemination, however, can mask a parallel process that is arguably at least of equal significance, but can be overlooked or underestimated by supervisors. Hand in hand with knowledge production is the production of a new kind of self: that of scholar or researcher. As a number of scholars have noted regarding the process of doing a research degree, knowledge production occurs with and through identity production (Lee, 2011; Grierson, 2009; Kamler & Thomson, 2006; Green, 2005). The implication of this is that you do not simply acquire a new set of skills and knowledges through the research experience, but become anew or renewed as a kind of hitherto unrealised self: a 'researcher self'. For the practitioner-researcher this formulation can be extended further to include the professional practice context to take the form of the 'practitioner-researcher-self'. This formulation gestures beyond the process of 'coming to know' involved in the doctorate to the broader ontological and identity issues involved in doing research and learning to be a researcher. The entailments of this conjunction, the 'practitioner-researcher-self', are not necessarily either consistent or without conflict, particularly in terms of becoming and being authoritative. Becoming authoritative is one of the key aspects of researcher identity development. As Lee points out, the process of doing a research degree involves "…becoming and being a certain authorised form of research(er) identity" (2011, p. 157). Kamler and Thomson (2006) also discuss this issue with respect to writing, making the point that supervisors often fail to recognise the identity issues inhering within the work of crafting a research thesis/exegesis and learning not just to write but to do so authoritatively.

One site of tension for the practitioner-researcher arises through having to move between two potentially contrasting modes of being: experienced professional on the one hand and novice researcher on the other. Where authority may be established firmly in ones' professional sphere it is necessarily nascent, or developing, within the research context. This can make moving between the two domains particularly jarring and fraught. It is important for supervisors to recognise the vulnerability implied in being a beginner, particularly for someone who is usually an expert or at least a highly competent professional. Resistance to being a beginner can also become a barrier to learning or discovery; what might be called the risk inherent to research. This manifests, for example, in the candidate who seeks through the research to more or less confirm what they already know. In this case authority is never relinquished, significantly constraining the potential of the research process to generate new knowledge and challenge established practices. This is particularly limiting when ones' own practice is the subject of the research as it leaves little opportunity for genuine discovery and insight. It also leaves little opportunity to contribute knowledge to the discipline or profession more broadly. One example of this is candidates who treat a research degree as an opportunity to document what they do in their professional practice. This overlooks the investigative and critical components of research, as well as the question of how ones' practice may contribute to broader debates, scholarship and practice in the area. Where one's own practice is the subject of the enquiry there is also a further dimension to contend with: What role becoming a researcher might play in one's ongoing professional practice? Will it make one's practice better, or increase one's authority as a practitioner? More specifically, how is the relationship between the two to be understood? Unfortunately, in Australia research degrees are not well understood or valued outside of academe. This ambivalence is evident in the words of this research degree candidate from the School of Architecture and Design at RMIT University:

> …I can't see a Masters would benefit me financially in my work at all. I mean I'm not going to be able to charge any more money because I've got a Masters, and I don't think anybody would say; 'we'll get her to do it because she's got a Masters' (Barnacle & Usher, 2003).

Such issues make the question of what it means to be a *researching professional* particularly pertinent for the researcher-practitioner.

INTEGRATING KNOWING, ACTING & BEING A RESEARCHER-PRACTITIONER

For a number of years now I have been working with Gloria Dall'Alba, from the University of Queensland, to re-conceptualise how learning and knowledge gets understood in higher education discourse and practice. We do this through what we have called an ontological approach to knowing (see Dall'Alba & Barnacle, 2007; Barnacle & Dall'Alba, 2011). One of our key moves in this work is to argue for a shift in the focus of higher education programmes from knowledge in-itself to learning and its enhancement. Accordingly, we refer to knowing, as a verb, rather than knowledge, as a noun, to make the point that it needs to be understood as enacted, or in terms of enactment, rather than possessed, or in terms of possession. We argue that the aim of all higher education programmes, higher degrees by research included, is to promote the integration of knowing, acting and being.

In a conventional account, knowledge and knowing are restricted to an ideal realm of thoughts, ideas and concepts; however, knowing can also be situated within the materiality, and spatial and temporal specificity, of embodiment. In this account, knowing is not treated as reducible to thought or the discursive, as is often the case. Embodiment refers to inhabiting the body within an historical, cultural and social place (although it is not determined entirely by this situatedness) (see Merleau-Ponty, 1962/1945). Knowing thus transforms from the merely intellectual, or something that can be accumulated within a (disembodied) mind, to something inhabited and enacted: a way of thinking, making and acting; indeed, a way of being. This way of reconceptualising knowing has the potential to transform the way that learning research is conceived, as well as the role of the supervisor. Becoming knowledgeable remains important but notions such as knowledge transfer or acquisition become of less use as they imply that content can be uploaded and downloaded, computer style; traded and exchanged; accepted or declined. This is the model of knowledge as commodity, such that, as I have argued elsewhere:

> Having and doing are distinct. Integration does come, but not until an appropriate practice context is identified. There is a temporal disjuncture, therefore, between learning and doing (not to mention being), such that knowledge gets treated as an instrument of convenience (Barnacle, 2005, p. 186).

Embodiment is a useful notion for reconceptualising what it means to become a researcher. It turns attention to aspects of being that can be overlooked when becoming a researcher is understood without reference to the identity and ontological aspects involved. These aspects include, for example, gender, desire, commitment, and resistance. As Nigel Blake and colleagues note in regards to the skills debate in higher education, a common propensity to reduce a range of human abilities and qualities to 'skills' or 'competencies' overlooks the engagement, commitment and risk involved: "what are commonly called skills are not activities to which we give anything of ourselves" (Blake, Smeyers, Smith & Standish, 2000, p. 26). Indeed, without commitment, or caring about the outcome, the development of important skills and knowledges like those involved in learning research is unlikely to occur at all, or will do so only in a superficial way. As I have argued, an instrumental account of knowledge:

> … situates the knower at arms length from what is known. Consequently, knowledge on this model does not produce hardship, struggle or grief. And

nor is it confrontational or difficult. Rather, knowledge is conceived as fundamentally plentiful, useful and productive. The knowledge worker is untroubled and the potential of their knowledge unlimited (Barnacle, 2005, p. 185).

When knowledge is understood as created, embodied, and enacted a shift occurs such that learning and becoming (a researcher) requires integrating ways of knowing, acting, and being within a broad range of practices. This approach seeks to engage actively the very real challenges of ensuring that 'having and doing' are indistinct. Arguably, the potential for such integration should be greater for the practitioner-researcher, straddling simultaneously, as they do, professional practice and research contexts. Perhaps this view underestimates, however, the challenges of inhabiting two potentially contrasting modes of being: experienced professional on the one hand and novice researcher on the other. In my experience, one of the key places that these tensions play out is with regards to the requirements of scholarly or research writing.

BECOMING RESEARCH WRITER

Writing tends to be fraught for most research students, but it is particularly the case if you are a researcher in the field of art, architecture and design undertaking practice-based research where the first language, if you like, is practice of some kind. It is tempting to refer to the making, designing, etc., that researchers in art, architecture and design do as their practice and treat writing as somehow distinct. But if by practice we mean, broadly, what we do, then writing is also, of course, a practice, or at least can be if one practises it regularly. The issue really for researchers in these fields is that writing does not tend to be a primary practice. One of the things that I am interested in as a supervisor and research educator is addressing such issues in discipline or practice-specific terms rather than through a skills-deficit type approach. This means exploring ways-of-being appropriate for a particular individual and their practice(s) as a researcher-writer.

Writing involves struggle because it is a site in which meaning is performed and brought into being: writing is meaning-making. Of course, not all meaning-making and thinking involve writing. If your practice is in the fields of art, architecture and design then it is likely that your primary mode of meaning-making is not writing. The problem, however, is that Ph.Ds. also require artists, architects and designers to become writers. Writing is also a useful research dissemination tool, enabling communication of the research process and outcomes to those who would otherwise find the disciplinary modes of research communication illegible. In the case of art, design and architecture researchers, however, the struggle to write becomes doubled: it is there in the meaning-making process that accompanies all writing as well as in the requirement to do so beyond one's primary mode of meaning-making. In fact, the struggle is tripled because it also inheres within the practices of the primary mode of meaning-making, but here I am going to focus on writing.

Writing can be fraught because it is not simply a matter of decanting the contents of one's head, or the 'what I want to say', onto the page: as if from a full vessel onto an empty page. Meaning is made through the writing process so it emerges through the doing of the writing act itself. This has a number of implications. One is the imperative to write from the commencement of candidacy and not leave the exegesis until the end. The notion of a 'write up' is really not helpful here, not least because it leaves the perceived hard work until last. More significantly, it treats writing as an exercise of reportage, that of reporting on what has come before, as if all the meaning-making has been done and all that is left is to communicate it, or tell the story, linguistically. If writing is meaning-making, however, then this exercise fails to engage the full potential of writing as a research tool or medium. It is not that writing does not, cannot or should not function merely as reportage; my point is that it has much more to offer the practitioner-researcher.

Research writing and practice can also be understood as mutually informing and transforming. Practitioners can feel somewhat daunted by the requirement to write an exegesis as they can feel that their capabilities as a writer are less developed than those as a practitioner. While this may indeed be true it can lead to the view that the writing process itself is of limited value and, in particular, as having little to offer the development of their practice-based research. This view implicitly neglects the meaning-making role of writing and treats it as a means to write-up and report on the practice-based work where the 'real' research occurs. If writing is merely a mode of communication then its research value, or potential to contribute substantively to a research project, is questionable indeed, but this is a view that I want to challenge: writing is research.

There is one final point to make on this issue: if writing is thought of as merely a communication or reportage device then the struggles of meaning-making can be confused with issues to do with being or not being 'a writer'. There can be a tendency amongst art and design practitioners to think of themselves as not very good writers and therefore to some extent confuse the hard work inherent to writing with some kind of skills deficit. I am not suggesting that what might be categorised as writing skills, such as knowledge of grammar etc., are irrelevant as they certainly play a part in writing struggles. However, it can be useful to recognise at the very least the 'double struggle' involved in exegesis writing as an exercise in both meaning-making as well as learning how to do research writing, or be a research writer, while bearing in mind that in practice, of course, the two are necessarily intertwined. Why this is the case becomes more apparent when writing is seen as a social practice, rather than just a technical skill, which involves, as Kamler and Thomson argue, "...meaning making and learning to produce knowledge in particular disciplines and discourse communities" (2006, p. 4). Novice research writers can be seen as becoming acculturated into the writing practices of their broader disciplinary or practice community. Writing any academic text, therefore, has two dimensions: the text work involved in knowing the genres, conventions and textual practices of one's discipline; and the identity work involved in positioning oneself authoritatively with respect to that discipline.

An added dimension is the professional circumstances of the practitioner researcher whose practice and research activities typically straddle both professional and academic spheres. In this context, finding your 'voice' as a practitioner-researcher-writer can be particularly fraught, particularly for experienced practitioners grappling with the genre of academic writing/research. It can be difficult, if not personally confronting, to accept that although you might be a good writer for professional purposes you are all at sea when it comes to scholarly practices.

BECOMING PRACTITIONER-RESEARCHER-WRITER

As discussed, writing issues are readily conceptualised in terms of some kind of knowledge and skills deficit in which technical training in, for example, sentence structure, grammar etc., is an appropriate response. This, however, can address the problem only in part. Also requiring attention is the question of what 'being a research writer' might mean for a particular practitioner-researcher; indeed this is a question for all researchers. Thesis writing hand books and the like are dominated by the social science model, which structures the thesis into a series of temporally distinct episodes comprising the research question, design, findings, analysis and conclusion, represented spatially as a series of chapters culminating in a conclusion. As others have also argued, such as Kamler and Thomson (2006), such theses tend not only to be boring to read because they contain very little argument, they also enforce a linear, and to a large extent artificial representation of the research process. In my experience, the reservations practice-based researchers can feel about research writing are often due to the mistaken view that they need to contort what they do to fit this model. Again, there is an issue here of what it means to become authorised as a researcher and what practices it is considered necessary to enact in order to demonstrate that authority; fitting into the 'strait-jacket' of the linear thesis becomes equivalent to donning the white coat of the lab-based scientist. As a supervisor, it is important to engage the question of alternatives with the candidate from the commencement of candidature. This is important not only from the perspective of allaying anxieties, but it also has the added advantage of ensuring adequate time is made available for writing exploration. If the researcher seeks research writing practices that are appropriate to the research practices then it makes sense for the two, practice and writing, to evolve in tandem. The question of how the research is to be conducted is just as pertinent to the practice-based component as it is to writing the exegesis.

Inevitably such questions will elicit different responses depending on the research practices involved, offering a number of benefits both for the researcher and the research. I would encourage supervisors and candidates to begin by exploring writing media and practices that are not as prescribed as thesis or exegesis writing practices. One option is the use of blogs and wikis. As emergent social practices they can be seen as offering greater freedom for exploration than the genres, conventions and textual practices of established forms of research writing. A research blog, for example, can be deployed productively in the research process as a site of experimentation as well as for the purposes of reflective writing. Depending on how it functions it can also form part of the examination package. Another model that may be useful to explore is designerly modes of writing, drawing on the work of scholars such as Nigel Cross (1999). Such writing integrates aspects of design practice into the writing process, concept development, and exegesis structure, manifesting in an iterative, often cyclical, approach to research writing that deliberately resists closure.

While there are inevitable challenges in exploring alternative modes of writing and representing research, these are mitigated to some extent by the liberation that can be experienced in finding alternatives to the 'strait-jacket' approach. Moreover, exploring appropriate ways-of-being a practitioner-researcher-writer makes writing itself less foreign to someone whose primary research practice is practice. Ultimately, what I am hoping to see as a supervisor is the emergence of a fruitful writing process in which the candidate is not continually struggling and is able to 'let things come'. As Winnie the Pooh would put it:

> And that's the whole poem," he said. "Do you like it, Piglet?" "All except the shillings," said Piglet. "I don't think they ought to be there." "They wanted to come in after the pounds," explained Pooh, "so I let them. It is the best way to write poetry, letting things come" (Milne, 2007/1928, p. 31).

Pooh is seeking to be receptive to the agency of the poem itself, or in other words, to the writing process. This is an important aspect of writing as meaning-making: letting go, and having the confidence to 'let things come'. It is hard to do this if the research writing genres, conventions and textual practices at your disposal are at odds with your primary research practice. One of the things I try to do, therefore, is encourage candidates to be experimental with the writing process and cultivate their own way of being a researcher-writer. This approach is conducive to what I would call an embodied writing practice, which integrates knowing, acting and being a practitioner-researcher-writer. If this works, candidates are more likely to avoid the problems of extreme responses to validation touched on in the beginning of this chapter. The temptation to defer too much to external sources of validation, whether in the form of adjacent disciplines or other scholars/practitioners in the field, is decreased when candidates have the confidence to assert a researcher identity that is appropriate to what they do as practitioners. Such confidence can also make the scholarly practices of engaging with the literature more appealing than it might otherwise appear. I think of this as a broadly phenomenological approach to research and supervision because it encourages researchers to cultivate attentive and responsive ways of engaging with what they do, through what they do.

CONCLUSION

Research writing is necessarily fraught but this is exacerbated in practice-based research where the research mediums are not singular and therefore the sites and intersections of meaning-making are multiple and diverse. Practice, within any field, is dynamic and complex and can be enacted in multiple ways. Moreover, practices are continually reproduced and renewed over time, so that supervisors need to be responsive and spontaneous in their approaches to each candidate, and within each candidature, during the various phases of a given research project. Barnett argues that one of the key roles of higher education is that of enabling students to deal with the dynamism and complexity of practice (2005). By promoting engagement with the specificity of the candidate's own art, architecture or design practice, supervisors have a key role to play in terms of encouraging their own candidates to encounter and dwell reflexively in such dynamism and complexity.

REFERENCES

Barnacle, R., & Dall'Alba, G. (2011). Research degrees as professional education? *Studies in Higher Education, 36*(4), 459–470.

Barnacle, R. (2005). Research education ontologies: Exploring doctoral becoming. *Higher Education Research and Development, 24*(2), 179–188.

Barnacle, R., & Usher, R. (2003). Assessing the quality of research training: The case of part-time candidates in full-time professional work. *Higher Education Research and Development, 22*(3), 345–358.

Barnett, R. (2005). Recapturing the universal in the university. *Educational Philosophy and Theory, 37*(6), 785–797.

Blake, N., Smeyers, P., Smith, R., & Standish, P. (2000). *Education in an age of nihilism.* London: Routledge Falmer.

Bourner, T., Bowden, R., & Laing, S. (2001). Professional doctorates in England. *Studies in Higher Education, 26*(1), 65–83.

Cross, N. (1999). Natural intelligence in design. *Design Studies, 20*(1), 25–39.

Dall'Alba, G., & Barnacle, R. (2007). An ontological turn for higher education. *Studies in Higher Education, 32*(6), 679–691.

Evans, T. (2002). Part-time research students: Are they producing knowledge where it counts?. *Higher Education Research & Development, 21*(2), 155–165.

Grierson, E. (2009). Ways of knowing and being. In E. Grierson & L. Brearley, *Creative arts research: Narratives of methodologies and practices* (pp. 17–31). Rotterdam: Sense Publishers.

Green, B. (2005). Unfinished business: Subjectivity and supervision. *Higher Education Research & Development, 24*(2), 151–163.

Kamler, B., & Thomson, P. (2006). *Helping doctoral students write: Pedagogies for supervision.* Abingdon, UK: Routledge.

Lee, A. (2011). Professional practice and doctoral education: Becoming a researcher. In L. Scanlon (Ed.), *"Becoming" a professional* (pp. 153–168). Lifelong Learning Book Series 16, DOI 10.1007/978-94-007-1378-9 8, Springer Science+Business Media B.V.

Merleau-Ponty, M. (1962/1945). *Phenomenology of perception.* London: Routledge & Kegan Paul.

Milne, A. A. (2007/1928). *The house at Pooh corner.* London: Egmont UK Limited.

LINDA DALEY

8. PEDAGOGIES OF INVENTION

SUPERVISING ACROSS PARADIGMS

Having been asked to reflect on my experience as a supervisor of creative research projects, I need to start with a disclaimer: my experience in supervising began only about five years ago. This was in the co-supervising of projects in graphic design, literary theory and in the pedagogy of an online design studio, and more recently in supervising creative writing projects. These projects, understood as research by creative practice or research by project are outside my customary field. Indeed, they are outside the paradigm of fields in which I was trained – the text-based world of the humanities. My research is generated from texts in order to make claims about their concepts, techniques and assumptions. This is especially at the intersection of philosophy and literary expression, and particularly where this intersection is generative of 'the new'. My training is viewed normally as being in some kind of distinction from 'creating' or 'creativity'. However this work requires the creating of my own texts from the resources within the disciplinary traditions in which I work. My doctoral research focused on a critical engagement with the concept of 'originality' and its sister terms, 'creativity' and 'creating'. The aim was to debunk the romanticism those terms convey while courting the irony – unremarked by my examiners – that like all doctorates, it was to be assessed according to its "*original* contribution to knowledge". My preference is for 'invention' and 'inventiveness' rather than 'originality', 'creation' or 'creativity'.

You could well ask, how does a professional background that does not include *doing* creativity but rather *knowing about* creativity provide a skill-set for supervising research candidates who are coming to their projects from a creative background? The quick answer is that *doing* creativity – making – is not the beginning and end to the research programme in which the making is situated. The longer answer will begin to be demonstrated in the rest of this chapter. Suffice to say here, making through a research programme requires an understanding of the thinking embedded in the creative practice. This should not only lead to a work, a thing or a produced outcome, but should also 'speak' explicitly to the professional practice and/or creative discipline in which the research more broadly, not simply the made work, might be located. As a research outcome, it speaks to the academy of the knowledge generated by the practice of making. *Research through making* requires the demonstration of two things in a research programme: the work/thing/product *and* the knowing extracted from the work/thing/product shown explicitly through an accompanying artefact. In the space between these two forms of showing, a non-practitioner supervisor can productively guide a skilled

B. Allpress, R. Barnacle, L. Duxbury and E. Grierson (Eds.), *Supervising Practices for Postgraduate Research in Art, Architecture and Design, 91–102.*
©2012 Sense Publishers. All rights reserved.

practitioner who is a research candidate, when they both understand that the margin between practitioner and practitioner-researcher identifies a skill-set that locates the academic outcome. The knowing that is extracted from the making, and is presented in the related artefact, is what locates the creative practice as research activity within the academy. It is the artefact that actualises the shift in the candidate from a practitioner to a practitioner-researcher.

I should note also that what I bring to supervision is a professional background that includes, while not being limited to, the training from within the field of the humanities. To be sure, that training among other things enabled me to think, for example, about concepts as having something like three-dimensionality to them. They could be looked at not only in their historical and theoretical context, but also viewed as pliable constructions of thought that are receptive to emplacement in new contexts, thereby making them anew. Concepts are not only tools of thought; they are also objects of thought that can do certain things when handled in certain ways. This way of thinking about concepts resonates with the practitioner-researcher who makes from the given resources and materials of their practice. The humanities is part of my professional background that also includes training as a teacher and experience in the academy as a teacher of pre-service teachers; the latter necessitating reflection on my own and trainee teachers' professional practice. To objectively view one's own teaching as a 'practice' had never occurred to me when I was working as a teacher. It was only when the simultaneous mirroring of, and distancing from, my own teaching with pre-service teachers occurred that I began to see it as having a knowing both embedded in it, and in excess of the doing of it, as a practice. The shift occurred when I located my teaching practice in the university with trainee teachers requiring me to relate the theory, knowledge and concrete experience of teaching to those trainee teachers: in other words teaching about teaching while doing teaching. I then began to see, and thus articulate, what had to that point been largely tacit: my job of teaching was a professional practice that was enabling of my agency as a teacher, to mobilise the conditions and assemble the resources within a given classroom setting, to achieve learning outcomes and to know what these might be in designing the process toward those outcomes. Teaching came to be more than simply complying with the guidelines, policies and rules set out by curriculum authorities, government agencies and the school board. Many aspects of my professional practice as a teacher carry over into higher (tertiary) education and research degree supervision.

A further professional experience within the academy that I bring to my supervisory skill-set has been my role as a postgraduate research coordinator. This has included membership on two research committees: the faculty ethics committee; and the university-wide committee approving examiners and examiners' reports. The academy often appears as a monolithic bearer of tradition and truth, a leviathan of uniformity that stands against the chaotic ground from which innovation emerges, before it is recognised and valorised as knowledge. From my membership on these committees, and as coordinator of postgraduate research programmes, I have come to value these opportunities as insights to the academy. The academy is an institution comprising strongly motivated individuals working toward consensus from a diversity of perspectives, fields and judgements. This consensus is fundamentally about knowledge production, its value and transfer within and beyond the academy. These research management experiences have enabled me to view supervision from a broad perspective within the academy and within the continuum of candidacy. This begins with the enquiry stage of struggling to articulate the reason why investigating a problem, a theme or a practice is a burning question for potential candidates. This applies from the beginning through to the discussion of examiners' evaluations of completed projects ranging from landscape architecture to nanotechnology. Usefully informing my approach to supervision is institutional knowledge of where candidates come from, their motivations for entering the academy, and how research (creative or otherwise) may be evaluated across diverse disciplines.

My main focus here is the experience of supervising candidates outside my own field that has given rise to an expertise that I have acquired by accident. This supervisory history is possibly quite common, but if not, it is likely to become more so for academics working in a constantly and rapidly changing sector. In higher education disciplinary mergers and institutional restructures occur with increasing frequency, necessitating agility by academics toward supervision practices and roles. In giving emphasis to this type of supervisory experience, I am also making a claim for a certain kind of pedagogy within supervision. By this, I mean supervision understood as a set of relations or a set of relays of knowing and unknowing held between supervisor and candidate of any research project, but especially when supervision of candidacy occurs across diverse paradigms. I am therefore staking the ground for a supervisory pedagogy that does not restrict itself to the idea that creative practice projects always and exclusively necessitate the skilled master-practitioner supervising the candidate who is a practitioner-researcher.

A supervisor without a practice-based background can offer productive and successful supervision if there is a focus on the relation between knowing and making in the candidature. Research in the academy produces qualitatively different outcomes from those of the conventional location of creative practice: the studio, the laboratory, the profession. Additionally, the outcomes of research in these locations are valued according to criteria that relate to market-place concerns and applications rather than the academic criterion of originality in the production of knowledge. Furthermore, if supervisors reflect on all the experiences of their professional and/or institutional expertise that contribute to their practice as a supervisor (for example, the scholarship of their teaching practice), they can guide their candidate to view his or her practice as research within the academy. I will illustrate this understanding of pedagogy as a relation of knowing and unknowing between supervisor and candidate at two distinct moments of presentation in candidacy. Firstly, at the start of candidacy there is the moment in the research statement where the candidate presents as a practitioner-researcher bringing their specific skills and knowledge of practice into the academy; and secondly, there is the accompanying artefact, usually called the 'exegesis', which as Barbara Bolt (2004) describes it, realises the knowing from the creative practice in and through 'languaging'. This is a mode of speaking to the practice of making, with the ideas, tools and materials that practice affords, through reflection on the concrete knowing emerging from their interactions. While these two moments of presentation are separated temporally in the candidature by up to a couple of years, they need to be integral to the thinking and making from the word go.

FROM PRACTITIONER TO PRACTITIONER-RESEARCHER

One of the first stages in the process for which I seek clarification from research degree candidates is the marrying up of their statement or proposal about their research intentions and what I call the 'presentation' of their research outcome. From the point of enrolment to the point of confirmation of their research plan – usually about one year into the three (sometimes four) year programme – fine-tuning the proposal involves the guidance associated with making the shift, previously referred to, from that of a practitioner to that of a practitioner-researcher. Too often the creative result or product is clear in the mind of the candidate at the start of candidacy, but the enquiry is not. The issue of enquiry – its significance and nature in relation to the practice – needs to be addressed in the proposal in order to clarify why the making is the mode in which this particular enquiry will unfold. While it might seem obvious to a fiction writer or a filmmaker, for example, to write a novel and make a film while enrolled in a research programme, often what is not obvious from the research statement is the nature of the enquiry that is motivating the making (e.g. of a novel or a documentary), and more so, motivating the making as a pre-determined form.

Part of the dilemma facing research students at the proposal or research intention stage is the institutional requirement of stating, in advance of the making, the outcome of their research enquiry effectively before the process has begun. This early-stage dilemma is compounded by an end-point dilemma that in order to be awarded the research degree, the outcome must (at doctoral level) fulfil the requirement of originality. Planning for originality is based on a faulty logic that has been thoroughly critiqued; the new cannot be known, intended or calculated in advance of its arrival (Derrida, 2007). The institutional demand on the research candidate to square the circle of the research before the research has begun places the candidate in a difficult situation. Their proposal either encourages grandiosity of claims about the intended outcome, or reinstates the faulty logic of originality. It does this by suggesting that the appearance of the work/thing/product equates to the appearance of an original contribution to knowledge in the academy. In other words, the appearance of work as such is viewed to be equivalent to knowledge understood as original.

For example, when they enter the programme some candidates who are clear that they are making a creative work, for example a novel, find there is a clear set of expectations around what the finished form of the research will look like. Often with creative-writer candidates, several thousands of words toward a draft manuscript have been completed already by the time of enrolment: setting and characters have been determined; a title to the novel has been decided; and the narrative voice(s) have largely begun to be explored in relation to the themes or images that have motivated the work. The fictional universe is often firmly in place. What remains to be determined for these research candidates usually is thought to be the question of how the novel raises 'literary' themes or issues. These can then be addressed in a series of two or three short essays that will ultimately comprise the exegesis, which is seen as the non-creative artefact intended for commencement after the novel has reached a standard ready for submission to a publisher. The goal of being ready for submission for examination largely focuses on the smaller artefact of the literary exegesis. Where creative-writer candidates are commencing their candidacy with their novel at a less advanced stage, the research aspect of candidacy is assumed to revolve around researching the facts that make the narrative plausible (such as, visiting a site for descriptive detail; interviewing a key 'witness'; or reading archival material); undertaking an editing course and writers' workshops where feedback on the writing is central; researching potential publishing houses, and so on. The exegesis in these cases is often viewed as a supplement or add-on to the creative work. It would involve a literary analysis of, say, a fiction writer's oeuvre, or an aspect of a key published writer's biography whose body of writings influenced the candidate to write the novel that they already have in their sights for publication. Through this process what results at the end of the research programme is the production of two only marginally related artefacts: one viewed to be creative, the other, not. Sometimes, it is the hardier creative-writing researcher who pulls themselves away from the novel to undertake the exegesis, the experience of which they find alienating because it is unrelated to their making. In these situations, the exegesis sometimes fills the role of the catalogue essay or functions like curatorial notes at the edge of a work or beside an artefact in a gallery or museum. Alternatively, it may function like a mini-literature thesis in giving focus to textual analysis and interpretation of canonical authors. While each of these versions of the non-creatively written artefact is permissible as submissions for the examination of a creative-writing research programme, I argue that they sell short the possibilities of the exegetical artefact. They also short-change the creative work produced within a research programme. Indeed, you cannot short-change one without also short-changing the other.

On this bifurcated view of research, the production of the creative work in the research programme is no different from the manner in which it was undertaken before entering it. Furthermore, the assumed validated knowledge production of the literary analysis exegesis bears only marginal connection to the creative work. Moreover, it rarely benefits the literary discipline to which ostensibly it is speaking. I do not deny the depth and breadth of research in and of creative-writing practice; however I do want to distinguish these two notions: research as a preparation of the ground for production of the work; and research in the academy. Perhaps it is a distinction that can be expressed as the difference between research and scholarship. If preparing the ground of the work's production is 'research', then how does the creative practice outcome produce scholarship within the academy? This is another way of asking: How can the candidate make the shift from being a practitioner to being a practitioner-researcher, and can the 'languaging' of that shift occur through the proposal statement, and the accompanying record of the creative research?

Paul Carter writes about creative research occurring through the explicit speaking to, and articulation of the techniques of invention associated with the "intelligence of the materials" with which the practitioner works (Carter, 2004, p. xiii). His views can be understood in context of the institutional requirements of proposing and presenting creative research. There we can view the statement of research intent to be less concerned with what the form of the making will be than with the techniques (tools, ideas and knowledge) of the practice, and how these techniques call to the material means by which something will be found or known through the enquiry (Carter, 2010, p. 16). He refers to the techniques of invention involving a conceptual and/or affective advance as a movement of thought that may or may not result in the making of something with a recognisable and completed form. The proposal should aim to articulate not simply what will be made, but more so, how this way of mediating the materials of practice offers a way of knowing.

SHOWING THE KNOWING FROM THE MAKING

Faced with practitioner-candidates struggling to make that shift of their practice into the academy, supervisors can ask: What is it for the candidate that makes doing this kind of research in the academy different from what they did in the studio, study, laboratory or profession prior to their enrolment in a formalised doctorate? How does this novel form, coupled with an intended exegesis, mark the shift from being a creative practitioner to a practitioner-researcher? How is their research problem coming from their specific practice as a writer (in the case of creative-writing doctorates) in a craft where language is the primary material, and the techniques of fiction (its capacities for dramatisation, multiple points of view, focalisation, dialogic and polyphonic voice and the different modes of narrative) evoke a problem that one can learn to address through making within the medium of their craft? Do the techniques of fictional language pose knotty, difficult problems for the writer that the research programme can address through offering space, focus and time? Too often, these questions return a blank look in response from an existing or would-be candidate, or there is the claim that being able to critique their writing with other writing candidates through a peer-to-peer workshop is precisely their reason for being in the academy. However, neither response addresses the necessary shift from practitioner to practitioner-researcher. As research candidates they have shifted the location of their practice and thus their approach to the nature of that practice. The primary shift is that the practice itself has become a question for the candidate, and its place within the academy brings with it the possibility of viewing it as another genre of knowledge production within the academy, not just another milieu in which a candidate's practice is possible. How then does a supervisor guide a candidate to make their shift into the academy enabling them to see themselves as practitioner-researchers, not simply as practitioners?

The kinds of questions that a supervisor might ask their newly enrolled candidate include: What is the problem, and why is it a problem, such that your act of writing a novel is a way of addressing it as an identified problem? How is creative writing a method of enquiry addressing a problem through a formalised process that your practice as a writer can both set and potentially solve? Is there an issue or debate within the history of the novel form, or of the particular genre in which you are locating your fiction, that you want to test, explore, describe, experience, and this can only be achieved by the practice of fiction writing itself? Is there a pattern of experience in your own writing of stories that keeps recurring as a problem of technique, or a problem of process in relation to say, the use of dialogue, the manner of characterisation, the modes of narration, points of view, and so on? If the writer-candidate cannot see their making of the fictional work within candidacy as research along these lines, then logic suggests that the research project is already clear about its outcomes in advance of the making, in which case one has to ask if it is research in the sense in which Carter puts it and the academy deserves. Alternatively, the making of the project may be masking the problem that the making is meant to expose, and explore, in which case the candidate still has to undertake more preliminary thinking in relation to the materiality of her or his practice.

Let me draw out what I am describing here, through providing an example of a creative writing candidate I recently encountered. He had been struggling to position his practice in the academy, and could not move beyond the drafting and re-drafting that had resulted in a couple of chunks of about 30,000 words towards his aim of a finished novel of 90,000 words. I made the suggestion that he think about giving up on the novel as the creative artefact. Instead of the finished form of the creative work driving the research activity, he could instead have two or three incomplete fictional artefacts that comprised the creative work(s). Instead of his intended exegesis being a literary analysis of his sources of influence (Franz Kafka and Peter Carey) alongside his completed novel, he consider exploring the composition of this particular kind of fiction he was working on as the problem itself. What was beginning to emerge in our discussion was the problem of how to incorporate two different levels of reality into the fiction: one that was realist in order to engage the reader into the narrative, and the other that was fabulist, somewhat like magical realism in that it drew on the myth and dreams of the subordinated culture that was being affected adversely by the events within story.

The problem that he was beginning to articulate is not new to literary analysis and interpretation of canonical authors' works, but is new when approached as a problem of composing from the position of a creative-writer and the disciplinary practice of fiction writing. What was emerging in our discussions was, firstly, an unlearning of the finished form that is valorised outside the academy, and secondly the driving of the project's progression within it. Then, subsequently, it was a matter of re-thinking the problem's enactment in order for it to be seen as a problem of composition; a problem of the material qualities of language that both conveys meaning transparently and resists that same transparency in all sorts of ways. These are qualities that some fiction writers aim to formulate as a theme of their writing. We began to discuss how this problem that designers call 'wicked problems', necessitated a movement between what these canonical and contemporary writers of fiction had articulated about this very kind of struggle with the materials, ideas and tools of their craft (language, narrative, representation) and their experiments in their fiction, and the candidate's own struggles and experimentation in his writing. What emerged from our discussions was not only how the problem could be seen, but also how it needed to be designed differently to be creative research. We could see the potential for episodic explorations of language and its techniques undertaken and reflected on by others interwoven with episodes of his own experimentation and reflection in composing fiction – a series of turns and counter-turns between knowing and making throughout the candidature. When the problem was reset in this way, the outcome of a finished novel looked unnecessary and the actualisation of artefacts would replace the single work in its finished form. This approach would produce a qualitatively different kind of doctoral research from what the candidate thought he needed to undertake and produce. Instead of conforming to fixed, familiar and finished conceptions of creative practice, the candidate was entering a different kind of relation to his practice in the academy.

Approaching the problem of the creative work in this way, the candidate seemed liberated, quite genuinely, from the anxiety of meeting the demands of a publishable standard of a work within the time constraints of his remaining candidature. It had not occurred to him that as a writer in the academy he had the opportunity to clarify this problem of competing modes of reality and thus competing modes of language usage and techniques. Furthermore, the difference between being a practitioner and being a practitioner-researcher was that the research programme gave him the space to explore that problem as a problem that faces a certain kind of fiction writer. He came to see that he had several ways of approaching his situation, and the least scholarly way of doing so was to think of it as the completion of a novel meeting a publishable standard within the time of candidature. What had been previously the burden of meeting market-place expectations about the creative work, and then adding on an artefact of literary analysis, which he felt ill-equipped to undertake, was inverted to become one that arose from his situated practice as a creative writer in the academy. The process of designing the problem from the materiality of the practice and seeking a solution to it in the movement through those materials would ultimately lead to a qualitatively different set of artefacts that arose from 'languaging' the writer's problem of language itself.

DIFFERENT GENRES OF KNOWLEDGE PRODUCTION

In the academy *knowing through making* is different from knowing through argumentation. They produce qualitatively different kinds of knowledge. While the former kind of knowledge production is relatively new within the academy, it is important that its value to the academy is not just assumed by creative practitioners because it has been traditionally excluded. That is, its value as a form of knowledge production must always ensure that it engages primarily with the criteria of the academy (i.e. not the market-place). Knowledge production within the academy should be measured by: the *validity* of the enquiry to a community of scholars; an *ethical* approach to designing the enquiry; the *rigour* of method in undertaking the enquiry; an *intelligence* in assembling the materials and resources involved in the enquiry; and an *integrity* in presenting the discovery of knowledge so that it complements the mode of enquiry. None of these criteria are exclusive to one domain of knowledge production over another – that is, to the conventional mode of argumentation (thesis) over making (creative practice) as a mode of knowledge presentation. In spite of, or rather because of the difference between these types of knowledge, presenting the *knowing through making* in a related artefact is imperative as a means of reaffirming the academy's need of this newer, less conventional form of knowledge production.

In order to meet that imperative, creative practice must recognise its activity as a mode of knowledge production that fulfils these generic academic criteria. It cannot do so without stating that fulfilment through the related artefact, the exegesis, which is the durable record of the knowing occurring from the making. Without an integrated artefact documenting the knowing, the explicit showing of knowledge generation by makers through their making results in the production of works that fall short of their being fully valued within the academy. The production of artefacts within the academy neither can nor should be excluded from their value and privileging within the marketplace. However, a valuable opportunity is lost if the creative practice within the academy leaves an account of the knowing through making either unsaid ('the work speaks for itself') or understated (the artefact that should document the making only marginally relates to that making).

The conventional presentation of findings in a thesis is a natural or physical science model of discovery and presentation of knowledge. This is somewhat modified within the social sciences from which the discipline of media and communication, my institutional location, has partially derived. Consistent with this form of 'discovery' and 'presentation' of knowledge there is, firstly, the idea that it has nothing to do with the elements that are ascribed to 'creativity' and, secondly, and in a related way, the researcher as knower is completely without implication in the knowledge that is 'found' and 'presented'. While neither the natural nor the social sciences hold onto this latter convention at the level of pedagogy, it remains an implicit assumption that the presumed neutrality of the knower in the enactment of knowing is replicated in the form of the presentation of knowledge. The presentation of the findings from practitioner-research, by contrast, should replicate the explicit conditions of that research. Such conditions suggest that it is a form of knowing mediated by materials and techniques where the embodied subjectivity of the practitioner-researcher is co-implicated in that mediation. Practitioner research findings should reflect the differently acquired knowing in the form of its presentation rather than mimic the form that belongs to another paradigm of knowledge production.

During the course of candidature I often hear students and supervisors describing the relationship between the creative work and the exegesis according to one of the following models: (a) two parallel projects that are met by virtue of a bridge between them (the figure 'H') such that essays may be written for publication about the creative work alongside the writing of the creative work itself; and, (b) the creative work is the dominant work in so far as its completed form consumes the major part of the candidature and the exegesis follows its completion such that the document of making is reduced to a 'writing up' of the process, much like a chronicle of a journey. The problem with both of these models of practitioner-researcher presentation of findings is that they each, in their different ways, miss the opportunity for demonstrating how this practice-based form of knowledge production is a crucial part of the academy's role as a site of knowledge production.

SPATIALISING THE THINKING ABOUT MAKING

There is a figure that comes to mind that may help in supervising the candidate who is a practitioner-researcher. I draw on it because I think it represents visually and spatially the relation between the creative work and the exegesis. It also figures other sets of terms that are assumed to be in harmony or unity but, also, can be productive of tension or opposition. Such terms are representative of binary thinking that underpins Western thought structures and therefore practices. Binary thinking always invokes a hierarchy where one term is privileged over another and often leads to detrimental consequences. As we are in the business of innovation we owe it to ourselves to interrogate where and how these structures are operating, and where and how we can think and make their subversion to introduce the new in whatever guise that might be.

The chiasmus is a figure of thought and speech that has been around since ancient times. Its traditional purpose was to bring harmony or continuity to a text through the inversion of two opposing or contrasting elements such as form and content or words and meanings as they move through the crossed lines of the chiasm (the 'X'). As a figure, it is supposed to show the unity at the heart of the difference within and between the two terms of a relation when the elements intersect and are turned back upon themselves in their passage through the intersection. Unity of opposing or contrary terms is a design feature of classical notions of truth. According to Jacques Derrida (2007) the figure of the chiasm entwines the appearance of a unity at the same time as it disengages that unity: one of the poles of the X is longer than the other. In the switching or crossing over of the terms through the intersection, one becomes something other than the inversion or mirror of what it was before that passage. One term exceeds and therefore deforms the unity in the swap over.

Where every text aims to unify or balance what it is saying (content) with how it is saying it (form), these poles or elements of a text never lead to the unity their intersection or encounter assumes. Something other than unity or harmony is achieved in the movement of crossing through a point of encounter between two different terms. That something other is not to be feared or avoided – as if that were even possible – as all writing goes through this gesture of aiming for the unity of its elements and missing the mark. Something about the terms resists their simple substitution of positions either that of content with form, or of the form within the text as a whole. It is in the resistance to this substitution, the necessary but fallible quality of substituting the positions of the terms, that Derrida locates the invention of something unexpected, unplanned for, something other in a text. Where others might call this something other, 'creativity' or 'originality', like Derrida, I prefer 'inventive', 'generative' and 'productive'. All texts display this generative excess, but some do so more than others, and do it more strongly or profoundly.

I am reminded of this figure not only in relation to text-based or language-based creative works. It is a figure that demonstrates that where opposites or contrary positions, say, between thinking and making, are intended to be unified, harmonised or solved through the research outcome, close attention to the movement of these terms reveals the element that is not going to unify. By virtue of that a third or other term appears that belongs to both and neither of the previous terms. This is the unknown, unplanned element that I think we can say is genuinely new or generative of what cannot be intended, and it takes a form or position that is always local and particular to the context or relation in which it arises. It is this *both/and* feature of making, a feature that participates in both sides of the division of binary thinking, that we call the invention of the research. When the invention is discovered or found, its originality confronts the researcher as if by accident rather than through planning.

CONCLUSION

The academy needs and deserves not only new modes of knowledge production, but also new perspectives on old modes. We need to ensure that the structures and conventions within the academy around what counts as knowledge are not simply the replication of the familiar, or the reappearance of the same. Practitioner research is not the only genre of knowledge production that has a stake in this matter, however, it is the very mode by which the stakes can be decisively shown and presented.

REFERENCES

Bolt, B. (2004). *The Exegesis and the Shock of the New*. Retrieved April 11, 2011, from http://www.textjournal.com.au/speciss/issue3/bolt.htm

Carter, P. (2004). *Material thinking. The theory and practice of creative research*. Melbourne: Melbourne University Press.

Carter, P. (2010). The ethics of invention. In Estelle Barrett & Barbara Bolt (Eds.) *Practice as research. Approaches to creative arts enquiry* (pp. 15–34). London: I.B. Tauris.

Derrida, J. (2007). Psyche: Invention of the other. In P. Kamuf & E. Rottenberg (Eds.) (Catherine Porter, Trans.) *Psyche. Inventions of the Other*. Vol 1 (pp. 1–47). Stanford, CA: Stanford University Press.

PIA EDNIE-BROWN

9. SUPERVISING EMERGENCE

Adapting Ethics Approval Frameworks toward Research
by Creative Project

INTRODUCTION

Writing a paper is a process toward discovery and clarity; it is a way to work out
how one could think and feel about something more clearly and also in ways that
emerge as part of that process. This is true of my own approach to writing, filling
me with both anticipation and anxiety as I started typing up notes for this chapter,
and it is what I tell candidates doing creative project-based research as they turn,
often reluctantly, toward writing their exegesis. This process is extremely
rewarding, but never easy – even for those more comfortable and at ease with
writing than others – and tends to involve some quite uniquely difficult challenges
for this mode of enquiry.

But this pales in comparison with the frustration that many creative researchers
experience in negotiating the ethics approval process. In what seems to be the
unanticipated product of considering creative projects as a research activity, ethics
approval frameworks impose a set of prescriptive conditions that unwittingly
threaten the fragile emergence of creative experimentation and discovery.
Evidence points clearly to the fact that the ethics approval process is not widely
viewed as having a positive effect on the area, because it does not adequately
accommodate the particulars of this mode of research activity, to the point, as I
will argue, that the process verges on operating unethically itself.

This makes it all the more important a problem for the supervisor, who has a
special role to play in leading positive change in practices. In what follows I will
offer three examples where my candidates have engaged with the ethics approval
process, and where each 'story' highlights a different issue, or problem, that
candidates tend to face. These stories provide a set of tangible examples through
which to address what I regard as the main problem in the tension we find between
university ethics approval processes and research by creative project: that the mode
of research enquiry in question pertains to a paradigm that can be understood in
terms of broad socio-cultural changes, and that a nuanced ethical framework is
demanded by those broad changes, neither of which have been significantly
absorbed within ethics approval processes. Working out how to deal with the
problems is not an easy or straightforward task. My hope is that this chapter might
help suggest ways that we might tackle the challenges, so that we can move
collectively toward the innovation clearly required in this terrain.

B. Allpress, R. Barnacle, L. Duxbury and E. Grierson (Eds.), Supervising Practices for Postgraduate
Research in Art, Architecture and Design, 103–116.
©2012 Sense Publishers. All rights reserved.

KILLING THE AH-HA: THE BAN ON RETROSPECTIVE APPROVALS

...it could be argued that through its very stringent processes of ethical regulation, the university ethics procedure introduces limitations that work against "cutting edge" research and mitigates experimentation at the heart of practice (Bolt, 2010, p. 127).

The first time I dealt with an ethics approval submission as a supervisor was for the master's thesis, in fashion, of RMIT candidate, Adele Varcoe (completed 2009), whom I co-supervised with Robyn Healy. Varcoe's research inhabits a fashion-art nexus. She was interested in the limits of fashion, in terms of the relationship between fashion, convention and belief: what counts as being dressed, or not? She would test this by doing things like wearing her pyjamas to work, and asking her class: Am I dressed? Is it possible to be naked and dressed at the same time? The story of 'The Emperors New Clothes' became a useful parable for the work, sketching out the idea that people will often see what they need and/or want to see, and that this is an aspect of social codes, conventions and pressures that impacts on what counts as being dressed or not. Certainly, an important part of this picture is what people find acceptable and/or are willing to accept. For Varcoe's research, a clear way to approach these issues was to explore a blurring of the boundary between clothes and the body, such that she was probing the limits of acceptability.

In undertaking this exploration, Varcoe developed a technique of skin-folding involving the use of latex, which became the focus of the masters. She set out to test the proposition that in making skin akin to a material fabric, this folding technique could become both a way of dressing and a new fashion. The technique emerged, as is most often the case in creative work, in a fairly unanticipated manner, initially through trial and error with experimentation on her own body, and as an extension of her studio experimentation with various plastics in casting objects and playing with materials. For instance, she made a mould of a pair of socks and cast it in red lipstick. This red lipstick pair of socks was something she then smeared on her face, asking: Is this a way of putting on my socks? She made an enormous array of material tests and objects, developing her sense of the character and tendencies of a variety of materials along the way. The skin-folding technique was something that emerged in the context of exploring materials and ideas in this playful manner.

While playing with latex on her own body allowed her to work out the technique to some degree, it was not until her boyfriend at the time became involved, and then some family members at home, that the potential of the technique became evident. At first, she was struck by the fact that skin is not a homogenous, predictable material. Rather, each person's skin presented different possibilities through their different degrees of elasticity, firmness, texture, etc. As such, she could see that this potentially offered a way of dressing that was fitted to the body in an entirely new way. Then, on seeing photos and demonstrations of skin folding, Varcoe was somewhat surprised at how many of her friends wanted to try it. Rather than searching for willing recruits, people were asking her to be folded. Not only did this point to pragmatic potential, it was pointing in the very direction she needed to explore: what people think is acceptable and/or are willing to accept. The fact that the work appealed to so many was unexpected, quite understandably; and the outcomes of the technique often seemed quite grotesque. Through a combination of evident appeal to others and the fact that it was unexpected, this technique sprung off the table of her many material explorations landing in the very territory she needed, as a definitive 'Ah-ha!'

However, because she was touching and manipulating bodies using a manufactured substance, in addition to photographing them, there were some pressing ethical issues. This made her ethics approval process arduous – it was classified as 'Risk Category 2'. She did a great deal of research so that dangers and risks such as latex allergies were thought through and ways of dealing with potential problems were worked out. None of these problems arose, but it was a worthwhile process, knowing and understanding the risks in some detail. Her application was not successful the first time, and there were several submissions required to get it through the approval process. As a supervisor, this was an eye-opener for me. It is not so usual to deal with Category 2 in a creative research context, so it was both a jump into the deeper end and an experience of quite some frustration, with progress delays and anxiety. Nevertheless, it helped produce a heightened sensitivity for both Varcoe and myself in understanding and managing risk.

In this sense, the process was positive and beneficial for all. However, much of the early folding work, before she really understood it to be anything more than playing around with latex on herself and a few people close to her, was very poignant in that these were the steps and moments through which the 'discovery' was made. Because the central ethics committee processes would not allow any retrospective approvals, these images or stories could not be used in her research. These poignant moments, which revealed something important in terms of how unexpected potential arises, had to be excluded. This was a shame, because they could have been valuable to others. This prescriptive application of particular rules and regulations of the ethics approval process arguably becomes a suppression of a particular kind of valuable contribution.

By its very nature, the emergent 'Ah-ha!' cannot be predicted; it has to arise through playful exploration. By banning the retrospective approval, ethics committees risk silencing discussion about moments and methods that are important for the fields to which contributions are being made. The ban seems in accord with the statement, from the National Statement on Ethical Conduct in Human Research (2007) that, "A judgement that a human research proposal meets the requirements of this National Statement and is ethically acceptable must be made before research can begin" (Australian Government, 2007, p. 8). But a hint about how the National Statement document as a whole might be less well acquainted with research by creative project can be found in the paragraph immediately following the working definition of research:

> To enable comparative assessment of academic activity, this definition sought to include the widest range of creative and experimental activities. Many items in the definition are uncontentious, but there may be

disagreement about some – for example, 'the invention and generation of new … images, performances, artefacts … where these lead to new or substantially improved insights' – since this could count poetry, painting and performing arts as research (2007, p. 8).

Aspects of creative work, such as how 'discoveries' emerge, may well "lead to new or substantially improved insights", but whenever there is an effective silencing of those emergent moments that make these creative activities count as research, the 'disagreement' referred to above looms painfully large. While Varcoe went to great lengths to research and manage risks, one has to wonder about the degree to which university processes are currently *able* to respond in kind, given the evident suspicion about this mode of research activity as acknowledged at the highest level of the National Statement. But if not, then I would argue that the ethics approval process itself is placed at risk of becoming somewhat and ironically unethical.

Now, I suspect there would be some who would argue that Varcoe should have applied for ethics approval before she tested putting the latex on her own, or her boyfriend's body. Firstly, there is a certain impracticality of this demand: Why would you spend that much time and research on something that may go no further than a half hour test, yielding nothing interesting? Such a requirement would bring creative exploration to an ineffective standstill. If that is the answer, then this is tantamount to excluding creative activity from academic research. But also, such a demand would be a complete misunderstanding of the nature of creative research, and its value. Before I move to my second account of an ethics approval process, I will argue this point in more detail.

NATURE AND VALUE OF CREATIVE RESEARCH
IN THE AGE OF EMERGENCE

The first thing to emphasise is that the greater recognition of creative activity as research, where it becomes an assessable part of doctoral degrees, can be understood as part of broader socio-cultural transformations. One can track these broad transformations against the development of creative practices as a valid component of doctoral degrees, which go back to around the mid-1980s, with more traction and familiarity emerging in Australia and the UK at least by the late 1990s and early 2000s.[1] It was also around this time that the term 'emergence' was starting to reappear in the title and subject matter of many books, indicating the rise in research activity around this concept. I would suggest that this is not a coincidence in that these developments are both part of the same paradigmatic shift, and that the past several decades, across which doctorates by creative project have been proposed, developed and formalised, has been a passage through the late phases of the information age and into what I refer to as 'the age of emergence'. This shift has also been remarked upon in some detail in the work of scholars such as Antonio Negri and Michael Hardt, and Paulo Virno. Earlier, Félix Guattari signalled the nature of these broad cultural shifts in his late work, *Chaosmosis: An ethico-aesthetic paradigm*, where he highlights the amplified significance of modes of knowing that operate at the heart of creative practices:

> The aesthetic power of feeling, although equal in principle with the other powers of thinking philosophically, knowing scientifically, acting politically, seems on the verge of occupying a privileged position within the collective Assemblages of enunciation of our era (Guattari, 1995, p. 101).

In the context of this chapter I cannot develop this connection in as much detail as I have elsewhere (Ednie-Brown, 2007). However, in pursuing the idea that the supervision of research by creative project is tantamount to supervising an emergent process and that this requires a shift in how we might approach ethics, I need to offer some background.

The term 'emergence' refers to a model of the complex operations of the world and is seen to be "a ubiquitous feature of the world around us" (Holland, 1999, p. 2). As such, emergence becomes the name for a contemporary understanding of the laws of nature. As a discursive construct it seeks to explain, often through mathematical frameworks, the way that complex, global forms of organisation come into being through simple, local behaviours and rules, in the absence of any apparent, centralised or dominant control mechanism. A significant feature of emergence is that it is no less applicable to economic systems, games and urban planning than it is to living and natural systems. With emergence, culture and nature are swept artfully together, providing a model that describes the nature and organisation of contemporary socio-cultural operations particularly well, and vice versa. In particular, in the context of this discussion, it provides a way to link the nature of the creative act – and the emergence of the new, such as in the 'Ah-ha' moments – with activities well beyond the doing of creative projects. In the context of this kind of transversal connection, accounts of the activity of generative, creative activity become of potential value to issues beyond themselves.

If processes of emergence are ubiquitous in the world around us, operating as part of the laws of nature, they are also integral to the way in which the world and life comes-into-being and endures. In other words, emergence is an issue of *composition*: the process and outcome of combining things to form a whole. The rise of doctoral research by creative project seems deeply linked to a movement therein toward the *generative* – not at the exclusion of the analytical or other modes of activity, but simply as an increasingly important activity that works with others. This is reflected in the widespread call to better understand 'design' and 'creativity' in the discourses of business, technology and innovation, where creative composition and emergent processes are seen to be more and more relevant to broader, worldly problems. As such, to exclude it from the academy due to the tensions arising with other models and protocols of research, seems counter to at least one statement of purpose in the National Statement, that of: "fostering of research that is of benefit to the community" (Australian Government, 2007, p. 7).

Interestingly enough, where sciences have tackled emergence and complexity there are many glimmers of recognition in this direction. One of the more cited publications on the subject is, *Emergence. From chaos to order* by John Holland, a professor of psychology, electrical engineering and computer science who is promoted as "the father of genetic algorithms" (Holland, 1999). At the end of his book, he outlines a series of obstacles standing in the way of a better understanding of emergence. But before he launches into this list he writes:

> There is one larger issue, however, that I will avoid. It may be that the parts of the universe that we can understand in a scientific sense – the parts of the universe that we describe via laws (axioms, equations) – constitute a small fragment of the whole. If that is so, then there may be aspects of emergence that we cannot understand scientifically (Holland, 1999, p. 231).

This gap in scientific understanding has a significant part to play in opening scientific paradigms onto the field of creative composition and aesthetic modes of knowing, an opening that Stengers suggests is embedded in the potential of complexity science:

> Physics and chemistry are thus no longer defined only by the power of their definitions; they can also explore the cases where this power is lost, where scientists' practical position in relation with what they address must change. The problem is no longer one of deduction but of wondering what is relevant and how. Scientists no longer address a system as explained by what they know about it, even if they know it perfectly well, because it is a model. Their questions imply an open situation: 'what will it be able to produce?' 'What kind of behaviour will emerge?' And the question must be asked each time, with each new situation (Stengers, 2004, pp. 92–99).

The defined age of emergence becomes a time in which the very situated, emergent nature of research by creative project seems especially pertinent. As such, if ethics approval processes premised on scientific models cannot adapt to acknowledge and accommodate the value, relevance and needs of this mode of research activity – by, for instance, working out how to deal with retrospective approvals – then one might question quite reasonably the ethics of that process.

ETHICS APPROVALS SHAPING CREATIVE PROJECTS

Olivia Pintos-Lopez, a Ph.D. candidate whose work I have been supervising, required ethics approval for an art and design project she was planning that involved human subjects. Pintos-Lopez's research has been exploring the design of structures of engagement through which to cross the producer-consumer divide, along the lines of trends in on-line spaces toward user-generated content, but with a spatial emphasis, i.e. how spatially implemented structures can be involved in this border crossing of mutual interest and benefit. Essentially, Pintos-Lopez's interest lies in trying to find ways of designing spaces that involve engagement of a more structured nature than most open public space, such that the public are offered the opportunity to engage collectively with new forms of creative agency. She has a particular interest in developing such spaces and structures of engagement in order to offer an alternative to the dominant structuring of public interaction around the imperatives of financial profit, i.e. the purchase of services and the acquisition of goods.

She was working with an idea for using a shop window and commercial shop space to entice passers-by to interact with a window display, where their actions would contribute to the production of a collectively generated short film. There were considerable challenges within this idea, implicit in the difficulties with the research aims. For the project to work she needed to produce a framework that would draw in the attention of passers-by, sustain that attention through some kind of playful and meaningful interaction, while offering an engagement that was not onerous or too lengthy such that people may become disinclined to continue. According to university protocols, this required ethics approval because it involved human participants.

When she moved to fill out an ethics approval submission, the challenges became magnified. If she needed to have each potential participant read a 'plain language statement' and sign a consent form, unavoidably the nature of the engagement was affected in a way that was difficult to see as positive. Apart from the unwieldy nature of bringing ethics protocols into the interaction, having elicited interest and before 'collecting data', the plain language statement and consent form presented a more profound problem; they implicitly situate the potential participant as a research subject, or at the very least, as someone participating in a process that involves risk. The National Statement (2007) suggests that:

> The relationship between researchers and research participants is the ground on which human research is conducted. The values set out in this section – respect for human beings, research merit and integrity, justice, and beneficence – help to shape that relationship as one of trust, mutual responsibility and ethical equality. For this reason, the National Statement speaks of research 'participants' rather than 'subjects' (Australian Government, 2007, p. 13).

Creative research methodologies in art and design rarely involve people, whether 'subjects' or 'participants', in the same way that other research methods do, through engaging them in interviews, focus groups, testing, etc. – but this is absolutely assumed in the way the ethics application form is structured. Sections of the ethics application such as: 'Methodology used for collecting data', and 'Explain how data will be analysed', are an anathema to the creative project, which does not tend to collect or analyse data in the scientific ways implied. Clearly, an aim of Pintos-Lopez's research was to engage people in a scenario that involved a sense of mutual exchange, and collective, creative agency. The experiment was to see if this particular set of conditions could generate this kind of exchange and atmosphere, and to see what else might (unexpectedly) emerge through the process. Part of the mismatch between the actuality of the project and the assumption of the ethics approval framework, is that it was not the participants themselves being studied *per se*, but rather a structure or spatial system of engagement, albeit one that involved participants as a crucial component.

Now, these problems might not be insurmountable, and the potential intimidation of the plain language statement and signing research consent forms could be dealt with in ways that might minimise damage, or indeed even be used carefully to foster a sense of ethically poised, mutual exchange. But it is certainly true that this added a degree of difficulty to the development of an already difficult idea, requiring her to incorporate this ethics-framework parameter in an inventive way such that it did not destroy what she was trying to achieve. There was also a lack of time, as she had the opportunity to use the space on particular dates and could not afford for this time-frame to be extended through repeated resubmissions.

As such, she made a strategic decision that would enable her to free up the potential interaction that was crucial to the project. Rather than set up an interactive window display herself, she decided to curate a group of artists to work in the same window display/shop space, each one having 24 hours to produce material that would contribute to the making of a single, animated film. Pintos-Lopez was offering each artist an advertised event, involving the provision of a site in which to experiment and develop their own work, the opportunity to become part of a bigger project, and engage with the public in ways they might find valuable. She became a curator, rather than a content producer, who then assembled and edited material generated into a single film. She chose artists that already had a developed interest in participatory practices, and with whom she could spend time explaining the research project without compromising or hindering the likelihood of their engagement in any way. These artists were not operating as research candidates so the specifics of their own work were not subject to the same ethics approval process. Rather, each artist signed a consent form prior to commencing, demonstrating their understanding of the project, its parameters, and the intended outcome of a collaborative, animated film, and the design of a system for collectively making a creative work. In order to get around any potential issues with public engagement, she proposed to use signage and clearly displayed plain language statements, and to request that public participants were not filmed.

So, this was her strategically inventive way through the problem. In many senses, this was simply good design, where given parameters were accommodated into a design outcome, not unlike negotiating planning guidelines and building codes in the design of a house, for instance. Both, after all, are about establishing principles of conduct that have a broad aim of collective social benefit and of helping to assist in negotiating and accommodating the often conflicting interests therein. These codes of conduct modulate behaviour and action in ways that, at best, ensure ethical outcomes. In the face of frustration, this can be a useful comparison for supervisors to offer candidates.

But just as planning guidelines and building codes are modelled around issues that are specific to the act of producing and inhabiting the built environment, an ethics approval process for research by creative project should be modelled around the paradigm it seeks to modulate. If ethics approvals shape creative projects, ethics approval processes need to re-shape themselves around the creative research project paradigm. It is ethical to expect that if one can affect, one should also be affected.

Pintos-Lopez's project was fundamentally about an explicit interest in developing ethical frameworks of engagement in collective, social contexts. The irony of this story is that the ethics approval process did not help her deal with that aim, because she sought a different kind of ethics.

SITUATED ETHICS: FROM THE VIRTUOUS TO THE VIRTUOSO

This different kind of ethics – what I would refer to as 'situated', is also discussed in a recent paper by Kate Macneill and Barbara Bolt on the subject of problems and tensions between research by creative project and university ethics. Their concluding sentence refers precisely to this term:

> What is called for is an environment that encourages a situated ethics of practice, one that responds to the particularities of each individual artistic activity and interpersonal negotiation, rather than regulating artistic activity through the external imposition of codes and protocols (Macneill & Bolt, 2011, p. 27).

But what does a shift toward a more situated approach to ethics really mean? As I alluded to earlier, this is linked to the broad implications of an emergent paradigm. In a paper titled, 'The challenge of complexity: Unfolding the ethics of science' Isabelle Stengers warns against compulsive reductionism and calls for scientists to take a more generative, risky, uncertain stance. This, she suggests, is an ethics that unfolds from complexity science itself:

> Complexity, as it started with the discovery and study of surprising properties, usually related to the irreducible importance of nonlinear relations … would produce the opportunity to entertain a different relation with the past, emphasising openness, surprise, the demand of relevance, the creative aspect of the scientific adventure, and not reduction to simplicity. True scientific simplicity is never reductive; it is always a relevant simplicity that is a creative achievement (Stengers, 2004, p. 96).

Related issues are explored through a remarkable little book called, *Ethical know-how: Action, wisdom and cognition* by Francisco Varela. He distinguishes between ethical expertise and ethical deliberation. Most Western writers on ethics, he claims, tend to focus on reasoning as the central issue (Varela, 1999, p. 23) wherein ethics becomes an issue of deliberation. Ethical expertise does not centre itself on rational judgments of reasoning or on how this may be applied as ethically instrumental. Rather, it is based on the inextricably specific tissue of circumstances – or situatedness. Sharing some affinity with Foucauldian and Spinozist approaches to ethics, as well as Félix Guattari's notion of the *ethico-aesthetic*, his notion of ethical know-how dwells in a "skilful approach to living … based on a pragmatics of transformation that demands nothing less than a moment to moment awareness of the virtual nature of our selves" (Varela, 1999, p. 75). To act ethically, one must be acting with sensitivity to the particularities of the situation where there is not a reliance on a set of rules:

> To gather a situation under a rule a person must describe the situation in terms of categories we may call cognitive. Instead, if we try and see correspondences and affinities, the situation at hand becomes much more textured. All relevant aspects are included, not just those which fit the reduction of a categorical analysis (Varela, 1999, p. 28).

As such, ethical activity becomes infused with a breadth of relevance, becoming situated in a field of potential such that the creative and transformative possibilities are multiplied and amplified. The kind of know-how being discussed here does not exclude forms of knowing that "fit the reduction of a categorical analysis". *Knowledge of* and *know-how* are not set up in opposition; know-how incorporates both rational forms of categorical analysis and the situated forms of aesthetically inclined knowing.

Theorist Mark C. Taylor, in summarising the moment of complexity writes that, "according to complexity theorists, all significant change takes place between too much and too little order" (Taylor, 2001, p. 14), resonating with Holland's suggestion that innovation requires finding an artful middle ground between the looseness of poetry and the tightness of science.[2] Along these lines, Varela has suggested that, "intelligence should guide our actions, but in harmony with the texture of the situation at hand ... truly ethical behaviour takes the middle way between spontaneity and rational calculation" (Varela, 1999, p. 31–32).

Ethical know-how becomes a measured practice of engaging with the world, of how we behave, and of what we acknowledge is at stake. Rather than being framed around the *virtuous*, ethico-aesthetic know-how is about the *virtuoso*: the skilled performer. This property of ethical expertise might also be called 'the art of emergence'. Steven Johnson writes that:

> We are only just now developing such a language to describe the art of emergence. But here's a start: great designers ... have a feel for the middle ground between free will and the nursing home, for the thin line between too much order and too little. They have a feel for the edges (Johnson, 2004, p. 189).

It would seem that the art of emergence involves what Varela calls ethical know-how. Stenger's assertion that an ethics unfolding from complexity science calls for a more uncertain stance can also be seen as a challenge to university ethics procedures: how can we develop a more nuanced, situated approach to accepting and managing risk and uncertainty?

Even if there are no easy rules or moral guidelines here, there is an important principle or navigational directive implicit to the art of emergence in that the performance of any act strives for a balance between affecting and being affected, between active reflection and the immediacy of embodied response, between sensitive responsiveness and determined agency. This is a politics of action that neither caves in passively to collective desires or beliefs nor holds to individualism, authorship or dictatorship as the power of truth. It is determined and respectful, pushy and playful. It involves the raising of thinking and acting to their highest powers, such that they affect and fold into one another.

If we can accept that the broader context of our activities is something like the general characterisation I made earlier about the age of emergence, and the importance therein of an emphasis on ethical know-how over moral guidelines, then it is important that the collegiate process of both engaging in, and overseeing university ethics approval processes also involves this striving toward affecting and being affected, with regards to "the texture of the situation at hand" (Varela, 1999, pp. 31–32). This becomes important when ushering candidates through the process, because it involves the potential to foster ethical know-how and to amplify the power of a creative event, however hard it may be to find a way through the layers of frustration. My next story is an example that points to how a highly situated ethics can surpass the ethics of care demanded by current protocols.

A CASE OF SITUATED ETHICS

The danger of the current system of ethical review, perhaps, is that the preoccupation with gaining ethical approval shifts debates away from genuine discussions of ethical dilemmas, negotiations and difficult decision making. We are encouraged to make our research appear ethical and discouraged from raising genuine ethical concern (Wiles, Coffey, Robison, Prosser, 2010, p. 13).

Another of my candidates, Pia Interlandi who, like Varcoe, was from fashion and also co-supervised by Dr Robyn Healy, becomes an interesting case for what she added to ethics protocols in a science context. Interlandi's research concerns dressing the dead, and ways in which garments might become part of fashioning the process of dealing with the deceased body. The project I will discuss here was being done collaboratively with a scientist, as part of an experiment designed through a conventional scientific framework. The project involved using 21 dead pigs, which were dressed in a garment, buried and gradually dug up to examine the decomposition of the fabric over time. The ethics approval for using the pigs was not difficult at all, because they were dead. In fact, all that was required was a submission of 'Notification of use of Animal Tissues or Carcasses' form to the Animal Ethics committee. This is Interlandi's description of the project on that form:

Within the next ten years natural earth burial (NEB) will be offered in Australia and it is foreseen that more people will opt to be buried in Natural Earth Burial grounds than are currently choosing to be cremated (which is the most popular method of body disposal in Australia). The general rules for NEB are that the body is not buried in a coffin or embalmed, and thus buried in a simple shroud. As such there is room for people to choose a garment or shroud that is personalised through print, embroidery and the placement of letters and mementos in pockets.

> The project investigates the effect of garments on the decomposition of carcasses, and the effect of decomposition on garments in a 'Natural Earth Burial' scenario. The carcasses will be washed and dressed just as a human body would be prepared for burial. The garments in which the carcasses will be buried consist of a hemp cloth (both printed and raw) and also include some polyester embroidery. Cellulose fabrics (such as cotton, linen and hemp) are thought to decompose rapidly, whereas fibres from a synthetic derivate will theoretically last longer.
>
> Over a period of 1 year, the pigs will be recovered and textiles samples analysed to establish the rate of decomposition. The aim is to use the data collected to create burial garments for humans which have a predictable rate of decomposition (Dadour & Interlandi, 2009).

Now, this is a good and fair description of the project. However, it does not indicate the importance Interlandi gave to the process of burying these deceased pigs, as part of the attentions and issues that her research was working with, nor does it indicate the degree of concern she felt about the sheer fact that 21 pigs were to be killed in order for this experiment to occur. She did not need to state this. From the point of view of procedures, the fact of the killing was not an issue. It was an issue for Interlandi, though, whose distress was palpable. She spent a long time deciding whether to go ahead with the proposed experiment, researching details such as which pigs would be killed (where were they coming from, would they be killed soon for other purposes, etc.), and the method and conditions under which they would be killed. For the thoroughly initiated, where animals are sacrificed for scientific experimentation on a regular basis, this is perhaps a dilemma that has been approached and processed such that when asked the question, as Interlandi was by a researcher at SymbioticA – "will you be able to forgive yourself?" – the answer is resolved to some degree. But for Interlandi, this was far from resolved. To her credit, Interlandi's process and attention to the ethical dilemmas of this experimental act surpassed the expectations of the ethics committee to a notable and explicitly stated extent. This becomes all the more interesting in terms of the relationship between ethics approval processes and research by creative project candidates because, as I will describe, it was her detailed attention to the aforementioned texture of the situation at hand.

Interlandi did this component of her research at SymbioticA: Centre for Excellence in Biological Arts, at the University of Western Australia, where artists work in scientific laboratories in collaboration with scientists in the production of artwork. She was offered a residency there to undertake this work, and collaborate with the forensic scientist, Professor Ian Dadour. SymbioticA encourages all of their residents to take the PAWES course (Programme in Animal Welfare, Ethics and Science), so she enrolled and attended. This course involved familiarising people with the handling of animals, and a family of mice was presented to the class. It turned out that ethics approval had been required in order to use the mice in this way, and that they would be 'sacrificed' after they had fulfilled this purpose. When a few people in the course asked if they could save the lives of the mice by taking them home, they were told this was not allowed. This significantly upset Interlandi, who felt she was implicated in an ethical dilemma: would she have done the course if she had known in advance that the lives of animals would be sacrificed?[3] This touched closely on her own ethical dilemma, which led to discussion about her project and her struggle with this situation.

This class discussion led to several people expressing interest in witnessing how she dealt with the pigs' bodies and for staff from the Research Ethics and Biosafety Office, as well as the Chair of the Animal Ethics Committee, to be in attendance in observing the pig burials. In directly confronting, acknowledging and respecting the lives of the pigs used for the experiment, Interlandi visited them all prior to their deaths. She named each one, had them washed, carried with care and respect, dressed and buried with ceremony. Details were designed, such as a name token to be placed around the neck of each, and the form and printed fabric of the garments, designed and carefully wrapped around each pig's body. There were certain pressures from some scientists present, discouraging her approach and arguing against these degrees of aesthetic attention and care. Far from being pushed, or forced by rules and protocols to treat the lives of others with respect and care, she had to assert her sense of commitment to this quite forcefully, in order to make sure it happened. But she refused to view this as simply an experiment using 21 homogenously treated carcasses, acting ethically in the sense that Varela meant, where "All relevant aspects are included, not just those which fit the reduction of a categorical analysis" (Varela, 1999, p. 28).

After this burial process was complete, Interlandi received a letter from the Chair of the Animal Ethics Committee. Her project had been discussed at a subsequent Animal Ethics Committee meeting, and on behalf of himself and the committee he was writing to commend her on her excellent attitude, and congratulate her on setting an example for others to follow. The example set was one of believing in one's ethical know-how.

This story points to an issue that is important for supervisors: that we might guide candidates, and ourselves, toward recognition of our own ethical know-how, and a willingness to be prepared to stand-up for the aims, aspirations, and kinds of processes we are undertaking as part of our research activity. Somehow, this needs to be asserted, rather than folding silenced actions under the templates of rules and protocols. The need for innovation in this realm is resoundingly clear, and all parties, candidates, supervisors, and ethics committees need to move together in enabling the emergence of productive change.

NOTES

[1]   For related histories see Krauth (2011); Allpress & Barnacle (2009).
[2]   Holland suggests that a yet to be formulated carrier model of creative process would pertain to the conjunction of poetry and physics. "In a sense," he writes, "the poetic framework is too loose whereas the scientific framework is too tight" (Holland, 1999, p. 219).
[3]   Interestingly, 'sacrifice' is the scientific term used to refer to the killing of animals for scientific research. One is not, apparently, meant to use the term 'slaughter'.

REFERENCES

Allpress, B. & Barnacle, R. (2009). Projecting the Ph.D.: Architectural design research by and through projects. In David Boud, Alison Lee (Eds.) *Changing practices of doctoral education*. London: Routledge.

Australian Government (2007). *National Statement on Ethical Conduct in Human Research*. Developed jointly by National Health and Medical Research Council, Australian Research Council, Australian Vice-Chancellors' Committee. Canberra: Australian Commonwealth Government.

Bolt, B. & Kett, G. (2010). The trouble with CARE: Creative Arts and Research Ethics Quality. In Margaret Kiley (Ed.) *Postgraduate Research: Educating researchers for the 21st century* (pp. 119–128). Proceedings of the 2010 Quality in Postgraduate Research Conference, Adelaide, Australia, April 13–15. Canberra: The Centre for Educational Development and Academic Methods, Australian National University.

Dadour, I. & Interlandi, P. (2009). Description of Proposed Study. Approval form, Animal Ethics Committee Notification of Use of Animal Tissues or Carcasses, unpublished document, University of Western Australia.

Ednie-Brown, P. (2007). *The aesthetics of emergence*. Doctoral Thesis. Melbourne: RMIT University.

Guattari, F. (1995). *Chaosmosis. An ethico-aesthetic paradigm*. Paul Bains and Julian Pefanis (Trans.). Sydney: Power Publications.

Holland, J. (1999). *Emergence: From chaos to order*. New York: Basic Books.

Johnson, S. (2004). *Emergence: The connected lives of ants, brains, cities and software*. NewYork: Schribner.

Krauth, N. (2011). Evolution of the exegesis: The radical trajectory of the creative writing doctorate in Australia. *TEXT* Special Issue Website Series *15*(1). Retrieved September 23, 2011, from http://www.textjournal.com.au/april11/krauth.htm

Macneill, K. & Bolt, B. (2011). The 'legitimate' limits of artistic practice, *Realtime Magazine* #104, Aug-Sept, 2627.

Stengers, I. (2004). The challenge of complexity: Unfolding the ethics of science. In memoriam Ilya Prigogine. In *E:CO* Special Double Issue *6*(1–2), 92–99.

Taylor, M. C. (2001). *The moment of complexity: Emerging network culture*. Chicago, London: University of Chicago Press.

Varela, F. J. (1999). *Ethical Know-how. Action, wisdom, and cognition*. Los Angeles: Stanford University Press.

Wiles, R., Coffey, A., Robison, J., & Prosser, J. (2010). *Ethical Regulation and Visual Methods: Making visual research impossible or developing good practice?* NCRM Working Paper Series. Canberra: ESRC National Centre for Research Methods.

PETER DOWNTON

10. BESIDE MYSELF

Scrutinising Decades of Supervising Designers

INTRODUCTION

A Ph.D. produces knowledge. A supervisor of a doctorate assists in this production and helps shape the form and presentation of the knowledge. For me, there is no single mode for this assistance, nor is there a means of providing it that is appropriate to all candidates. People undertaking doctorates have differing needs and these may mutate across the course of their candidature. Patterns of need become more visible the longer one supervises; perception of, and reaction to differing needs colours the nature of supervision. This does not differ with the mode of doctoral study. It is complex in the case of project-based doctorates because there is a sizeable spectrum of activities involved in the way the research is presented as well as in the way in which it is conducted. The projects entailed in a project-based doctorate may or may not be more complex than the research undertaking involved in any other Ph.D. (For instance, some projects entail the construction of buildings or other designed entities, and this could be equated reasonably with the development and use of equipment in scientific research. In either case, other people will probably undertake construction under the direction of one or more researchers.) The doctoral content really revolves around understanding, theorising, and conveying the processes and outcomes of whatever work is involved.

I will draw some ideas from the very nature of project-based doctorates in the postgraduate programme in architecture and design at RMIT, and it is worth articulating their constituent parts as I see them:

1. the work undertaken, and the knowledge embodied and revealed in projects;
2. an accounting and contextualising of this through an accompanying exegesis;
3. the presentation of this to examiners through: (a) spoken words and gestures, and (b) an exhibition of the project work – this is not simply an assemblage, but is in itself designed to tell intended tales;
4. responses by the candidate to the enquiries and clarifications of the examiners.

All of these parts are essential to the whole. Components one and two are presented as a durable record – first to the examiners and then, post successful completion, to a wider audience in an archival form. The third and fourth components are photographed and filmed to record the examination event as thoroughly as possible; they form a further archival part. Together with the

B. Allpress, R. Barnacle, L. Duxbury and E. Grierson (Eds.), Supervising Practices for Postgraduate
Research in Art, Architecture and Design, 117–130.
©2012 Sense Publishers. All rights reserved.

research process and conduct, they are the doctorate. They are not a separate account of the doctorate.

Supervision in these doctorates is provided to assist and shape the candidate's investigations as they are undertaken – which is a process paralleling supervision in a thesis – and also to advise and assist on the production and delivery of all components of the whole Ph.D. Supervision does not take place without both a supervisor and the supervised. To consider supervision, it has to be realised that it is processual, and that it is an excellent example of a second order, cybernetic system, in which the first-person observer (observing the process and reporting on it to enable a chapter such as this) is part of the system being observed, described, and analysed. The process of supervision cannot therefore be abstracted and bottled as a distilled essence.

To tease out some of what I consider important, and to give the reader an idea of how I came to these views, I start this chapter with some personal postgraduate history before considering what I try to do as a current supervisor, and the roles a supervisor plays for a candidate. Next, there is consideration of supervision of individuals and small groups by one or more supervisors. Then, because practice-based doctorates are focussed on producing knowledge through the work done, I turn next to issues of guiding and forming these doctorates and to issues of the speculation entailed in them. In any doctorate, necessary 'good' practices can be helped by a supervisor, and I consider this prior to some thoughts on guiding the dissemination of research knowledge by candidates. To end, there are thoughts about the relative appropriateness of forming a doctorate as a thesis or a project.

A LITTLE LIGHT HISTORY

Like any practices, those of an individual supervisor are shaped by their prior experiences and opportunities. So, mine are entwined inevitably with my personal history, and they have also been shaped by those I have supervised, and they have grown with the times and places of my supervising. The ideas of the last sentence are elaborated over the next few paragraphs as a way of conveying and considering some of my specific supervisory traits.

It was 1976. As a Ph.D. candidate at the University of Melbourne, I was supervised by professors who lacked doctorates, but possessed research experience. The previous year as a research fellow, I had started my first efforts at supervising higher degrees although I had yet to complete my own Master of Architecture degree. Higher degrees in architecture were being invented on the fly; there was little disciplinary specific tradition, and supervisory practices were not well established. To supervise, I drew on some years of experience as researcher and part-time design studio tutor; inevitably, I also drew on the experiences of being supervised. By then, I had learnt from four very different supervisors. (They kept abandoning me, their research candidate, to accept professorships elsewhere.) At the commencement of the 1970s, research (including higher degrees) in architecture was very limited in Australia – there was historical work, socio-psychological-anthropological investigations of people with respect to architecture, and assorted variants of building science. There was little focus on researching design procedures until the dawning of design methods, and certainly no concept of researching through the practices of designing itself. Fundamentally, the researching then current was operating in a paradigm at odds with the projective nature of designing. When I wanted to examine designing and behavioural ecology for the Master of Architecture degree, I was initially deemed to be attempting nonsense. Only through the gracious agencies of my first supervisor was I permitted to start in 1970. After becoming involved in an international research project with a later supervisor, and converting to part-time student status, I began an intense initiation to supervision when I was employed to provide considerable consulting on research strategies to a collection of 35 master's degree candidates and 25 honours students beginning in 1975. I was also the supervisor for several of them.

On moving to RMIT, in 1977, my activities lessened to supervising a straggling handful of candidates over the next decade until the numbers began to increase. My supervising practices were concocted prior to 1990 and refined subsequently. This has involved establishing ways of supervising people engaged in research that is centred strongly on designing, whether that research is examined ultimately as a thesis or through the presentation of projects. Research that teeters in the realm where it is debatable which preferred mode of telling the research story is worth scrutinising when reflecting on supervisory practices. This consideration is discussed below.

Design studio tutoring preceded supervising for me, then paralleled it, before becoming an intermittent activity. What is gained from studio tutoring is experience in helping people bring their investigations and designs to fruition. Because such experience is concerned with designing, it is more-or-less immediately transferable to project-based higher degrees. In my case it was over a quarter century between starting to tutor design and first supervising a project-based higher degree, but for many in design schools the transfer of such skills is more immediate.

As a supervisor, I have been blessed by a preponderance of candidates with considerable extant experience and expertise in their research areas. This assists my learning with respect to topic-specific material. I play the role of a more experienced colleague – at least with respect to supervision – not a dictatorial expert. However, there have been times when I would have been aided by a dictator's power to enforce an injunction to have the prescribed ideas dealt with in the way I suggest, and completed promptly by Tuesday. While my personal research area, and therefore a good deal of my supervising, eddies around the nature of designing and making, I might be described as possessing a sufficiently ratty assemblage of knowledge, in that it can be brought to bear on a range of topics. I can also offer a sceptical headset that can be deployed to evaluate the plausibility of arguments, visual, verbal and aural.

The brief history above tells us something of the experiences of the particular supervisor I construct as 'me'. There are also characteristics of personality and style that make me variously suitable to interact effectively with any particular other person – in this case one whom I am endeavouring to assist. Constructive, destructive, exciting, or dreary supervisory relationships hinge at least partially on these personal interactions. They are significant, although they are more nearly a given rather than a learnable set of abilities to be sought by an inexperienced supervisor.

WHY HAVE A SUPERVISOR?

Supervision is minimally a joint process. The supervisor is not the sole possessor of the one right answer; rather, answers are arrived at collectively, often at the time of supervisory meetings, sometimes through the subsequent efforts of the candidate to use the ideas generated from a supervisory conversation, or perhaps through wakeful second thoughts by the supervisor.

In all instances, my emphasis as a supervisor is on overall encouragement; this does not mean all my utterances are benignly flattering – to get to a good end, backtracking and abandonment of that which is not productive may be necessary. Suggesting this is appropriate can be done with greater and lesser care and be fitted into an overall pattern of encouragement rather than one of confrontation and bullying.

As a supervisor, my principle concern is to see research candidates engage with their chosen topics in ways that excite and inspire them. I see my task as a supervisor as being focused on enhancing the thinking and abilities of my research candidates, to assist them in their learning as researchers. Given the experience and competence of many of those I have supervised, my most significant activity with them is to promote incremental development of existing competencies. As far as I can tell, I operate in the same manner with less experienced candidates. It seems to be held by some others that one cannot instruct a colleague who is a senior lecturer, associate professor, or senior professional in a significant design office or government department, in the same way that might be appropriate for a twenty-something year old with limited experience. I hold that the same supervisory concerns and courtesies apply to all candidates. I hope to enhance my researching colleague's journey – to support, to nurture, to excite and to, if necessary, re-direct. I must convince, not tell. It is necessary to form persuasive arguments and present coherent and convincing reasons to develop the research, re-cast the writing, or elaborate the project in a direction I argue to be appropriate. A candidate may find my suggestions unconvincing; I have to earn respect for my view if it is to be considered by those I supervise. My model is that the higher degree in design areas is a learning journey, but a journey with an end that is, at the outset, ill defined. I have no interest in producing clones of myself, the researcher. I hope to help people undertake very different journeys and end in places sometimes removed from the intellectual place I occupy. I enjoy grappling with an unfamiliar view or approach and being convinced by a candidate that their position or approach is fully thought through. If what is being put forward by the candidate is the outcome of an unchallenged belief, then it is still my supervisory responsibility to question and test, to check its robustness. We journey together. I learn considerable amounts as the accompanying person on the research journeys of others. This is an exciting and delightfully rewarding experience for me.

Along the journeys, the roles I have found myself needing to play have varied greatly. I cannot identify a definitive list; the interactions between the candidate, his or her research, the cultures of their disciplines, the culture of the parent school, and the character of their interactions with me, all vary and evolve. I can recall occasions when my most useful role has to been to irritate or goad. At other times I have needed to console, to support, or to bolster. It probably continues to surprise me how often the supervisory role is to aid the candidate's confidence. Most successful doctorates were nearly abandoned at some point. Supervisors and people close to the candidate all help to keep it going during such crises. However, ongoing, chronic confidence issues need to be dealt with constantly and possibly informally in passing social meetings in corridors and lifts. I assume these are no more likely to happen in design areas than in any other research realm, but they require significant input from supervisors. The ability to suggest an alternative approach to a research issue at such moments is very useful. It may not matter if the alternative idea is of much value as long as it offers a direction for the candidate, a way of continuing beyond the current, confidence sapping stumble. In trying the idea suggested, hopefully something of greater value will occur. Some confidence issues I found to be helped by presenting once again documented peer evidence to a candidate that they are 'better' than they think.

Depending on the other supporting structures within a research community, the supervisor's role may include some very basic matters such as an introduction to doctorates, a commentary on what they look like, how to research in the discipline, or introductions to exemplars and gurus. Certainly, I have offered much of this guidance over the years of Ph.Ds. developing in design disciplines. This class of advice is still necessary; often it is required to overcome preconceptions by dispelling persistent myths. It morphs into what I have found to be a significant supervisory contribution: consistent focus on research thinking, the building within the candidate of a self-expectation to think more richly, more deeply, more rigorously. The word 'more' is important here – there is no correct amount or level, rather, an expectation to exceed prior efforts. I think we can be roughly confident that a certain level of thinking and engagement will be sufficient to pass a doctorate; however aiming for the best that one can achieve currently will result in something of greater value.

Over the years, I have had conversations with candidates in which we have discussed how good they want their doctorate to be. Do they want to take the piece of paper and get on with their research careers? Do they want to polish up the work beyond its current standard? This becomes a very pertinent conversation for busy part-time candidates with substantial job loads and responsibilities in addition to the activities in the rest of their lives. Some level of balance needs to be attained. It is unlikely that any active researcher will look back on their doctorate a few years after its completion and find all of it satisfactory, so is it necessary to strive for perceived perfection at the point of submission? This perspective may temper the need to over-achieve at the time of doing the Ph.D. I have yet to get genuine agreement with this view from any candidate with whom I have had such a conversation, even when they are battling time problems. Such is the masochistic character of doctoral candidates in design. This seems to be bred from the absence of 'stopping rules' in designing. An answer may be arrived at, but would more time result in improvement? Usually the termination of design activities is driven externally by clients, budgets, and the evaporation of time.

The role of exemplar is not an easy one for a supervisor. There has to be a level of 'do as I say not as I have done' involved if the supervisor is to claim to have learned from the experiences of researching and being supervised. The supervisor must therefore pick apart the past to distil lessons that he or she believes can benefit current candidates. Therefore, the very nature of supervision can become somewhat anecdotal. In my case, this is not altogether relevant; my own doctorate is elderly, and from the time of thesis only. I am better served by referring to familiar recent examples, but as these mostly involve me as the supervisor, there is rich potential for constantly repeating the same mistakes. Self-evaluation is thus vital. A supervisor may, however, be an exemplar in a more generalised way through a public presence as a researcher, exhibitor, and writer.

THE MODES OF SUPERVISION I HAVE EMPLOYED

Reverting again to some personal history, it is worth reflecting briefly on a seminar for postgraduate candidates that I offered from the late 1980s, in several different guises, as it suggests some models for small group supervising. Initially it was cross-faculty, later it was single faculty, but embroiled a number of design disciplines. It masqueraded under a number of names, but the most explanatory and longest lasting was Design Research Methods. In this seminar, I choreographed discussion and debate about design epistemology. I sought ways to inform the seminar through input from all of the participants, and to bring their varied disciplinary perspectives emanating from their different design disciplines to bear upon the central theme of researching through designing. This theme is likewise central to my supervisory practice. When research has been understood in design as it has been in sciences, then it is viewed as an activity necessary to aid design, to find out the things designers needed to know to enable and facilitate design. This can be termed research *for* design. Sometimes research is turned on design itself and the nature of design is enquired into, as research *about* design. This might encompass enquiries about designing and about the history and sociology of designed entities for example. Both research *for* and *about* design are valid realms of research. The central project throughout the seminar was an exemplification and investigation of designing as a way of enquiring, a way of knowing and of producing knowledge; this is research *through* designing.

While I could vary the envelope shaping the seminar, its success has always been extremely dependent on its participants, their group chemistry, and the generosity of their participation. My role was to guide the enquiry, to inject enough new material and concepts to ferment debate, and to expect it to be debate of quality. Student feedback in both the seminar and in my supervision has enabled me to maintain currency of content and to develop iteratively in terms of style, mode, and means of assessment, to match the evolving needs of research candidates.

In evaluating the approach to the seminar it is evident that it was always somewhat of a knife-edge process dependent on my being able to be especially alert and well informed about wide-ranging material – there was never precise control of scope and sequence. These seminars were always inherently dependent on the qualities of the participants, and on my ability to get them to talk and think. I had no magic formula. I offered responsiveness, a range of tools and techniques that experience had shown to work and which could be adapted to new circumstances, and finally, an enthusiasm for constantly learning and developing with the other participants. This was placed within the overarching programme of establishing a new epistemology of design.

Broadly, the same suite of approaches and attitudes is applicable to group supervision. The content of the occasion is less likely to be determined by the supervisor as it usually hovers around individual presentations of projects. What presenters draw on, when all goes well, is a range of comments and viewpoints requiring sieving and digestion. Too many ideas can become disruptive for the candidate and those lacking confidence can attempt to incorporate everyone's views or to substantially reshape their research directions. To help filter what is of value, the supervisor needs to review the suggestions a candidate receives.

When either group or individual supervision is undertaken with more than one supervisor present, the supervisors may of course view the presentations in much the same way, or they may express divergent views. My experience is that a collective discussion of differences is more constructive for the candidate than when each supervisor is approached separately by the candidate who can then be cast as a go-between. There can be value in separate discussions with a single supervisor when this supervisor possesses specialist knowledge pertinent to (parts of) the Ph.D., but not shared by the other supervisor, however my preference is for meetings with both supervisors present.

Returning to group supervision, it is particularly suited to design areas when candidates are exploring through work, as their familiarity with visual and public modes of presentation easily enables others to access the research. I will share an account of one set of exemplary group supervision meetings. The participants comprised of five Ph.D. candidates each more than half way through their candidature, and me. Two were associate professors and three were senior lecturers. In various ways and groupings, each had worked with at least some of the others over a number of years. They had all supervised higher degree candidates and undergraduate designers in their own fields. This was a group with the confidence in themselves and in the views of the others, to operate constructively without posturing or fear. They were inevitably polite. They each endeavoured to provide helpful ideas, supportive encouragement and praise, or advice, references, and contacts for the others. They were in fact, very generous. When they deemed it necessary, no one was shy in suggesting that they considered major change was necessary in another's work. Much that was valuable was thus put forward. In such a group, my role was similar to that of each of the other participants although I was their supervisor.

Despite the power and value of the ideas put forward, most, if not all of them, found that the principal benefit emerged from witnessing the approaches adopted by others and their accounts of what was, and was not, successful. Each participant at some point abstracted another's way of researching to his or her own ends. This is an extremely potent characteristic of group supervision. Another is that where there is trust in the others, the group offers a vehicle for testing ideas semi-publicly and fairly 'safely'.

On one or two occasions, another (much less experienced) candidate and her supervisor joined in too. Each new person was well known to the existing members. The group proved robust enough to continue to function well. Such group dynamics cannot always be achieved, I presume. My other collectives have involved participants with much less experience. Candidates have been mostly younger and the groups started soon after the doctorates commenced, for nearly all participants. While those involved have displayed most of the interpersonal characteristics of the exemplary group described, they naturally cast the supervisor in a more central role with more likelihood of shaping the conversations and directions of the work. While I have not had a sustained group that has continued from commencement to completions, if the energy can be maintained, such a group should be able to forge a collective approach and potentially shape their respective work into at least a partial whole.

THE PRODUCTION OF KNOWLEDGE THROUGH WORK

This section is not a debate about the possibility or otherwise of such production. The production is taken as a given that I have argued elsewhere (Downton, 2003) and quickly outline here. From a supervisory point of view, adding to knowing through works entails promoting strategies of introspection. These are to do with examining one's own processes (in the case of makers such as designers and artists), understanding intentions and motivations, and evaluating both the processes and the outcomes (Downton, 2004). This interrogation of self must be carried out with realism and rigour; it is insufficient to simply construct a list of sequential activities, although this may be an interesting and valuable foundation upon which to build an investigation. A subsequent scrutiny of one's own thought and production offers a more privileged reading than that available to outside observers, although it has a sense of being by a person who is different from the one originally doing the work. It is reasonable to think of this as an eisegetical process. Although eisegesis is derided typically by exegetes because it entails a personal reading of a text – usually criticised as a 'reading into', which I would argue is all that is possible. In the context of scrutinising one's own production, eisegesis is required, as there is no possibility of an impersonal reading by a third party. Any idea of objectivity is illusory; this is a fully subjective process, no matter how carefully and thoughtfully carried out. It is eisegesis in the service of an exegesis.

Processes of knowledge production require revelation to self and others, and the establishment of a rich inter-linkage between their explication in words and what is conveyed through the project work. The knowing produced will be presented to examiners through the written exegesis, spoken words, 2D or 3D visual material, and possibly aural material, all of which build and convey knowledge in manners detailed below.

Much of the debate concerning design and its relation to research can be addressed by an examination of knowing and knowledge. At the centre of research is the idea of enquiry aimed at the production of knowledge. With an epistemological focus, any process of designing can be seen as having two components to its outcome: (1) personal knowing for the individual designer where there is a change to that individual's mode of designing, to their suite of stored knowledge, and to their beliefs about designing and its context; and (2) an embodiment of knowledge (which is constructed at the level of a collective) in the design work produced. That which will be constructed as knowledge is stored and transmitted by this embodiment. In time this embodied knowledge is propagated through a community of interest, brought into some sort of relation with knowing(s) embodied in individuals, and is shaped hence as learning by designers and others. This is not in principle different from the embodiment of researched knowledge in perhaps a formula, a table of data, or an explanatory text.

Designing is thus a producer of knowing and knowledge through researching. Practice-based researching through designing is different from research in science. Its outcomes are assessable by criteria different from science,[1] but this does not make it a lesser form of knowledge; and I engage those I supervise in an ongoing conversation about this suite of ideas.

GUIDING SOMEONE PRODUCING KNOWING THROUGH WORK

While research is carefully constructed and conducted enquiry, there is a considerable spectrum of ways in which this might be done – even in practice-based research. For a supervisor, responsive guidance is necessarily tailored by the existing competencies of a candidate. Individuals have greatly varying knowledge of where and how to look for ideas, precedents, and potentially fertile concepts. Early in a candidature, I usually regard it as my role to promote divergence, to encourage casting a fairly wide net when trawling through the world of ideas. For designers, this is not only concerned with what others have done, but is an exploratory process in which they converse with their own design ideas, evolve them and evaluate them (Schön, 1994). Toward the end of a candidature, the supervisor's task is to promote focus and to lie outrageously by assuring the candidate that they have found everything possible that could be useful in their work. While both parties are aware, quietly, of the artificiality of this conceit, if it is not employed the Ph.D. is unlikely to reach completion.

Along the doctoral way, candidates must be guided in how to scrutinise and evaluate the work of others. In particular, they need to be helped to reveal new knowledge through the assembling and consideration of the pertinent enquiries and production of related researchers. This is similar for theses and projects. In my experience, nearly everyone engaging in practice-based research requires challenging in order to engage with their own production in rigorous and insightful ways. At the outset, some candidates simply do the work they do and present the outcomes of their practice. This may be celebrated work, but no matter how good it is, this is not a fully doctoral activity. The work requires positioning and at least minimum levels of exegetical accounting. Closely examining the entrails of one's own work is also inadequate as it too easily becomes research about what one has done, not researching through doing. While recording and reviewing what one is doing is necessary, it is not, in this case an end in itself; it is there to support theorising and reflection, which is work usually done in the medium of words. I aim for candidates to undertake this as a parallel activity, not through 'writing up' their more-or-less finished research. Initially, it is usually necessary to move candidates away from ingrained views that words carry ideas that are then illustrated by the project work, or from the symmetrically erroneous view that words are there to explain the works undertaken. I strive for an approach where the words and the works are both regarded as powerful ways of investigating the same issues, and that these investigations should be conducted in parallel in the two different modes.

Candidates are expected to speculate. Projects are vehicles for speculation through designing. Written work, whether it is a thesis or the exegetical component of a project, enables language-based speculation. Either mode of speculative undertaking may comment on the other, illustrate, amplify, or explain it. I try (with troubled success) to get candidates to engage in parallel explorations, investigating the same topic area via differing means. Pure theses are denied this extra richness, but often they are aimed at revealing some set of conditions or events and having a (possibly speculative) view of them, as in history, rather than engaging in projecting knowledge forward, as in design. It is worth noting that some candidates who successfully resisted my injunctions to conduct these activities in parallel are now, post successful completion, loud advocates for this approach.

GUIDING THE FORMATION OF A PROJECT-BASED DOCTORATE

How to reveal knowing to oneself as a candidate is a significant question. How to make such knowings available to others is another. This includes ways of revealing and ways of disseminating. A supervisor can guide the candidate towards appropriate answers to these questions. I use the plural term 'answers', as I consider that different research undertakings need to be conducted and produced in very different ways. The idea of a single prescriptive envelope suitable to all doctorates suggests that only a precisely described and constrained undertaking will form an acceptable piece of work that will glide over the doctoral hurdle. Too many texts on the production of theses presuppose narrowly conventional outcomes.

In the end, what is presented for examination in a Ph.D. tells the story of the research undertaken by the candidate. The way in which to best tell this story has to be designed, whether the appropriate vehicle is a project or a thesis. Mostly the decision to undertake the Ph.D. by project or by thesis is made at the outset; sometimes, however, I have worked with a candidate to re-conceptualise an emerging doctorate as the story is not being told as well as might be by the initially-selected format. (The final section engages further with this.)

Candidates, even experienced ones, typically need help and support with the skills of structuring the doctorate and finding the appropriate means of telling the story. Rich and rigorous thought and incisive modes of visual and written communication are all implicated and intertwined in such story telling. Considerable refinement of skills results from searching for, and finding, a good way (arguably a 'best' way) of telling their doctoral tale.

While Ph.Ds. are often limited or even narrow in their topics, the way in which they are approached, conceptualised, and dealt with, should not be. I encourage flexible and broad thinking. This is not superficial thinking; I try to prod candidates into thinking with care and clarity, and to continue to polish their doctoral work until we are satisfied that these aims are attained. The expression of care and clarity, whether in words or a visual medium, should be evident to others.

GUIDANCE ON BEHAVING WELL

Whether the research is in the form of a thesis or a project, a supervisor helps a candidate to adopt and continue orderly research behaviours appropriate to the nature of the work being undertaken. As always in higher degree research, this involves surveying appropriate sources (which might include pictures, sounds and people, not only published literature), logging data, findings, sources, influences and behaviours. In the realms of research considered here, little use will be made of statistical analysis of data. What serves an equivalent role to numerical data upon which statistical manipulation can be performed is often visual or behavioural, and may be personal. Just as statistical analysis can be used to reveal information from a sea of data, here scrutiny of collected material must be made to produce patterns of significance. Close recording of moves in designing and making must be carried out to support understanding. These records, however they are made, must be logged and stored in appropriate media to enable concurrent and subsequent evaluation. There is a notable difference in making an evaluation at the time of the doing, compared with producing an evaluative account later in the research when the context is enriched by a greater amount of work. Both are valuable. The differences between them enable further understanding and reveal more of the processes of designing, so I have been requesting candidates to be thorough in their compilation and manipulation of 'findings' about their own production of research knowledge.

The sweep of behaviours sketched above is, at an abstract level, necessary for any doctorate. There are overlaps and differences across research fields, but the principles of orderly operation are followed sensibly if a candidate is to avoid dramas and anguish at various stages of the candidature. My success as a supervisor in enforcing such sound behaviours is questionable, however I have obtained unequivocal assent from those I have supervised when they supervise others.

GUIDING WAYS OF CONVEYING THE RESEARCH
AND THE KNOWLEDGE PRODUCED

For a doctorate to be convincing, just the right 'voice' needs to be found for the words, and just the right approach must be found for images, models, sounds, and their curated presentation to others. A mismatch between the research and the way it is conveyed quickly reveals weaknesses in the research. A substantial part of the message is genuinely in the medium of its presentation. A candidate who professes one thing and undermines this position through the media of presentation has not fully thought through their research and the ways in which new knowledge is revealed; they have probably retreated to words alone to carry ideas and meaning. Either it is a whole with holes in its fabric, or more likely, they have not yet woven a genuinely whole piece of research.

Supervisory advice on finding a voice for the written material or on ways of devising an image approach draws largely on experience of what has 'worked' or not when used by prior candidates. I derive a greater breadth of knowledge from chairing project examinations than from prior supervising, as I have chaired more than 100 exams. This knowledge needs to be tailored to suggest modifications where it is deemed appropriate. It also serves as a ground from which to prompt a candidate to conduct a thorough evaluation of proposed ideas.

Similar guidance needs to be offered on exhibition and the performance of the candidate in the examination. Design of both is important, particularly in a design school where examiners have design in the forefront of their thinking. The effectiveness of both as communication is important, but their integration in the whole that is the doctorate is of greatest significance. Some candidates are inclined to present everything; some savagely edit their output. The selection of the 'right' components presents difficulties and, I find, leads to considerable discussion. Again, precedent is informative, but selections must be judged finely to reveal and explicate the research. There are no formulaic answers.

I frequently advise candidates to begin to design the end presentation means of a project (and even a thesis) more-or-less at the outset of the candidature, as it contributes to forming a rich understanding of both the whole undertaking and of the best way to tell the tale. Candidates have to be comfortable that their concepts and intentions will keep changing. This is a sign of progress, not necessarily an indication of confusion.

THOUGHTS ABOUT TELLING DOCTORAL TALES AS THESES OR PROJECTS

The way in which a particular doctorate is best presented to examiners and others is shaped by the material and by the candidate. Personality and style mean that some candidates are more comfortable speaking about, and to their research work; others want to unfurl an argument in an orderly manner that they consider can be best attained and sustained through a text of greater magnitude than the word limit prescribed for an exegesis. Project exams enable a presentation of the research in a largely parallel, rather than sequential, manner. The works are available for scrutiny immediately and concurrently. The way in which the candidate tells the story of the research is obviously sequential as this is the nature of human story telling – minimally we have to say one thing prior to another and the choice involved establishes some epistemological niceties. Sometimes material is revealed as the presentation proceeds; sometimes it is present throughout, but highlighted as the story progresses. When the latter is the case, it is easy to see members of the examining panel scanning differing material as the candidate speaks, making their own sense of the material, asking and answering their own questions. Thus a project examination of this form enables rapidly sequential, not truly synchronous, presentation of knowledge. This is all that is attainable by a human perceptual system.

Judgments by candidates and supervisors of the most appropriate form for the research presentation need to be made with care. The best answer is not necessarily clear. I offer four examples from the last few years: (1) Doctoral research in which all the projects had been publicly exhibited, and this had been documented and evaluated, was finally presented as a thesis to allow the candidate to explore some rich writing and theorising of the value and context of the works, their production processes and other material; (2) research in which all the projects (one resulting in a book) had had performative and activist public existences was examined in both a performative exegesis and a performance event that was, of itself, what the research was, and not a detached reflection upon it; (3) research in which all the pieces had been publicly exhibited – often a number of times – and had also taken their place in a larger context of related research projects, was curated into an exhibition with a detailed exegesis of intensity that was comparable to the works, then presented to, and discussed with the examiners.

As a fourth example, consider research consisting of spatial, sound design works that had likewise had public installations and performances interwoven with the establishment of a studio and its culture. Although all project-based, these works were deemed best presented collectively as a thesis with detailed audio accompaniment. The sound projects had a total duration of more than five hours. Sound and film present similar issues as they unfold in time and must be sampled selectively to conform to the dictates of a project examination. Regardless of the care with which this is done, a type of violence results when work is sampled. We are more able to deal with the substantially synchronous availability of visual works, although in the case of architectural works, for instance, it is representations of the works, not the works themselves, which exhibit these characteristics.

Because I have supervised or worked with candidates across architecture, communication, fashion, interior design, industrial design, landscape architecture, and less defined design disciplines, in some art areas and in parts of engineering, I have tip-toed across the strictures of enshrined practices and developed a personalised eclectic set. This has necessarily evoked scrutiny of my own practices, and ruminations on the nature and techniques of supervision in a generic, rather than specific, sense. Fundamentally, I advocate flexibility and responsiveness to individual candidates, to their needs, and to the characteristics of their research. In collaboration with the candidate, I must come to understand what these needs and characteristics are, how they differ from other supervisory processes, and hence how my supervisory role is evolving.

NOTES

[1] One considerable difference is the preparedness of sciences to accept as knowledge that the outcome of an experiment is 'failure' and that something can be shown not to be the case. Designers and artists do not accept 'no outcome'; they simply regard some outcomes as not their best work. That they learn from this is an indication that knowing is entailed in such productions.

REFERENCES

Downton, P. (2003). *Design research*. Melbourne: RMIT University Press.
Downton, P. (2004). *Studies in design research: Ten epistemological pavilions*. Melbourne: RMIT University Press.
Schön, D. (1994). Design as a reflective conversation with the situation. In *The reflective practitioner: How professionals think in action*. London: Ashgate.

DAVID THOMAS

11. HOW TO WORK BETTER

Supervising for Ph.D. Exhibition

INTRODUCTION

In 1991 the Swiss artists Peter Fischli and David Weiss produced a collaborative artwork, a text-based wall painting in situ onto the external wall of an office building in Zurich-Oerlikon. Employing simple turquoise blue capital letters, it was entitled: *How To Work Better*. The building is visible from the train that travels to and from the airport to central Zurich carrying travellers and business people. The work consisted of a list of ten points or rules:

HOW TO WORK BETTER

1. Do one thing at a time.
2. Know the problem.
3. Learn to listen.
4. Learn to ask questions.
5. Distinguish sense from nonsense.
6. Accept change as inevitable.
7. Admit mistakes.
8. Say it simple.
9. Be calm.
10. Smile.

Upon first sight this work functions as text, literally as a how-to-do list. It contains common sense ideas and humour. This is an artwork functioning within the context of contemporary art and society revealing physical, conceptual, political readings and implications generated by, and of specific sites and cultures. To my mind its usefulness, its 'artfulness' lies in its ambiguity, in its ability to move between stable or fixed readings; its meanings remain slippery. As a list the readings appear to shift from action to quiet resignation, from doing to feeling.

The work functions in the ambivalent space between rationalist management solutions of the didactic 'how-to-do' kind and the ironic space of questioning, giving us the opportunity to spend time with these issues and interrogate our own values, in order to become aware of our constructions of meaning. As a work it eschews simplistic answers. Its messages are complex, ironic, even contradictory but not aggressive. The work's role, therefore, to my way of thinking is not to provide an easy solution, but rather provide questions and critique regarding

B. Allpress, R. Barnacle, L. Duxbury and E. Grierson (Eds.), Supervising Practices for Postgraduate Research in Art, Architecture and Design, 131–146.
©2012 Sense Publishers. All rights reserved.

particular assertions and habits: to question 'can't', to turn certainty into a relativist reality using the clichéd tropes and language of bureaucratic kitsch. To put this in another way, it reveals the complicated reality of things.

In employing a tongue-in-cheek strategy, the artists generate readings and the forms that are contingent, elusive and allusive. The work's reception or success relies upon the viewers' understanding, experience and perception as much as the artists' deadpan expression. By creating a work that generates a consciousness of its context in the viewer, Fischli and Weiss manifest content that roams between politics, advertising, conceptual art, text art, site, time, space and the specifics of narrative that offers a broad range of readings and associations. Their message (and that of much contemporary art) is that reality is complex; as viewers and makers we have to negotiate not only knowledge and content but understand our own mechanisms and reasons for doing so, amid a fluid thing called life.

Fischli and Weiss are able to assert the importance of understanding complexity while avoiding the trap of obfuscation. The work itself demonstrates not only a conceptual reality via text but does this by existing as a physical reality in the actual world. The artists employ physical means that are deceptively simple: text on a wall; but they manipulate the scale, surface, style of lettering, colour and location to enable shifts in the readings to occur. So what does this work have to do with supervising practices of exhibiting at Ph.D. level? A lot I think, for Fischli and Weiss through this work ask us not to take things at face value. They demonstrate how we can address and manifest complexity simply and directly.

Every one of the rules listed is a generalisation requiring clarification and interpretation in specific contexts. From a certain perspective, the generalised nature of the list can be seen as one of work's strengths, for it permits us to have fun in imagining how each rule could be used by each of us in particular situations. In this way the list is inclusive. We can project our imaginative experience onto it.

The rules noted are ones that any Ph.D. candidate or artist will have used. Every researcher and artist will have experienced the 'smile' whether one of resignation, of joy, or exasperation, or the smile as an indication of a problem seen or solved. In the artwork, however, the type of smile is not specified, but left open for our interpretations.

For me, the important message of this work is not simply to look at the work as a guide of how to do things better. *How To Work Better* in its own succinct way recognises the work of art as a composite, a multiplicity. This work therefore, can be of use in helping us understand the nature of the contemporary artwork, a Ph.D. by project and the practice of supervising.

In the following section I will discuss the Ph.D. exhibition and its supervision and relate this to the heterogeneous nature of a composite, as it exists in the fine art context in three ways:

- considering timing and the composite by looking at the work of Jacques Tati;
- exploring my interpretation of Henri Bergson's ideas of duration and the composite applying them to Ph.D. supervision in fine art practice;
- looking at a specific case study in section three of the chapter.

IS A LAUGH A MINUTE NECESSARY?
MONSIEUR HULOT, BERGSON AND SUPERVISION

A Ph.D. by practice is a phenomenon consisting of artwork and exegesis. In it practice and exegesis are manifest and intertwined. Both engage in research through questioning, evaluating and presenting outcomes. The exhibition is an embodiment of these factors.

Practice in contemporary art is informed by history, ideas, theory, experience, and by intention and sensibility. A studio-based fine art practice and exhibition is based usually on phenomenological methodologies of action-based research and employs heuristic approaches. There are many forms of practice for the contemporary artist. Even the definitions of practice and of studio need to be flexible and fluid in order to accommodate new understandings and discoveries. As the research can lead us into unknown territories we must be cognisant that new approaches different from those originally intended may be required.

It is in the practice of 'doing' that we can understand the function and the specificity of the artwork and exhibition, and this like knowledge and life itself is one of recognising 'becoming'.

Les Vacances de Monsieur Hulot, 1953, Cady Films, by French filmmaker and comedian Jacques Tati, is a work I often discuss with postgraduate candidates. I find it can assist in our understanding of timing, duration and the composite. We can become aware of how his structuring of the film enables content to unfold and change over time. *Les Vacances de Monsieur Hulot* illustrates and manifests duration in a composite form where knowledge and experience, technique, sensibility, seriousness and humour intertwine.

Jacques Tati made this film during a time very different from our own. Life and art had a pace different from that of the early twenty-first century. The film follows an innocent well-intentioned bumbler who upsets the 'normality' of the holiday period by the sea. Day to day working life stops for the vacation in France, which was and remains a continuing tradition during summer. The ritualistic calmness of the vacation remains sacrosanct. Hulot disrupts this in his role as the clown, the outsider, and the comic innocent, as the man who does not fit the norms of polite society.

Although the setting for *Les Vacances de Monsieur Hulot* occurs during the annual holiday in a northern French seaside resort over 50 years ago we can still laugh, but not if we apply the wrong rules. By this I mean that we should not apply to this work the same expectations regarding the speed of delivery as we do to much of contemporary comedy. From our temporal and cultural distance Tati's humour and actions may happen more slowly over a longer duration than we are accustomed to. If one is in too much of a rush and does not engage with its timing, we miss its spirit. The work can introduce us to the importance of slowness, of patience, of waiting and of anticipation. Not everything has to be, or can be, recovered quickly. Some readings, understandings, ideas, sensations and experiences in life take time to unfold and to recover and some things are not able to be approached directly but need to be suggested obliquely.

Understanding the idea and application of appropriate timing is critical if we are to understand both the film, the nature of artwork and exhibitions in general. Supervision requires a similar sensitivity to timing. We need to understand the contexts, manners of the period and culture in which they occur. Then there are also the more general principles that seem to transcend the specifics of culture such as slapstick. Structurally, Tati employs pictorial composition, duration and deferral to enable his content to be recovered. Many of the most important events happen on the periphery of the composed image screen or frame in order to enable the surprise of discovery to occur. Tati's jokes are often sonic, disrupting or complementing expectations in relationship to images to events. Natural action disrupts mechanistic behaviour. Some of Tati's humour is satirical in a gentle way; it is culturally and politically specific, commenting upon the class structure and attitudes in France at the time.

Experiences, ideas, actions and narratives unfold in time, over an extended duration. The work therefore, can be seen as a composite in the Bergsonian sense of the word. If we apply the understanding of complexity to Ph.D. supervision we see that it has many of the same properties: a composite that unfolds in time and place and engages with particular fields of knowledge. A Ph.D. by practice and its supervision has its narrative, its material, conceptual and linguistic components. Its outcome, the exhibition, is filtered through the perceiving agency of the viewer. The understanding of the viewer is dictated by perception, and perception is dependent upon intention.

One of my favourite quotes on this comes from Henri Bergson, the French philosopher, who said the following regarding the experiencing of complexity or the composite:

> When sitting on the bank of a river, the flowing of the water, or the gliding of a bird, the uninterrupted murmur of deep life, are for us three different things or a single one, at will (Bergson, 1922, p. 67).

The role of supervision (itself a composite) should aim at assisting the artist/candidate in recognising how complexity functions in addressing their own research, practice, exegesis and exhibition. To supervise this appropriately requires an understanding by all parties involved, of how learning and the project moves through diverse stages and requires differing approaches. I discuss this in more detail later in this chapter. In many ways we supervise from our own experience. My Ph.D. research asked several key questions via the practice of painting/installation, and in the exegesis, regarding the historical and theoretical origins of the idea of duration as applied to painting and painting/installation practice in the twentieth century. I examined which artists applied the principles of duration, how they had been employed and how the principles of duration could be applied to my work. I explored these issues in order to find out how I could enable various meanings to unfold in time, and in turn affect the perception of content in a painting and/or painting/installation. I employed the principle of duration in order to reconcile heterogeneous experiences and codes that would, while retaining complexity, manifest in a succinct way contemplative imagery.

The project was predicated upon my understanding that making art is a form of research practice different from writing about art. Practice here is not simply doing, but is a complex, informed, physical, theoretical and intellectual activity where private and public worlds meet. Art practice is the material outcome of intertwined objective, subjective, rational and intuitive processes. Considered in this way, art is a discipline informed by the conceptual and linguistic conventions of its own culture and history. These understandings have informed much of my approach to supervision of practice.

ENDURING DURATION

My interpretations of Henri Bergson's ideas of *durée* (duration) have informed my practice and subsequently my supervision. Bergson was in many respects a precursor to the continental, poststructuralist thinking that contributed to a paradigm shift from modernism to postmodernism. Nick Mansfield distinguishes this change as:

> The shift from the structuralist belief in a stable or fixed relationship between the signifier and the signified, to post-structuralism's understanding of the unpredictable and unstable nature of that relationship ... therefore disrupting hierarchical principles of essence and identity into ones of paradox and relational becoming (Mansfield, 2000, p. 124).

Hopefully my previous description of Fischli and Weiss' work demonstrates this adequately. When we consider supervision and the Ph.D. by exhibition as being amid the process of becoming, of manifesting, they exist in time as a flow of relationships. This means we need to be sensitive to the dynamics of the situation. Certain moments require appropriate approaches. We need to employ both traditional tools and new combinations of technologies that can expand possibilities for learning and discovery. This approach requires that we need to understand specific contexts, concepts, intentions and cultural frameworks in order to make something meaningful.

Bergson's belief in the movement of meaning and his critique of the spatial in favour of the temporal, along with his ideas on the complexity and embodiment of experience, appealed to me for I had discovered similar recognitions through my own practice as an artist and a teacher. It was in my interpretations of Bergson's writings that I found an appropriate terminology and a useful model in sympathy with the holistic nature of practice-led research and exhibition in the visual arts. His approach embraced both an analytical method that had as its basis a Cartesian rationalism that asks questions outside of content from an objective, empirical position, and an experiential method that stated that certain fields of activity needed to be taken as a whole over its putative parts (Moore, 1996, pp. 17–18). Bergson's philosophy and method were rooted in the concrete experience of time as embodied in a living being.

SUPERVISION AND PRACTICE AS COMPOSITES

Two aspects of Bergson's model of duration are relevant to this discussion of the practice of supervising for exhibiting. They are:

- the composite as a model or idea composed of different components;
- multiplicity, which aims to reconcile the heterogeneous nature of experience (moments) within the unity of the continuum of time as a complexity.

Bergson stated, "Temporal structure is not a matter of putting together given, discrete items. On the contrary, so-called discrete items are only apparent when we have a need to pluck them from our continuing experience" (Bergson in Moore, 1996, p. 55). Duration was understood by Bergson as consisting of many durations (Bergson, 1911, p. 55). There are virtual and actual durations: the duration of matter, actual, measurable and fixed; and our own duration, virtual, internal and moving. Temporal awareness is not just an instant or a stretch of time, but an unfolding of various rhythms, hence my citing as examples the works of Tati, and Fischli and Weiss.

The recognising of interiority is critical if we are going to retain the specificity of art at the Ph.D. level and not create a pastiche of it as an illustration of *a priori* ideas. Here in the internalised continuum of lived space is located the actual. Knowledge of the external facts of the world is, for Bergson, an abstract representation, an idea, and therefore fixed and intellectual only; it separates the brain, body and the world. Bergson defines reality as a composite mixture of things that are different in kind: duration (temporal) and extensity (spatial), as a mixture of experience and representation: a composite.

I can think of no better definition of a work of art, exhibition, or Ph.D. by practice than this. It is through the unpacking of these mixtures in the studio over time, one by one, artificially fragmenting the whole in order to reconstruct it with greater clarity and impact that one can assist the candidate in preparing an exhibition. Bergson insists that images exist before they are perceived. Intention assists with perception. The French philosopher, Gilles Deleuze states Bergson's position:

> Perception is the object of perception minus everything that does not interest us. Memories exist only when they are recoverable in the present ... we do not move from the present to the past, from perception to recollection, but from the past to the present, from recollection to perception (Deleuze, 1997, p. 63).

This dynamic linkage between the virtual and the actual through the interval of recollection and selection enabled me to recognise similar relationships and potentials through the use of diverse signifiers in my own work and in my supervision for exhibition. It is a strategy often employed in visual arts, where the conscious and intuitive use of timing and memory enable discovery and shifts in reading through the choice and manipulation of image and structure. Dualisms, for Bergson, can be reconciled in the time of experiencing. It is not as though dualisms stop existing, but they are reconciled over time and placed in relation to broader contexts. As such, duration can be used as an operation to reconcile things different in kind; ideas, feelings, disparate visual languages, techniques and practices. This recognition is critical if we are to make an exhibition function or to supervise effectively.

SUPERVISING FOR EXHIBITION AMID COMPLEXITIES

As supervisors we need to assist students to learn how to learn. We need not simply tell them what is possible or correct, as if we could know, rather we need to give them appropriate tools to make their own choices in order to understand what they have done, what they are doing and what they may be able to do.

One of my first doctoral candidates used to quote from a text saying that during the first part of the candidature the supervisor has the knowledge, by the latter part of it the candidate has become the expert in their field. This conscious understanding of field is important: it is what makes postgraduate study different from ongoing practice. Although most of the artists I know are questioning their work and their context and wanting to amplify their practice, the Ph.D. and the exhibition in particular requires one to be conscious, even self-conscious, of the research questions and methodologies (this does not mean we cannot play or intuit, they are in fact some of the methodologies available). At particular stages we need to be rigorously analytical and at other times intuitive, in order to understand the field of knowledge that one is contributing to and the new possibilities that may occur.

The practice, exhibition and exegesis need to be seen as interconnected and need to be managed by the candidate and the supervisor. It is important to reflect on the key questions being addressed and if the exhibition enables these to be recoverable. To my mind, the role of the proposal is critical in assisting this, as its purpose is to define the limits of the project and hence the exhibition; it is not to attempt to do everything (a lifetime's work) within the timeframe of the Ph.D. project. Setting limits is crucial.

If we truly are going to assist fine art candidates in proceeding to make contributions to their field as artists and academics, we must not lose sight of the particularities of the discipline. Times, spaces and resources need to be clearly negotiated. Again, smaller steps may be required rather than rushing to mega conclusions. A simple example: rather than making a full scale, full sized installation, understand how the signifiers might function by working in a limited zone such as a corner or a table top rather than a gallery. Once it is recognised what is needed, then go for it. So that this does not cause frustration it is important for the supervisor and the candidate to recognise the intentions of the candidate and to make sure the intentions are in line with the questions being investigated.

Not only must we question and evaluate outcomes in light of the research questions being addressed, but also we must use the languages, methods and methodologies appropriate to the field. Hence we need to understand that the studio, the role of the exhibition and the exegesis go hand in hand. To state the obvious, the physical studio environment and equipment need to be adequate for the research intentions.

The exhibition is not an illustration of a thesis, nor is the exegesis an irrelevant add-on to the practice. Surprisingly even at the doctoral level many candidates in the fine arts see practice and theory opposed rather than integrated. I believe a good supervisor should demonstrate how they are interconnected. All art worth its salt is historically and theoretically informed, and a Ph.D. candidate needs to understand this if they are to contribute to their field. They need to be theoretically, artistically and physically equipped in order to achieve this. The exhibition and exegesis are the culmination of this at a certain point in time only. It is not the end point for further development; they have the rest of their lives for that.

In order to supervise, and this might appear self-evident, one needs to understand and get to know the candidate as well as the field of knowledge. This is not to be confused with being friends with the candidate, although this happens; we need to understand and trust each other professionally. I let students see my work, know my views and prejudices; in fact many approach me at this level because of them. Although I teach *from* these positions I do not teach them. I want my candidates to make their original contributions to the field; they do not have to agree with me.

It is important for me to realise the individual needs of and experience of each candidate. How are they and we different? How do their projects differ? In what ways must I supervise in order to assist the recently graduated young candidate to understand the role and complexity of the practice of exhibiting? How can I assist the experienced exhibitor to question habits? How do I assist the non-Western candidate to understand the role of the exhibition within the Western albeit globally orientated academy?

Supervisors, therefore, need to unpack their expectations along with those of the candidates and outline their (the primary, secondary supervisors and candidate) collective and respective roles. To do all of this effectively we need time, space, knowledge, sensitivity, timing and flexibility. We need enthusiasm, mutual encouragement and honesty; however, in reality all this is dependent upon the individuals concerned and there are no magic formulae, despite what Fischli and Weiss pretend to say. But if we start an honest discussion early as we start down this road of supervision, everyone can be aware of his or her responsibilities. Tati teaches us to slow down. Bergson teaches us about the composite and duration.

Too often everyone is in a rush to finish a Ph.D. before they start, to do the proposal ... next ... to do the confirmation seminar ... next ... to do the completion seminar ... next ... to review the work ... next ... to present it ... next ... ? The process can get in the way of why we are doing this in first place and what we are really trying to achieve, which is fine art practice-based research. We need to take our time, step by step. Often the best things we can do for a candidate are the small things that demonstrate this and that engender trust and confidence. To stop, listen and spend time with their work is a good start, mentioning their research to some external individual or institution, showing them where to get particular materials and sources. Appreciation and encouragement is what we all wish for. Obviously this is not a substitute for honest and rigorous analyses, but it compliments it, personalises it and humanises the joint enterprise. It helps to laugh with each other. Too often the contemporary university appears like a bureaucratic machine: our role, our very research practice through exhibition is to engage with values and understandings that humanise our world. We should demonstrate and celebrate those human values we cherish including: openness, tolerance, curiosity, creativity, intelligence and sensibility.

One has to learn to ask the appropriate questions as one works as a supervisor and as a researcher. For the candidates readying themselves for exhibition, it is important to realise that this process takes time, requiring an appropriately structured work plan that enables trial and error to occur, and that includes focused studio work, individual and group evaluation, intelligent thinking and sensing. While listening to the radio many years ago I heard the chairman of a multinational corporation say: "You have to kiss a lot of frogs before you get a prince". But I would like to add this: before you find the frogs you have to find the pond.

The supervisor can assist in making an exhibition successful by encouraging the candidates to keep stretching themselves, by building from one work to the next using the criterion of the proposal; encouraging the candidate to attempt yet another variation or effort; reinforcing the need for practice for making and re-making. By doing this time and time again we are consciously constructing an unfolding set of experiences that address the candidate's intentions through the artefacts or forms that are appropriate to their field. By spending time with the work and exploring variations, this enables the recognition of new opportunities to arise, discoveries to be made, and solutions to be questioned and reinvestigated. Time management and planning are necessary. But critically important also is the time of sitting, reflecting, musing and doing nothing. Many works have been destroyed by overwork or new opportunities lost by rushing. I often encourage the candidate to do nothing. A candidate needs time and space to find their pond, their frog and their prince, and so does the supervisor within the act of supervising. Sometimes we need to let the candidate get on with it alone and we should do nothing.

SOME STRATEGIES AND METHODS OF DOING NOTHING
MAKING SOMETHING

These comments apply to the act of supervising as well as to the specifics of making work for a practice-based Ph.D. by project. I have found the following points are useful to consider in relationship to assisting a candidate to engage with their research questions. So in the spirit of Fischli and Weiss:

- See what is there in relation to intention. What are the actualities of the work in relation to your aspirations? What is your candidate really doing in relation to their intended outcomes? Are the choices of materials and forms appropriate?
- Make time and space for reflection.
- Sit, look and experience before the time of feedback. Using diverse means of feedback from formal tutorial to informal peer discussion, both as a group and

individually. Ask for written descriptions and understandings of what is said at key tutorials.

- Ask different external experts for their opinions at times in order to obtain a differing perspective throughout the candidature.
- Use direct and indirect play, testing variations and possibilities without intentions. Then apply your criteria to them to see if the unexpected assists in new discoveries.
- Be quiet: recognising the importance of doing something and saying something, and of doing nothing and saying nothing, or the importance of silence and the importance of talk. This is a matter timing and judgement.
- Actions speak louder than words. Do!
- Encourage the candidate to generate exhibitions, small, large, inside or outside the institution to explore different ideas and aspects of their research, including the forms of installation (size, scale, formats) prior to the final presentation.
- Use documentation of the work as a tool to both record and generate new imaginative possibilities, such as shifts in scale or adjustments to size through projection.
- Ask the candidate to consider how the experience of the viewer is being addressed by the work itself. Is the installation of work their choice, or is the combination of media assisting or confusing in the recovery content?
- Think backwards from your practice of supervision and in the candidate's case the practice of making.
- Define and redefine what you both understand.
- Don't waffle, be direct, do not fear theory; 'pointy headed' theory is fine if it is real and relevant.
- Maintain ongoing contact.
- Use and develop professional networks.
- Give yourselves permission to learn together and have fun.
- Encourage the candidate to be ambitious for the work and be responsible for it; to own it and know how the systems we are living in work – social, educational and ecological.
- Understand why both of you are doing what you are doing: what is its value? Is it necessary? Is it relevant?
- Ask if your fine art or design practice is being undertaken for the approval of others? This may have underlying and complex reasons, but we don't talk about them much. Why should people like or engage with our work or ideas either as supervisor or candidate?
- How does our work contribute to the body of knowledge, experience and feeling? Does it make us wonder or feel alive?

Perhaps a direct way of presenting these issues is to take an extract of my previous writing on complexity. These considerations are relevant to my practice as an artist particularly concerning values in art, but if I insert the words supervision or exhibition, I believe it generates the type of comments and questions that may be useful for supervisor and candidate alike.

CONSIDERING COMPLEXITY STATED SIMPLY

I exist amid a complex world... my ideas, language, art practice are the outcomes of intertwined objective, subjective, rational and intuitive processes. They are the result of a complexity of interwoven cultures, histories, places, biologies and intentions.

As an artist I exist amid a body of knowledge and experience. I find this both serious and humorous. In the scheme of things if my work was to simply tell what I know already it would be even more minimal and limited than it is. When I work I try to be open, not fearful... to reach beyond my comfort zones, beyond what I know. This is problematic in its own way, for I know that it is absurd to make things about which one knows nothing or little... there is enough of that around also... so my work moves around, between the known and the unknown, the realised and the unrealised.

In making I ask ... what might happen if? I ask ...how and why is this work necessary? What is its value? Why show it? To be of value my work cannot just be about me; it must in my mind contribute to the body of knowledge, to cultural experience, to shared feeling. Specifically...

I want my art to engage with the viewers' experience and negotiation of meaning... To engender curiosity... to create wonder... to celebrate and at the same time question the realities that confront us. ...

Art for me is important because it is one critical way through which I can reflect on life, on being, or more accurately on becoming. Art can do this self-reflexively by creating an awareness of what constitutes the art I am engaged with. What is it that I am engaging with? What are the concrete, imaginative, and intellectual realities made manifest by the work? What decisions have been made to create its aesthetic, political and ethical complexities? How fast or slowly are these revealed; why are they constructed thus and how does this affect my responses to the work? Art for me is not about fashion, entertainment or the new although it can be fashionable entertaining and new (Thomas, 2008).

This is the order of questions and considerations I bring to supervision. I ask candidates to engage in similar enquiries regarding their own projects.

AN EXAMPLE:
LOCAL AMID GLOBAL. GLOBAL AMID LOCAL.
DIFFERENCES AND SIMILARITIES

In this section I would like to look at a specific example of supervision; I learn as much from candidates as they do from me. Dr Chen, Shiau-Peng was a candidate at the doctoral level from Taiwan. She was immensely talented, hard working and had to negotiate her studies in her second language. Chen's work dealt with abstraction and representation with a focus on colour and sign. She explored painting as object that carried readings regarding place, experience and history and extended space and time of painting into installation. Chen had studied in highly reputable art schools in her own country and in the USA and she was developing a growing international reputation as an artist.

As supervisor and candidate, we became interested during the course of her research, of the growing interactions, similarities and differences between East and West in the use of colour. Dr Chen produced work that respected both cultures, explored their diverse traditions and attempted to create a relevant contemporary practice that would bridge and celebrate difference.

In the course of my supervision I had to learn about and encourage her to investigate, while in Australia, some of the pictorial and spatial devices that were part of her own cultural tradition. Some were not necessarily seen as fashionable, contemporary or relevant in her homeland, where Western, in particular North American, modernism and postmodernism were admired by her generation. The tropes and energy of contemporary American culture had informed her practice as a dominant culture when she had studied there and these had been investigated thoroughly by her. The question for me was how to encourage her to move beyond this hard won knowledge and enable her to use those aspects of her own tradition, of European and Australian culture that she would find relevant. How could we expand our horizons in order to make an art that was global, local and relevant?

By reinvestigating the work of traditional and contemporary artists of her homeland and by employing Norman Bryson's pivotal essay, 'The gaze in the expanded field' in Hal Foster's *Vision and Visuality* (1988) we created useful starting points from which we could compare Eastern and Western approaches to looking. Bryson's essay focuses on the decentred gaze as a metaphor for a mobile conception of self. This approach, plus studio experiments, expanded her understanding of multi-layering and extended the paintings into the space of installation in original ways.

After describing Sartre's and Lacan's decentring of the gaze, Bryson uses the Zen master Sesshu's paintings to consider the concept of *sunyata* "blankness" and how Chan Buddhist flung-ink painting extends the viewer's perception of the work beyond image, to apprehending the painting as actual fact, as part of the world of events and matter. He compares these with Western, perspectival, scopic regimes.

Bryson then focuses upon the interaction of Western and Japanese philosophy between the wars, on Kitaro Nishida and in particular Kieji Nishitani, a student of both Nishida and Martin Heidegger, with reference to an expanded field of relations, where the figure-field relationship is one of mutual permeability. "What appears to be x is the difference between x and its surrounding field, and as the field is in continual mobility individual objects are constituted by *différance*, deferral in time" (Bryson, 1988, pp. 98–101).

Everything is 'becoming' to use a Deleuzian term. Over time we began to realise that the connections between certain Western streams of thought and older Eastern traditions had points of confluence. Both were able to deal with ideas of complexity paradox and movement of meaning within multilayered constructs. This then became a point where we discussed the composite both in its ability to reconcile different codes, materials and techniques but in the way we could use this principle to generate different working methodologies and methods. These understandings were evidenced in the studio work itself as well as in theoretical and historical research.

We clarified questions by asking, how does the practice contribute to the body of knowledge? I consistently asked myself how I could assist the candidate in managing her time between the written exegesis and the project. We both needed to negotiate the time required to make things, discover and evaluate. The time frame needed to be organic but useful as a guide to planning and progress. We let the project grow from what was known to what is not, both in its material reality and its coding. We questioned habits. As supervisor I was questioning how I should supervise; and the candidate was questioning in order to make work. We both had to make judgements questioning our accepted habits using the research questions; the aims and rationale of the project as criteria rather than personal preference. Sometimes our habitual way seemed correct, at other times we needed to alter our approach. The act of supervision and the candidate's practice were seen as a whole – both needed to be flexible and both needed to be reflected upon and managed in light of our intentions.

We recognised the value of approaches that contained the organic, intuitive and subjective as well as rational empirical procedures. We said: "Lets try, and then evaluate". We asked, "What if?" At a certain moment in a Ph.D. by practice the process of doing needs to be evaluated against intentions. This conscious recognition of the key questions is what makes this practice into research. We were able to organise ourselves and maintain it over the long term of the study, viewing the exhibition as the culmination of these understandings in its own terms as art, contextualised by the exegesis.

The visual arts and the plastic arts are by their very nature a unique combination of the conceptual, the expressive and the physical realities of the media employed. So experiments in colour mixing, scale, surface and placement were as important as library research was. We developed flexible working structures, parallel or simultaneous projects and methods to realise that there were many ways of addressing similar issues. This approach enabled us to become aware of multiple possibilities and to evaluate choices as they arose. We let movement occur in the early stages of the project, a movement in meaning so that we did not hang onto things or invest ownership of the outcomes too early. We tried not to pre-empt either with the supervision or the work. We questioned the idea of a signature style of the artist. This is a very difficult thing in our global culture. So often art students get style confused with identity and content, for example, "this manner of working is me". We attempted to remain open to new possibilities in the work … where one starts will not be where one finishes. We develop and change.

The importance of understanding how to use the studio flexibly, as a working place, as an exhibition place and a site to understand context, became important. We also realised that the work needed to be seen outside of the studio, so the transition of the work from studio into the world became important. I encouraged her to test the reception of the work by receiving and evaluating feedback in various locations from the formal exhibition space to the informality of her studio environment.

We became aware of new examples of works that extended our habits of working, which can also help one become aware of realities of practice. I looked at traditional Chinese Gardens as models of the composite and complexity. Chen studied relevant European works and writings including those of David Batchelor on colour. We compared understandings and experiences.

When these expansions in thinking and practice occur, we gain confidence, we realise key things about ourselves and the role of contemporary art. That our function is not simply to tell things or show things but one of the key roles that we use art for is to engender curiosity. This is, I believe, a gentle way to describe research and it is the thing I hope my students take with them when they graduate.

As a supervisor I must assist the student within the studio context to understand and define their field, and in this case realise the transcultural aspects of the content and methods. Simplistic assumptions abound and must be interrogated by candidate and supervisor. Take for example the use of colour. If we assume that colours have universal readings we can create great confusion. What does a colour signify? If I were to paint the sun as a young Western child might, it would most likely be coloured yellow. If I was to paint the sun in the way of a young Chinese person, most likely it would be red. Both colours represent attributes of the sun; light and energy. Both have symbolic readings that are culturally specific. This description, however, does not reveal the specific nature or sensation of the colours. What type of yellow or red do I mean? In painting we can be specific about this. Colour symbolism is not the only way to experience or use colour, but it is a useful way to introduce the relational aspects of culture to each other, and it reinforces that the understanding of such complexity and difference is important for our mutual cultural comprehensions.

So when we express complex concepts regarding ideas of time, of nothing and something, things become even more complex. Is nothing the same as nihilism? How do these concepts differ in different epochs in East and West? We need to understand and attempt to create a common terminology. Some non-Western students have an oversimplified view of the West as simply materialist, positivist and rationalist, and in doing so they miss an equally old and alternate tradition that students need to know about. Equally the East is not all lotus flowers and meditation or pollution and merchandising as some Western students think.

It is important for students to realise that they do not have to make work in the manner of their supervisor (Dr Chen had an independent attitude, due to her personality and diverse range of educational experiences). The independence offered at postgraduate levels of study can come across as a shock, as in certain Eastern and Western cultures the candidate may be used to the master-student tradition of the atelier model where one expects to work like their teacher, and often if they do not it can be considered disrespectful. Yet in the School of Art in which I am working and from which I speak, there is a focus on student centred learning, rather than teacher directed instruction. These attitudes and methods need negotiation between the parties involved. So communication must encourage a full understanding of this.

We are not just making things; we are attempting to negotiate and communicate original understandings and approaches and not simply to achieve expected outcomes. We need to demonstrate the need to interrogate issues with flexibility and an awareness of the differing contexts in which the candidate is and will be placed.

When students return home they may have changed; their homelands may or may not have changed in different ways. They will need to be flexible enough to know how to use their skills and to adapt them if required to re-enter their societies. Fine art as a research practice can assist in this understanding of flexibility while still retaining clarity of purpose and focus. What we as supervisors can do, I believe, is to prepare our students to understand change and to meet change with appropriate flexibility and optimism.

The Ph.D. by practice is a relatively new occurrence in the fine art academic context and it must not lose sight of its uniqueness. I believe art and by implication, design, is important because it gives us a way to reflect on life, on being, and to negotiate meanings in the world; it combines experience with thought via matter in time in place; and it is a site where the subjective and objective meet.

Here lies the rationale for my emphasis in this chapter and the point where an art and/or supervisory practice concerned with the ideas of the composite, complexity and multiplicity meets the ideological. We are living in a time where simple answers are being offered to culturally and politically complex questions. We need to be wary of this; we need to understand complexity. Art has a role in assisting this process.

REFERENCES

Bergson, H. (1965/1922). *Duration and simultaneity* (Leon Jacobson, Trans.). Indianapolis: Bobbs-Merrill.

Bergson, H. (1978/1911). *Matter and memory* (Nancy Margaret Paul & W. Scott Palmer, Trans.). London: Harvester Press.

Bryson, N. (1988). The gaze in the expanded field. In Hal Foster (Ed.) *Vision and visuality* (pp. 86–113). Seattle: Bay Press.

Deleuze, G. (1997). *Bergsonism*. New York: Zone Books.

Fischli, P. & Weiss, D. (1991). *How To Work Better*. Mural, office building, Zurich-Oerlikon.

Foster, H. (Ed.) (1988). *Vision and visuality*. Seattle: Bay Press.

Mansfield, N. (2000). *Subjectivity: Theories of the self from Freud to Haraway*. Sydney: Allen & Unwin.

Moore, F. C. T. (1996). *Bergson: Thinking backwards*. New York: Cambridge University Press.

Tati, J. (1953). *Les Vacances de Monsieur Hulot*. Paris: Cady Films.

Thomas, D. (2008). Unpublished writing for an exhibition.

LAURENE VAUGHAN

12. DESIGNING A PRACTICE AND PEDAGOGY OF POSTGRADUATE SUPERVISION

INTRODUCTION

> I sat down one spring day to write a book about walking and stood up again,
> because a desk is no place to think on the large scale (Solnit, 2000, p. 4).

As I sat down to write this chapter I found myself reflecting on Rebecca Solnit's statement in the opening pages of her book *Wanderlust* (2000) and I wondered, why did this text and this statement come to mind now? Here I am sitting and reflecting on my practice of postgraduate supervision and a text about walking comes to mind. I was introduced to the work of Rebecca Solnit by one of my supervisors when I was undertaking my own Ph.D. As a creative practitioner I had been exploring walking as a means of conceptualising the creative process, and I had yet to discover the world of theory in this area. In contrast, my interest in the practices of walking was founded in a framework of experiential knowing, grounded in proposition and a critique of other creative artists such as Richard Long, who walked as a means of creating. Reading Rebecca Solnit's text my world opened up, as I discovered another way of thinking and found a community of scholars to whom my work connected. (I must admit that I was also a little envious and wondered why I should go on when she seemed to have said it all.) Thinking about it, I have come to realise that it is not really such a surprise that this text and this statement should come back to mind now. This text, and my engagement with it, represents for me the richness of what begins in a Ph.D., and what goes on once the examination is over.

On reflection, I can see that my supervisor had an insight into what I needed to do next in my project and offered me a way through a text to begin my journey into the next phase of the doctoral investigation. The text itself has gone on to become a research companion in my continuing forays into walking; this is a research method that encompasses what it means to be *in* the thing that we are investigating. Often I have drawn on this statement in conversations with students and colleagues about the nature of knowing in practice, and the need to be both *in* the practice while looking *at* it. We rarely know what we will need to discover when we set out on the journey of a research degree; we discover things about the content of our research, and also much about ourselves. A research degree is what Jack Mezirow calls a transformational learning encounter (Mezirow & Assoc., 1990). Such learning encounters, involving critically reflective practices that occur throughout the research process, can result in a transformation of the students' understanding of themselves including their beliefs, values and subsequent actions. This process

B. Allpress, R. Barnacle, L. Duxbury and E. Grierson (Eds.), Supervising Practices for Postgraduate
Research in Art, Architecture and Design, 147–162.
©*2012 Sense Publishers. All rights reserved.*

results in transformed meaning encompassing the students' "schemes and perspectives" (p. 18), as well as eliciting a new body of deep knowledge in their area of investigation.

Academics have numerous practices that we draw on in the various aspects of a working day. One of mine is postgraduate supervision. It is a practice I have been engaged in for 15 years. I stumbled into it and over time it has become the focus of my academic teaching practice. Through this engagement my particular pedagogy of supervision has emerged.

HOW DID I GET THERE? AN INVENTORY OF PRACTICE

Since 1996, I have been actively engaged in a range of different disciplines, roles and approaches to supervision at RMIT University. This has included the role of postgraduate coordinator in the (then) Department of Fashion and Textile Design (1999–2001) and in the Communication Design programme (2005–2007). In the School of Education, 2002–2005, I was employed as a postgraduate supervisor and supervised students in the Master of Education and Ph.D. in Education through workplace practice or project. This programme was an innovation in the integration between practice-based knowledge and workplace learning projects. Since 2005, I have been employed in the School of Media and Communication where I currently supervise master and Ph.D. candidates from across the school's practice-based domains (communication and interaction design, networked media, documentary and no-budget film production).

This practice of postgraduate supervision has been evolving for 15 years. It has spanned more than 16 different disciplinary areas of enquiry and resulted in 35 submissions; at the time of writing three more are under examination, plus there are the nine students with whom I am currently working. Of the completions, 18 have been noted as early completions and six have been commended for being outstanding. Through this time, I have worked as a first supervisor, co-supervisor and second supervisor with 15 colleagues in three distinct educational units while also contributing to the broader university through colloquia, publications, policies and committees.

This equates to a little more than a seventh of a lifetime, with quite a number of people across a range of ages, locations and contexts, and a diversity of fields of practice and enquiry. In essence these are 47 different scenarios and approaches to research and their subsequent outcomes; these have included thesis and practice-based or project submissions.

I am an interdisciplinary practitioner and educator, with design as the cohesive thread that holds it all together. Some of the areas my students have been investigating include: communication design, fashion history, fashion practice, textiles history, adult education, land care engagement strategies, library management, community health, interaction design, health care, networked video, media studies, radio production, service design, education management, organisation design, digital archives and social sustainability. This list will no doubt leave some of my academic colleagues feeling a little ill at ease, for it challenges some of the conventions of postgraduate education.

The practice of postgraduate student supervision traverses the academic fields of teaching and research; with student outcomes being counted as research achievements while the reality of the research project and investigation is nestled in the realm of learning and teaching. Over recent years this practice has been named "research training". In my academic career I have endeavoured to extend the postgraduate research student experience from that of learning specific skills and competence in a topic area, to one of enabling students to discover research driven and rigorous approaches to lifelong learning that is informed, critical and creative; while at the same supporting students in their career development, and introducing them into local and broader communities of affiliated practice.

This is the foundation and context for my supervision practice. In the following pages I discuss why I am committed to the perspective of postgraduate supervision as a pedagogic practice, providing some of the structures I use to enact this process. In the remainder of this chapter I discuss four aspects, which as a result of this inventory of practice, I have come to know and continue to explore in this practice:

- postgraduate supervision as a pedagogic practice;
- postgraduate studies and communities of practice;
- working within frameworks of expertise;
- ethics and research and ongoing practice.

POSTGRADUATE SUPERVISION AS PEDAGOGIC PRACTICE

Bob Smith (2001) argues in his essay, '(Re)Framing research degree supervision as pedagogy', how it quickly becomes apparent when undertaking a survey of the literature on postgraduate supervision, that there are two dominant bodies of writing on the subject, both of which have the intention to enable better outcomes for students and universities. The first body of literature is framed around the concepts of quality and effectiveness. The focus of the discourse is on the institutional and procedural aspects of research candidature as realised through the various stages of the investigation from enrolment through to submission. The proposition of these texts seems to be that a well-structured system comprising checklists, clear definitions and statements of accountability will ensure a successful student outcome by empowering the supervisor to be effective in their role within the research degree process. Although I do support the need for sound administrative and procedural structures and codes of conduct, I think the belief that such structures will ensure a quality learning experience is to deny the messy realities of a two to eight year journey that a student and supervisor will undertake in the course of a research degree. Over the years my students have married, divorced, had babies, been promoted, changed jobs, had deaths in the family, or long-term illnesses themselves. Institutional procedures help to manage the details of enrolment in such situations, but they do not engage with what it means for the student's learning.

The framing of supervision as a pedagogic practice presents a second and less dominant body of literature than the discourse on quality and supervision. That said, there are also those working in the space of research on research, and critically exploring the pedagogic basis of higher degree supervision. A pedagogic conceptualisation of supervision calls us to perceive the acts of supervision as more than an act of transmission, where knowledge is passed from master to novice. The pedagogy of supervision involves a more complicated integration founded in practices and relationships underpinned with issues of power (Simon, 1992). With power come notions of authority, which I would argue are far more complex than teacher and student dichotomies. It is from this basis that supervision can be conceptualised as a critical pedagogic practice, where issues of morality and power extend beyond ethical and political assumptions and the organisational conditions that support them (Smith, 2001, p. 29). In this way Simon (1992) argues that critical pedagogy is founded in cultural politics while also being framed as a pedagogy of possibility. Enacting these theories in practice has been a central facet of my supervisory approach.

I have always perceived postgraduate supervision as a teaching practice. My initial bachelor's degree was in education and, since the age of 21, I have been engaged actively in teaching and education predominantly in the fields of art and design. I have taught all levels from Montessori kindergarten to Ph.D., including teaching at primary and high schools, technical schools, and Technical Advanced and Further Education (TAFE), community education and workplace training. In the university sector I have taught undergraduates and postgraduates, coursework and research degrees. In reflecting on this inventory of an entire teaching practice, it became apparent to me that in addition to my 'designerly' approach to knowledge production and dissemination, the consistent thread across these various educational contexts is my belief that my role as teacher has never been simply to deliver content, rather I have been committed to teaching and enabling students to learn how to learn. My rationale is based in this: content comes and goes, topics and areas of interest change, and information about them is increasingly and easily available, therefore teaching others how to find, critique and engage information is the most useful and sustainable aspect of educational practice that I as a teacher can do; that, and instilling in students the value of learning as an ongoing life practice. Enabling students to create their own knowledge practice of discovery and application is my ambition no matter the age or the context of the student with whom I work.

It is from this perspective that my pedagogy of postgraduate supervision is perhaps best framed as one that sits in the space of a phenomenologically critical educational approach. This is a pedagogy that is socially and culturally situated, and one that explores and is responsive to the social and cultural contexts of the student and supervisor(s). Max van Manen (1982) argues that a phenomenological pedagogy is a "situated pedagogy" where the teacher perceives themselves as a "pedagogic being" (p. 285). Although van Manen's argument conceives of the learner to be a child, and the teacher as literally being a teacher or a parent, I translate his argument and conceive of it as the relationship between supervisor and student, or even mentor and mentee, and hence embrace a more adult teaching and learning relationship such as that found in postgraduate research and supervision.

A phenomenological pedagogy embraces the learning context as being 'ever new', always in a state of development and evolving from each situation. "Pedagogy is not found in philosophy, but like love or friendship it is to be found in the experience of its presence – that is, in the concrete, real life situations" (van Manen, 1982, p. 284). In this way pedagogy is enacted rather than theorised or predetermined; and pedagogic competence involves the anticipatory and reflective capacity of the teacher whose focus is on fostering, shaping and guiding the student in the development of their own learning (p. 293). This conception of the learning relationship between teacher and student provides a useful means for me to articulate the student centred and responsive model, which I have endeavoured to adopt as an approach to supervision. It requires a mix between the formality of processes, dates and stages of the research degree process (including the requirements for submission and examination), while acknowledging the fundamental individual nature of research discoveries and the individualised experience that this needs to be. At times this perspective has been challenging. The diverse groups of students I have worked with, their varying levels of academic and research experience, and the professions they have been aligned with, have required dexterity from both supervisor and students, as we have worked to align their particular views and experiences of the world, and their desires and fears, in relation to the research process and requirements of the academy.

In reflecting on this process, I acknowledge that the 'looseness' of this approach has been challenging and sometimes alienating for some students. A phenomenological pedagogy reinforces, or perhaps forces, the student into the independent learning that is a research degree. For some students this brings freedom, for others uncertainty. I have acknowledged this and in the various contexts of my supervisions have utilised different devices to help structure the experience, without compromising the student's need to quickly transition into a state of safe uncertainty in relation to their research project. The safety is found in the community of researchers that they are a part of, through the support of their supervisors, and the understanding that the open-ended nature of research investigations requires a delicate mix of planning and open-ended discovery. This is particularly true for those students from different cultural and learning backgrounds, and those who have not been involved in educational institutions for quite some time.

POSTGRADUATE STUDIES AND COMMUNITIES OF PRACTICE

For many, undertaking a postgraduate degree can be a distinctly lonely and isolating process. This loneliness can be physical where the student is locked away with books and computer diligently working away; and it can be intellectual, where the only conversations they have about their research are in occasional meetings with their supervisors or at academic conferences. Many students, whether they are local or international, move cities to take up postgraduate research positions in universities, resulting in being distanced from many of their usual social support structures such as friends and family, which can add to the strains of their experience at their new university. For they not only work to find their way into their studies, but also to find a place in the local community. Many students in my fields are enrolled part time and work remotely from campus, adding to their dislocation from others in the academy. Intellectual loneliness and isolation effects most students, as the specialised nature of research education can tend to alienate us even from our loved-ones. Mature age students often have the added pressures of family and professional demands from fulltime employment.

Concerns about this isolation and loneliness are among the key drivers for many university processes and regulations regarding frequency of contact between student and supervisor, and the development of research student support programmes in universities such as writing groups, training programmes, and social activities.

One or both of these two contexts of isolation, the physical and the intellectual, are likely to affect all students at some stage; as a teacher I am concerned for the wellbeing of my students and know that this kind of experience does have a significant impact on students, on their quality of life during study, and their academic outcomes. I have always told my students that all research degrees are challenging in a way you never know in other forms of study. One thinks they are investigating a topic, they discover that they are actually learning a lot about themselves, their practice, and also how they are in the world. I believe that in a master's degree one begins to see who they are and how they operate, and in doctorates one is confronted by this at the core. From my own experience, I hold that a Ph.D. is one of the hardest educational undertakings one can do, and I am glad that I made it through.

Throughout the evolution of my supervisory practice I have worked to address the challenges of isolation and to draw on the benefits of community in a postgraduate context. During my time as postgraduate coordinator in fashion and textiles I introduced a seminar programme where students would present their research in development on a rostered basis. Part of the session time was spent in presentations and the rest was spent talking in an informal environment with refreshments. This was not a formal requirement of their candidature at that time, but having been a student in the programme myself I was aware of the limitations and challenges of working on my own, and as a supervisor and programme coordinator I was attempting to build a community across the programme.

Between 2002 and 2005, I was employed in the School of Education at RMIT to work as supervisor in their Master of Education by project programme. This was an innovation in the school's research degree offering, where they were embracing the university's 'by project' model and adapting it to workplace contexts outside the creative industries fields. The programme had a large enrolment and students were located in clusters in Melbourne, Sydney, Adelaide and regional Victoria. Students were drawn from a broad spectrum of industries including such areas as

TAFE, nursing, fire fighting, ambulance driving, library services, journalism, social work, farming and land management. Workplace learning and change management were the themes that were the common element across all enrolments, plus the understanding that the research would be undertaken within the students' workplace and the outcomes of the research would address or be applied to that workplace. Action research was the proposed methodology that all students would use. This resulted in many students working on strategies of engagement for their respective colleagues, students or constituents, or implementing proposed change with these professional communities.

Employed in the programme for my experience in practice-based research in design, I was a member of a six person supervisory team comprised of the programme coordinator, two Melbourne based supervisors (including myself) and three regional supervisors (two located in Warrnambool and one in Albury–Wadonga in regional New South Wales and Victoria). This six person supervisory team was a community of practice in itself, with each member having different expertise that they could bring to both their own students and to the broader community of enquiry that the programme was to become.

My role was to be the senior supervisor for the Hamilton and Warrnambool clusters in regional Victoria. Together with two local supervisors, we developed a model of team and peer supervision that was structured around monthly cluster meetings and individual supervision sessions. In between cluster meetings students were encouraged to meet with their local supervisor(s) for individual consultation and then informally as research communities to discuss their projects and experiences in the programme. The initial cohorts had enrolled at the same time and hence were progressing through the first phases of their research candidature together (proposal writing, confirmation of candidature and ethics approval). This consistency across the group allowed us to set readings, run discussion groups and presentations, with each student learning from others, even when there were significant differences between their research investigations. Over the course of my involvement the groups transformed. There were new enrolments and one student transferred to a doctoral enrolment. This had not only a slight fracturing effect on the groups, but also started to create a mentoring model between the more experienced and new students.

These clusters were formal communities of practice, where research through practice using the framework of action learning and action research was the common element to the various projects. It was an interesting integration of the individual and community. Both clusters were located in regional cities, and outside of the programme or their places of employment (one cluster was comprised of staff members from one TAFE institution) the students were members of a community, some had known each other their entire lives and many had connections through community organisations or through their children. The research cluster was a sub-community of enquiry within their broader everyday life community. Many of the cluster members were women, and they had varying levels of undergraduate education.

The structures of the clusters and research communities supported the students and created a framework for discussions across the community. The spirit of the groups, as members of regional communities, supported a culture of peer learning. Authentic good-will for their peers was a normal part of their everyday lives. The various challenges of their degrees were heartening to me as an educator. A number of students at the Hamilton cluster established a regular morning coffee meeting to discuss informally and share their experiences. In a group session with the supervisors, one of the students reflected on how much this research had made its way into their everyday life. That week during their coffee meeting the conversation had traversed the complexities of planning their daughters' debuts at the local college, and what do you think they (one particular author) really mean when they argue for a paradigm shift in practice. At this point the supervisory team was assured that no matter what the academic outcomes, the learning had broken out from the boundaries of the academy and was taking a life of its own.

In 2005, I commenced work as postgraduate coordinator of communication design at RMIT. The model of supervision that had been undertaken by the previous staff member, Dr Lisa Grocott, was similar to that described previously as she had been using group supervision in conjunction with collaborative design briefs as a pedagogical method. Again the majority of the students were working as design professionals and design educators, and were undertaking their research through practice. The context of the investigations was less focussed on a site of work as the Master of Education students had been, and there was a focus on research through design and reflective practice. This was a strong community of disciplinary peers who had great respect for the departing supervisor. The spirit of the group was of critical collegiality and good-humoured friendship and was similar to the collegial experiences in the clusters with which I had worked in Hamilton and Warrnambool. My challenge was to transition into this community and to find an approach to working with these students, in a manner that would not undermine what they had and what they were doing, yet would find a way to make a particular contribution to their research projects.

My approach to this research community was not significantly different from that undertaken by Dr Grocott. We shared a belief in the value of peer learning and of critique as a method of exploring design investigations. Unlike the interactions of the Master of Education students where we created a community of practice, this group was already firmly connected and my concern was to challenge them in their research projects while not alienating them. Again group meetings and the use of a reading group model of co-investigation was an effective method for creating a shared yet individual discourse. Students in the programme were also used to participating in the School of Architecture and Design's bi-annual Practice Research Symposium (PRS), formerly known as the Graduate Research Conference, which is a public review of student work in progress where a panel of reviewers critique the candidates' research investigations. Typically panels include external critics; I had been one such critic prior to my commencement in the programme.

Continuing to use these tools for peer enquiry was important for ensuring that the community of practice not only continued, but also flourished. Over the next four years the programme has grown to include Ph.D. completions, a greater number of international students, and a number of students on scholarship working on funded research projects as part of the community, which we have since named the Media Communication Design Studio (MCD Studio). Our collaborative research enquiries now include exploratory collaborative design projects; we have been on a three-day design retreat, travelled to conferences, co-authored publications and facilitated streams in conferences. The community has also expanded from being comprised only of communication design students, and now adopts a broader media and communications focus including film, networked media, and associated communications areas. The majority of students continue to undertake their research through practice with some students electing to submit a written thesis.

COMMUNITIES OF PRACTICE POST RESEARCH DEGREE

Ensuring the longevity of a research community is a significant issue for me when designing such communities of research practice. I believe that a community of practice must exist past the enrolment period, for it is in this way that the real learning of a student can continue to manifest once the degree is over. This is, however, impossible to ensure. For the students who were enrolled in the Master of Education programme, their pre-existing membership in a local community was advantageous for my ambition of longevity. Their time in formal study, which manifests as specific communities of research practice, could be seen as just a phase in the life of their community. The formal structures of the community have changed, but the people (students and local supervisors) continue to be part of the everyday landscape of their community life. Three of the graduates of the Master of Education programme have gone on to do Ph.Ds. in other schools at RMIT, and although undertaking more conventional supervisor and student arrangements, members of the original community continue to support and encourage them through their studies. They do this not just as friends, but as informed researchers who have an experiential understanding of the challenges of completing higher degrees by research. In this way an informal community of practice continues.

Similar outcomes have occurred in the MCD Studio cohort through a mix of formal and informal methods. An email list maintains ongoing correspondence between current students and alumni. Some master's alumni have gone on to undertake Ph.Ds. in the group; some are staff members in the school and now supervise or are on the way to becoming supervisors of future students in the studio. The supervision model of the studio is no longer focused around my supervision (or the lead supervisor) who draws on external critics for a broader influence. We are now a community of researchers (students, supervisors and external critics) who use the studio model of critical experiential learning with public critique and dissemination (publication) as a means of participating in research discourses across the media communication and design fields.

There are three key strengths for utilising a community of practice model of supervision. Firstly, it supports the research supervisors in the supervisory process of a postgraduate degree. Secondly, it enables students to learn from and with peers and provides a context through which they can find their voice and their way into a research community. And thirdly, if sustained over time, the community then provides the context through which graduates find an ongoing community of research practice even when they have formally left the academy. This is especially important for non-academic research practitioners who are endeavouring to apply what they have learnt within other professional contexts.

WORKING WITHIN FRAMEWORKS OF EXPERTISE

The conventional model of the postgraduate student and their positioning within the arts, social sciences and humanities disciplines in the university is that of the lone, keen, and young student working under the guidance of a supervisor who is an expert in their field of study. This student is fulltime and undertaking their studies as the first stage in their long term academic career. However, in my own supervisory practice, this is the student I have yet to meet. My students have come from what some name as the minor professions (Glazer, 1974). Most have been working professionals in their fields, have been employed in the area they are investigating, and many have had standings in their field outside of their postgraduate investigations. At least 20% of them have been older than I am, thereby raising challenges to notions of authority and expertise in traditional, master-student pedagogical models.

This is not an unusual scenario for postgraduate students, especially for students undertaking research through practice. The majority of my students have been undertaking research through practice and most have submitted their research outcomes under the 'by project' classification at RMIT. These students have been practitioners undertaking research through practice, with the location for the practice-based investigation being their workplace, which operates typically as their design studio. These contexts or locations of enquiry, which are often clustered as 'real world' research, create interesting questions and challenges for the academy with regard to the expectations and notions of rigour and form when undertaking research.

Earlier in this chapter I raised the issues of power and authority and the ways in which a critical pedagogy demands that we acknowledge and investigate notions of power in the student-teacher relationship. When a student is a leader in their field, a CEO of a regional library, or in senior management of an educational institution, a research active academic colleague, or a nationally recognised innovator in their field, the expectation that the academy and its agent, the supervisor, is the holder of power and authority in the research context is challenged. For in such a situation, where does the expertise lie in regard to the research investigation? There is a challenge to the conventional idea of the supervisor as topic expert in situated research projects. When the site of investigation is a student's day-to-day practice, and those outside the academy already validate this practice, it is essential that notions of expertise be transformed. This situation has emerged many times throughout my academic career.

My experience of working with students in the Master of Education by project programme was my real training ground for confronting any expectations or delusions I may have had about topic expertise. My experience in this programme provided strategies I have used since with students in my return to research degrees in the creative industries. The Master of Education was very structured with a strong focus on methodology from the first stages of enrolment. The focus on action research emphasised a distributed model of expertise and contribution, both in the individual student projects and across the cluster in which the student was enrolled. The team supervision model enhanced this distributed model. Each of the supervisors had diverse and complementary expertise and attributes, which we exploited in our dealings with students. At times, I would think of the adage that 'it takes a village to raise a child', and in this case it was a team of supervisors to lead a community of individual research completions. This team model in conjunction with structured peer learning supported the recognition of the diversity of expertise within the group and the valuing of each type of expertise to ensure successful outcomes. The student was typically the content expert and the supervisors, drawing on differing skills and perspectives, were the experts in turning this situated knowledge and expertise into research that was aligned to the expectations of the academy at master's or doctoral level.

Since leaving the Master of Education programme, I have continued to draw on this experience of co-developing a distributed model of peer supervision in my supervisions over the past six years in the School of Media and Communication. The co-development of the MCD studio as a community of practice was a crucial aspect of this approach to distributed supervision. In this context the domains of expertise across the student community are less diverse, although disciplinary and cultural diversity is a rich aspect of the research projects of which the studio is comprised. Although I am now working in a field where my content expertise is more aligned to what my students are investigating, and a number of students have been undertaking studies either directly as part of funded research projects or in areas aligned to them, this distributed model of expertise continues to be my modus operandi. One of the key reasons for this is the combination of the situated nature of projects and the use of practice as the methodology for the enquiry. The nature of situated research is that each event within the situated context of enquiry is unique, and each person's experience of these situations is of equal particularity. When you couple this with individual practice as the method of enquiry, the research student must be the key expert when it comes to understanding and analysing what has happened, what it means, and how it relates to their overall area of enquiry. The supervisor cannot be the expert of the student's experience; they can however facilitate the student's discoveries through critical and reflective conversations and critique of project artefacts. In this way, the supervisor partners the student in the discovery process, and as an outsider the supervisor may see, hear, or notice things that emerge from the artefacts and the conversations that the student may be unable to perceive. The supervisor is able to use their distance from the student's lived experience as a kind of mirror that can reflect back to the student so that they can better see the situation. This process of reflective conversation is a means to enable the student to notice what is happening in their research. From there my role is to guide and sometimes co-design with them the next actions of their research enquiry. This process is similar to my supervisor's suggestion to me to read Rebecca Solnit; he did not demand it of me, but from his distance from my study, and drawing on his expertise, he was able to direct me towards new possibilities in my research understanding.

When practice is the research method and methodology, and the expert knowledge is embedded in the research actions of the researcher (in this case the student), the boundaries and classifications of expertise are challenged. For my part, this is the only way I am able to address issues of expertise from the perspective of a critical and phenomenological pedagogy, an approach to supervision founded in a questioning of power and authority (Freire, 2005). However, this is not to deny the vital contribution that the supervisor then makes to the research enquiry. The supervisor (which may be a supervisory team including a community of peers) must work with the student as an external agent who is able, firstly, to assist the student to reflect critically on their research as it progresses; and secondly, guide them towards external sources that will support them to further and extend their enquiry and their practice. Often, when conceiving of the position of the supervisor in relation to the student, we see the supervisor located either opposite the student as an intellectual opponent, or in front, leading the student along the path of enquiry. The critical pedagogical approach to supervision is one where the supervisor sits beside the student, drawing on their experience as a researcher, critically supporting and enabling the student in their discoveries and their journey through the higher degree process.

Reading back over this I am struck by how easy, smooth or un-confrontational this approach sounds. I cannot leave the reader thinking that this is so. Throughout my time as supervisor, many students have cried, some have stormed, some have left and some have refused to see or hear what is emerging in our conversations, not wanting to heed the expertise of the supervisor as a researcher or to learn from their own situated knowledge. The other aspect of the situated praxis of my supervision practice is to expect a reciprocal relationship of respect between my students and myself. There is a reciprocal process at work here: as I must respect and heed their expertise in specific domains of practice, so too they need to acknowledge mine with regard to the requirements of a research degree and submission for examination. Although I work within a community of practice model of enquiry, the intention of this community is the successful examination of all research students for their respective research degrees. These projects are practice enquiries where the successful completion of an academic degree is the intended outcome. One of the challenges for students in this mode of enquiry is to design a submission that has relevance and integrity to the content of the research, the field of enquiry, and the context of the situation within which it has been undertaken, while also meeting the expectations of rigour of the academy.

ETHICS AND RESEARCH AND ONGOING PRACTICE

Practitioners entering the academy face many challenges. Universities are bureaucracies that serve and report to many masters, and over the years many processes and practices develop, which are integral to its workings and its contribution to society. As much as universities work to ease their confusion, students continue to have tales to tell about enrolment mistakes, email and other information system meltdowns, and mythical classrooms they have been unable to find. A considerable amount of a supervisor's time in the early days of enrolment can be spent helping students to find their way into the institution and then, finally, we can start on the research and the first stages of proposal development, endorsing a student's reasons for being there. Those early days of the supervisor-student relationship are when we are coming to know each other, with the supervisor starting to understand how the student works and thinks, their strengths and weaknesses, and with the student doing the same in developing their understanding of the supervisor. From my experience, introducing the student to the academy is an important aspect of this process. This must move quickly from issues of the what, when, and who of physically being in this place, to introducing the world of academic research.

For a practitioner-researcher, the process of transitioning from research as something they do in their practice to being the context they are practising within can be difficult. Discussion around ethics and ethical research is one such issue. It is unfortunate that our conversations around ethics and research focus on the university requirements for a student to receive ethics clearance before they talk to the subjects of their study. In this way, conversations about ethics that focus on ethics clearance as a compliance process are perceived as a hurdle to be overcome and a barrier to progressing with the work. I too have done this with my students, and reflecting on this has left me realising how I really have not served my students well in this process, and have not made the most of the opportunities that exist in this stage of candidature. We need to shift the conversation from one of 'doing ethics' to one of how we can be an ethical researcher and an ethical practitioner.

The RMIT submission guidelines emphasise that a student who submits by project will be able to evidence a shift in their practice as a result of undertaking their study. The aim of most practice-orientated research is to critically explore the practice and agency of the practice in particular contexts. If these objectives are to be met and graduates of research degrees are to be transformed as a result of their academic endeavours, then new discourses around ethics and research need to be embedded into our research communities.

CONCLUSION: DESIGNING A PRACTICE AND PEDAGOGY
OF POSTGRADUATE SUPERVISION

I think it is safe to say that those of us who are practising researchers are people engaged in discovering things; our inquisitiveness leads us into contexts of discovery and experimentation, and at times our interests are broad and at other times they are narrow and deep. For my part, I am one of these innately inquisitive people, curious about many things, but not all things. One of my areas of enquiry is in the design of discovery, exploring and gaining a deeper understanding of the how and the what – of what it is we are seeking to know or do. As a phenomenological and critical teacher and learner, I find each student's research project to be an opportunity to explore and develop methodologies for discovery. It is my commitment to the ongoing design of discovery throughout a research project that has enabled me to work outside and across disciplinary boundaries in my postgraduate supervisions (and in my own research projects).

Over the past 15 years, in working to design a practice and pedagogy of postgraduate supervision I have used design methods and strategies to realise this practice and to achieve the outcomes for my students. In particular, in drawing on design's ability both to solve and create problems, as in many contemporary perspectives on human centred design, I place the person at the centre of the process. It is this designerly approach to knowledge creation, with all the diversities and complexities this entails that enables me to work across the various disciplines and fields of practice, from history to theory, and 'real world' applications in which my students have been actively engaged.

Design is the constant and ever present thread in my supervision practice. It is design that enables me to think through each student's particular situation and focus of their study. The human element of supervision is the core of this practice. Too often supervision is framed only in terms of content expertise, but the two to eight year relationship that is the basis of any supervision is a human one. In my experience, occasionally this relationship has been one between novice researchers who are nascent in their field of practice, but typically my students have been older and wiser, and often leaders in their field. In both cases, my role is one of critically introducing them into the world of research, research practice, and ultimately the submission of research outcomes that will make a contribution to their particular field. RMIT University's practice or project model of submission has been an important enabler in this. Although many conceive of this model as being for the creative arts, and architecture and design, it extends well beyond these disciplinary boundaries. To practice is to participate in a profession, and each profession has its process and artefacts. Utilising methods of critical reflection and enquiry in these practices has enabled me to move across the disciplines in a supervisory capacity.

From my experience in the creative fields, as a practitioner and educator, I am at ease with the logic of the RMIT three-part project submission comprised of project artefacts, a text, and an oral presentation. These are the norms of art and design disciplinary domains. Thus it makes perfect sense to me to translate them into a research submission that honours the multifarious ways we know and articulate professional outcomes to audiences. There is no reason why a research submission embracing multiple literacies of practice and communication in a field or discipline would be any less robust than the literacies in a conventional academic thesis, for the form of the submission is not the measure of the rigour in the enquiry. The rigour is to be found in the content and how it is articulated.

This inventory of my supervision practice has provided me the opportunity to realise that the pedagogical basis of my actions and my commitment to quality learning experiences that will connect to the world outside the academy has been rich, varied and consistent. Perhaps it is my origins in the creative arts that have enabled me to move across boundaries, to see each situation as being ever new, and to know that it is through a focus on being in the situated contexts of discovery that this varied richness and consistency can happen.

REFERENCES

Freire, P. (2005). *Pedagogy of the oppressed*. New York: Continuum.

Glazer, N. (1974). The schools of the minor professions. *Minerva, 12*(3), 346–64.

Mezirow, J. & Assoc. (1990). *Fostering critical reflection in adulthood*. San Francisco: Jossey-Bass.

Simon, R. (1992). *Teaching against the grain: Texts for a pedagogy of possibility*. New York: Bergin & Garvey.

Smith, B. (2001). (Re)Framing research degree supervision as pedagogy. In A. Bartlett & G. Mercer (Eds), *Postgraduate research supervision, transforming (r)elations* (pp. 25–42). New York: Peter-Lang Publications.

Solnit, R. (2000). *Wanderlust: A history of walking*. New York: Penguin Putnam.

van Manen, M. (1982). Phenomenological pedagogy. *Curriculum Inquiry, 12*(3), Autumn, 283–99.

KEVIN WHITE

13. THE FLYING DOCTORATE

Doctoral Supervision by Distance in Hong Kong

DEPARTURES

It was 1996, and I was sitting on the right hand side of the plane on my first trip to Hong Kong, glued to the window as the plane made a steep right hand turn on its final descent towards the runway at Kai Tak airport. I found myself looking at the private dramas playing out from the windows of the tenement blocks of Kai Tak that seemed to delineate one side of the runway, with Hong Kong harbour appearing perilously close to the other. In Hong Kong it seemed one landed in the thick of it. This chapter chronicles my experience of supervising Doctor of Fine Art candidates in Hong Kong by distance education. It addresses what 'distance' means within the context of a cross-cultural educational experience, and how this distance is navigated and negotiated both by candidate and supervisor.

The genesis of this adventure is part of a larger picture of RMIT University School of Art's engagement in art education in Hong Kong, since 1997. I first started flying to Hong Kong on a regular basis in 1996, accompanying the then Head of Department of Fine Art, who was keen to look at the possibilities of delivering a Master of Fine Art programme there by distance education. At the time, calls to internationalise the curriculum were by no means the clearly defined objectives that have found their way more recently into every university's strategic plan – perhaps as much for economic survival as for more purely educational motivations. At the time there were few, if any, tried and tested models of international engagement that one could look to, for direction or advice, and no requirement to submit a carefully constructed and considered business plan before proceeding. Attempting to work 'off-shore' had a more pioneering ring to it, whereas now it forms an increasingly visible aspect of many university's strategic, political and policy directions. A journey to supervise students or deliver a programme away from one's home campus is now, more than ever, an accepted part of tertiary education's broader international engagement in the changed political landscape of a global economy.

It is in the context of a global, and transnational, educational environment that the term 'distance education' is perhaps both misleading and problematic. What do we mean by distance education? The term has been a convenient way of identifying teaching activities that occur in an offshore location, which essentially is apart from the university's geographical and physical location and even somewhat separated from its core business. While the term, 'distance' is perhaps a

B. Allpress, R. Barnacle, L. Duxbury and E. Grierson (Eds.), Supervising Practices for Postgraduate Research in Art, Architecture and Design, 163–172.
©2012 Sense Publishers. All rights reserved.

convenient descriptor for this other activity, it is, in my estimation, essentially redundant, as we increasingly navigate permeable and multiple sites of educational engagement. Furthermore, today the flexibility of the virtual is increasingly as important as the physical attachment to place, in both a pragmatic and philosophical sense. Distance is, of course, a relevant notion, but distance from what or from whom, one might ask. It might be considered ironic that what we define as distance education is in many ways a form of engagement that has the inherent potential to dissolve physical and philosophical barriers, and encourage greater interaction and understanding. Such qualities are of increasing importance in an often fractured and intolerant, global, political environment. However, this does not, and neither should it, imply a desire for homogeneity. Rather, it should be more a recognition of what knowledge of differing cultural perspectives can bring to an enhanced understanding of the specific identities of local communities of arts and cultural practice. This involves recognition of how such knowledge can negotiate specific cultural meanings within a broader, global community.

The concept of distance, often referred to as the tyranny of distance, has particular resonance with many Australians. We live in a very large country where the majority of inhabitants hug an eastern seaboard, and where it is not uncommon to find many who have no experience of visiting the vast interior, and have little knowledge of the Indigenous and migrant communities who may live there. Distance, both real and perceived, can offer continuing challenges and can have a profound impact on people both within and beyond national boundaries. The various ways such physical and metaphoric boundaries are navigated can be both confronting and liberating.

CUSTOMS

When travelling internationally, the act of negotiating customs marks a very real transition from one set of reference points to another. Possessing a valid passport is an essential requirement at both the point of departure and arrival providing evidence and proof of identity, and granting permission to move from one set of reference points to another. In a similar way, studying to attain a doctoral degree might be considered a kind of identity formation in process, providing a passport into a state of 'mastery' of one's professional life, and granting permission to enter new locations and experiences. Apart from the physical restrictions on the amount of baggage one is allowed, there is an imperative for the supervisor to 'pack' wisely, and for multiple and various contingencies. Such restrictions place a very real demand on being able to think on one's feet in circumstances that are often unpredictable and unforeseen. Flexibility is therefore of prime importance for travellers in both a physical and metaphoric sense, as is also sensitivity to differing cultural norms and expectations. Such qualities of flexibility and sensitivity to difference are important for all travellers. However, they attain a rarefied significance when both candidate and supervisor have a shared desire and expectation of travelling towards a successful completion of a scholarly doctorate programme, but may not always share the same ideas or reference points about ways to undertake the journey, let alone arrive at the destination.

In the context of doctoral supervision by distance, the idea of going through customs is as much about what one can bring in as it is about what one hopes to take out, and is circumscribed by the particular and prevailing political and cultural conditions of the time. In this context, it is significant that experiences of teaching in Hong Kong commenced for the School of Art at RMIT during the time of Hong Kong's transition from British colonial rule to its establishment as a Special Administrative Region of the People's Republic of China. In his essay, 'Between East and West: Negotiations with tradition and modernity in Hong Kong art', David Clarke discusses how Hong Kong might be characterised as a neutral arena in which Western and Chinese elements come into contact with each other. He writes:

> Such a characterization of Hong Kong is by no means unique to art: the notion of Hong Kong as the place where 'East meets West' is an enormously widespread cliché, and one which manages to deny any separate identity to the colony, to reduce it to a 'gateway' or 'bridge' through or over which Chinese and Western influences pass (Clarke, 1996, pp. 73–75).

It is of interest to note that many of the doctoral candidates in Hong Kong have sought to address issues of cultural identity through their practice. They seek to give attention to the specific contingencies of Hong Kong's modernity, and its states of cultural change between its Englishness and Chineseness. In the same essay, David Clarke writes:

> But if Chineseness is an identity which is difficult for an artist to sustain in the face of Western modernism's challenge, then Hong Kongness faces even more obstacles to its existence. Not only does Hong Kong lack any high cultural tradition of its own which can serve as a resource, it also lacks support from either an ethnic or a national narrative in a broader sense. These two most powerful sustaining forces (present even in the case of the more liberatory narratives of identity) are not available to Hong Kongness, and indeed may be said to be actively ranged against it. This is true in the sense that most Hong Kong people (artists included) have their ethnic and national identifications invested in China – and yet it is above all from Chineseness that Hong Kongness must distinguish itself. No easy demonization of the other, such as might be employed by a white racist in England for instance, can be drawn upon to shore up a sense of a distinct Hong Kong identity (Clarke, 1996, p. 76).

The notion of what it means to be Hong Kongese has formed a recurring backdrop to much of the research of the Hong Kong doctoral candidates. This occurs alongside investigations of the social and physical condition of a densely populated and constantly changing modern metropolis.

Figure 1. Drift City by Kacey Wong. Copyright the artist.

Artist, Kacey Wong was one of the first Hong Kong doctoral students to complete his Doctor of Fine Art (2003). Wong's doctoral project, *Perceiving the concept of home inside a city*, investigated an extensive range of perceptual concepts inspired by the idea of the home and its relationship to and within the dynamic modern metropolis of Hong Kong. Wong asserts that:

> The City of Hong Kong extends far beyond the simple notion of East meets West. The complete hybridization of the Chinese and British cultures and the consequent political and social development produced a unique urban condition worthy of intense investigation (Wong, 2003).

Wong's research resulted in a number of linked projects that explored and commented on the social and cultural fabric of Hong Kong. In his 'Drift City Photography' project, which the artist commenced in 2000 (and which continues until today), the artist curated an exhibition, *Personal Skyscraper,* where he constructed a skyscraper suit, or wearable building, out of foam board and documented himself in various locations that were of architectural significance within Hong Kong, and other selected sites, on his international travels. In his documentation of 'Drift City' the artist describes the project as follows:

> This is a story, a story about the city. The main character in this tale is a not so significant and soon to be forgotten skyscraper. It does not remember when it was constructed and it does not remember the faces of those people who once lived there. In its lost memory there seems to be a mission, yet it cannot remember exactly what it is. It drifts in space between reality and utopia, endlessly searching for an ideal city (Wong, 2003).

IN-FLIGHT ENTERTAINMENT

The methodology of supervising distance doctorates involves a mixed-mode delivery. This includes digital communications, such as Skype and emails, as well as seminars and conferences, and face-to-face visits in studios. Supervising students in their own studios in Hong Kong requires a great deal of travel both within Hong Kong island, across the harbour to Kowloon, and further afield to the New Territories. Many supervisory visits are adventures in their own right, requiring the negotiations of a complex, but seamlessly efficient, public transport system in all its various permutations, from the clattering trams and Mass Transit Railway, through to high speed ferry rides to the outlying islands. Finding one's destination can be as much of a challenge as it is invariably exciting. Also, it can provide a space for preparation, or reflection on the forthcoming meeting with the candidate. One's 'office' can be anywhere and this can be both liberating in its flexibility, and also limiting because of restricted access to the resources of a 'normal' office in the environs of a university campus.

Many students in Hong Kong have their studios in converted warehouses, and indeed the School of Art's involvement in arts education in Hong Kong has made a significant contribution to an arts-based recovery of decaying industrial areas such as Fotan. Galleries have followed and established themselves in the same industrial complexes adding further impetus to this urban regeneration. However, many vibrant small industries continue to co-exist in these buildings. A visit to a studio may well entail the need for a cautious footing, if it is situated next to an adjacent barbecue pork factory, giving rise to a need to negotiate the trail of accumulating fat in a corridor! For other candidates a studio might be simply a space within the family home. Visiting candidates in their own intimate spaces provides an important opportunity for the supervisor to contextualise the candidate's practice with reference to their personal environment and is often as revealing as the candidate's work itself. A candidate's studio might consist of little more than the opportune use of the kitchen table once the children have gone to bed. What continues to impress is that work of such exceptionally high quality and often of a large scale emerges from such confined and restricted spaces.

The delivery of the Doctor of Fine Art programme in Hong Kong is managed through four supervisory visits each year, where candidate and supervisor meet for approximately two hours to discuss and evaluate progress. This usually happens in the candidate's studio, but often this may occur in a coffee shop or restaurant, where a candidate might find time to take an hour or two away from their employment. Most of the Hong Kong doctoral candidates are employed professionally in a range of demanding occupations and their lack of time is frequently an impediment to progress, or at the very least, something to be overcome through consideration of appropriate and possibly new approaches to working.

As important as an understanding of what the local condition is within distance education, the programme aims to locate the local within the broader regional and international arts and cultural communities. This thereby reduces the perception of distance, as it builds and extends community beyond the student's immediate sphere of engagement. In each of the three years of the doctoral programme, a doctoral seminar is conducted. Due to local Hong Kong regulations that define the operating parameters of distance education, these doctoral seminars are conducted outside Hong Kong, but within the immediate South-East Asian region. These collegial seminars not only encourage dialogue between a group of candidates and supervisors, but also help to build an active network of contacts with public and commercial institutions, galleries and other practising artists within the region. To date, these doctoral seminars have been held in collaboration with a number of cultural and educational institutions, which include the Macau Museum of Art, RMIT Vietnam campuses in Hanoi and Ho Chi Minh City, and more recently the College of Fine Arts at Seoul National University, South Korea. At each of these locations the seminars have been held with the staff and students from both institutions participating by presenting and critically discussing their work. The seminars coincide where possible with significant art events, such as the Guangzhou Biennale, Shanghai Biennale, and in 2011 the Korean International Art Fair. Seminars have been conducted in Beijing with visits to the 798 (Dashanzi) Arts precinct, Caochangdi Art Zone and artists' studios. These visits form a significant adjunct and stimulus to the practical work conducted in the candidate's studio. Encouraging a community of scholars among the candidates themselves, and within the broader artistic community of the region, is a way of affirming the integrity of each candidate's personal artistic practice while locating it within a wider communal and collaborative environment.

The seminar programme is evolving into a new formulation in 2012, with the advent of an Asian-based, postgraduate, Practice Research Symposium (PRS) in a tri-partite collaboration with the RMIT School of Art and international partners, LASALLE College of the Arts, Singapore, and the College of Fine Arts, Seoul National University, South Korea. This PRS involves academics and students from each institution with postgraduate candidates presenting their work in progress to groups of critical respondents including peers, supervisors and experts in the field. The 2012 Practice Research Symposium will be held at Seoul National University after which it will rotate between the three partner institutions on an annual basis thus ensuring a strong practice-led research presence in the region.

ENCOUNTERING TURBULENCE

A completely smooth doctoral journey is rare. Distance education is, as its name implies, education at more than the usual arm's length. Turbulence can occur at any stage of the programme, from the very beginning when a candidate might be struggling to formulate a clear proposal; crises of confidence as the work progresses (or perhaps doesn't); and poor time management and writer's block, to name but a few obstacles that can become evident along the way. While technologies such as email and Skype allow us to keep in touch on a regular basis, face-to-face visits are highly valued by the candidate and form an integral part of the supervisory process. It is through the frank discussions, which can occur on a face-to-face basis, that candidate and supervisor both build and maintain trust, and this process can nurture the creative process. While Skype and email technologies may allow us to fill in the gaps, they generally do not expose the subtle shifts in a candidate's mood or reveal the nuances made visible through viewing the actual artwork under production, rather than looking at a flattened digital image of the artwork on a computer screen. Face-to-face visits help to minimise turbulence and keep the candidate focused.

Making the best of a supervisory visit is as much the responsibility of the candidate as it is the supervisor. From a supervisor's perspective, sometimes it may be frustrating to arrive at a meeting only to find that the candidate has given little thought to the research, or may have very little to show, particularly when, as supervisor, you have travelled so far for this meeting! It is perhaps in these circumstances, more than any other, that distance education leans more heavily on the trust that candidate and supervisor must establish. Feelings of self-doubt are not restricted to the undergraduate, and are perhaps more alarming for the doctoral candidate who is expected to be an independent and self-critical learner. It is also on these occasions that one may become aware of cultural differences in approaches to learning, and how the anticipated nature of the relationship between candidate and supervisor is interpreted. Therefore, it can be useful at the very beginning of the journey to have a conversation about how you might work together most effectively, with the expectation that this will be reviewed and fine-tuned at regular intervals.

The Doctor of Fine Art programme has been popular in Hong Kong over the ten years since its inception. To date, 13 students have completed the programme and a further five are engaged currently in study. Many of them work professionally as teachers and lecturers in various schools and universities, as well as in other professions such as architecture and design. The popularity of the Doctor of Fine Art programme owes much to its emphasis on the professional, studio-based project. While the required length of the accompanying exegesis is less than that of a Ph.D., it is in many ways no less demanding. While in the context of fine art practice there is a shared understanding between candidate and supervisor of a visual language, which is forming the basis of the research, the written defence of the project or exegesis can be a stumbling block for the candidate whose first language is not English. As stated earlier, most of the candidates in Hong Kong are working professionals and, therefore, the time that many of them can allocate to their doctorate is often compromised. In this context, candidates frequently privilege the production of visual work and neglect the requirement of writing an accompanying exegesis alongside the studio-based research. Candidates may need to be reminded frequently of the need to be engaged consistently in researching, and in drafting proofs of their exegesis. A useful strategy to assist in alleviating this problem, and to ensure that the exegesis does not become an insurmountable and miserable footnote to an otherwise productive journey, is to encourage the candidate to write a little, frequently.

Many candidates are not engaged regularly in writing and therefore they can be fearful of their ability to do so. Making writing both a familiar and enlightening part of their practice and discussing their visual work with reference to their writing is an essential process of a creative doctorate. In this context, translocation of meanings is significant and often problematised by the difficulty of expressing complex theoretical and conceptual issues with candidates for whom English is a second language. This can be particularly pertinent not only for the candidate, but also for the supervisor in the reading of the exegesis, where there is often a need to clarify with the candidate that the language used faithfully reflects their intended meaning. In such a situation the supervisor needs to resist any rush to make assumptions on the candidate's behalf, instead seeking clarification from the candidate through discussion. This process can usually be undertaken quickly with the achievement of desired outcomes; however, there are instances where the complexity of the issues being discussed can require considerable patience in bringing a successful resolution. What is of paramount importance in this situation is to retain the authenticity of the candidate's voice when it may appear easier to impose one's own.

ARRIVALS

The doctoral journey might well be considered the educational equivalent of a long-haul flight. There is the initial excitement of getting on the plane, frequently followed by periods of boredom and frustration intermixed with some wonderful vistas, some entertainment, rest and reading, and finally, the promise of arriving at a new and exciting destination. However, towards the end of any long-haul flight there is also a desire for it to be over as quickly as possible.

A consistently recurring need towards the end of a candidature to refine the exegesis, select and prepare work for presentation in order to ensure the highest quality end result, can be an infuriating process for even the most disciplined of candidates. It is at this point of wanting to get the whole thing over with that the candidate needs to take a deep breath, take stock of the mileage they have travelled, and not give in to a temptation to parachute out altogether. It is important for both candidate and supervisor to realise that a doctoral project should be of a certain containable size: not too big and not too small. As the research flight comes to an end, it is tempting to put more and more into the project, whether conceptually in one's head, physically in the studio, or textually in words on the page.

At this point of arrival, candidates generally come to realise that it has been as much their determination and persistence as any innate creative talent, which has enabled them to reach their destination. Although they may have struggled to find the enthusiasm to write the exegesis, each of them comes to recognise the confidence gained through the process of writing about their research in an intelligent and cogent manner. They then gain greater confidence in sharing their research journey with others. In selecting work for their final presentation they may have encountered some difficult choices, particularly the need to resist exhibiting as much work as possible, rather than selecting and editing to express the project with both economy and authority. However, with the exegesis completed and the final work selected for presentation they can be said to have arrived at their destination. Now they have achieved the recognition of being experts in their field, they can be confident and able to undertake further journeys, and assist those who might be setting out on similar adventures.

DEALING WITH JETLAG AND LOOKING FORWARD

After such a long-haul flight there is often the problem of coping with jetlag. While the thrill of having arrived at one's destination can be palpable, the physical and mental demands of a doctoral journey can leave many candidates exhausted. A short and well-earned rest is perhaps all that is required before considering what happens next.

Most candidates are already thinking of future projects, and are considering ideas for exhibitions, residencies, post-doctoral research, grant applications, and industry contacts. Studying for their doctorate has enabled them to shine a more intense light on their practice, and it is important to consider how this achievement can be sustained as well as providing a springboard for new opportunities. A doctoral candidate should be well placed to deal with this. They have had to be methodical, critically rigorous and reflective, as well as coping with frustration, successes and failures. They have had to set and meet the challenges of bringing research skills to bear upon their creative fine art practice. They have studied and worked as art professionals and have achieved the authenticated standard of becoming a doctor in their specialist field. Now they can look forward to new vistas. Having a forward plan after the completion of the doctorate enables the candidate to build on their hard-earned momentum. It sets a new goal. It allows them to look up at the night sky, trace the patterns in the stars, and realise where they have been and where they might be going.

REFERENCES

Clarke, D. (1996). *Art & place: Essays on art from a Hong Kong perspective.* Hong Kong: Hong Kong University Press.

Wong, K. (2003). *Perceiving the concept of home inside a city.* Unpublished Doctor of Fine Art by project, RMIT University, Melbourne Australia.

INDEX

Lightning Source UK Ltd.
Milton Keynes UK
UKOW06f1022280116

267280UK00001B/65/P

9 789462 090170